The Best American
Travel Writing 2013

P9-CQL-474

GUEST EDITORS OF
THE BEST AMERICAN TRAVEL WRITING

The Best American
Travel Writing™ 2013

Edited and with an Introduction
by **Elizabeth Gilbert**

Jason Wilson, Series Editor

A Mariner Original

HOUGHTON MIFFLIN HARCOURT

BOSTON • NEW YORK

Copyright © 2013 by Houghton Mifflin Harcourt Publishing Company
Introduction copyright © 2013 by Elizabeth Gilbert

ALL RIGHTS RESERVED

The Best American Series® is a registered trademark of Houghton Mifflin Harcourt Publishing Company. *The Best American Travel Writing*™ is a trademark of Houghton Mifflin Harcourt Publishing Company.

No part of this work may be reproduced or transmitted in any form or by any means, electronic or mechanical, including photocopying and recording, or by any information storage or retrieval system without the proper written permission of the copyright owner unless such copying is expressly permitted by federal copyright law. With the exception of nonprofit transcription in Braille, Houghton Mifflin Harcourt is not authorized to grant permission for further uses of copyrighted selections reprinted in this book without the permission of their owners. Permission must be obtained from the individual copyright owners as identified herein. Address requests for permission to make copies of Houghton Mifflin Harcourt material to Permissions, Houghton Mifflin Harcourt Publishing Company, 215 Park Avenue South, New York, New York 10003.

www.hmhbooks.com

ISSN 1530-1516
ISBN 978-0-547-80898-7

Printed in the United States of America
DOC 10 9 8 7 6 5 4 3 2

"The Pippiest Place on Earth" by Sam Anderson. First published in the *New York Times Magazine*, February 12, 2012. Copyright © 2012 by Sam Anderson. Reprinted by permission of Sam Anderson.

"Dreaming of El Dorado" by Marie Arana. First published in *Virginia Quarterly Review*, Fall 2012. Copyright © 2012 by Marie Arana. Reprinted by permission of Marie Arana.

"The Wild Dogs of Istanbul" by Bernd Brunner. First published in *The Smart Set*, February 29, 2012. Copyright © 2012 by the Smart Set. Reprinted by permission of the Smart Set.

"The Bull Passes Through" by Kevin Chroust. First published in the *Morning News*, July 13, 2012. Copyright © 2012 by the Morning News LLC. Reprinted by permission of Kevin Chroust.

"Pirate City" by Rich Cohen. First published in the *Paris Review*, Summer 2012. Copyright © 2012 by Rich Cohen. Reprinted by permission of the author.

"The Way I've Come" by Judy Copeland. Published in *Legal Studies Forum*, Volume 36, No. 1. First published in the *Florida Review*, Volume 28, No. 2, under the title "The Art of Bushwhacking." Copyright © 2012 by Judy Copeland. Reprinted by permission of the author.

"Caliph of the Tricksters" by Christopher de Bellaigue. First published in *Harper's Magazine*, December 2012. Copyright © 2012 by Christopher de Bellaigue. Reprinted by permission of Christopher de Bellaigue.

"Babu on the Bad Road" by Jesse Dukes. First published in *Virginia Quarterly Review*, Winter 2012. Copyright © 2012 by Jesse Dukes. Reprinted by permission of Jesse Dukes.

"Vietnam's Bowl of Secrets" by David Farley. First published in *Afar*, May/June 2012. Copyright © 2012 by David Farley. Reprinted by permission of David Farley.

"A Farewell to Yarns" by Ian Frazier. First published in *Outside*, November 2012. Copyright © 2012 by Ian Frazier. Reprinted by permission of the Wylie Agency, LLC.

"Bombing Sarajevo" by Dimiter Kenarov. First published in *Outside*, January 2012. Copyright © 2012 by Dimiter Kenarov. Reprinted by permission of Dimiter Kenarov.

"Blot Out" by Colleen Kinder. First published in *Creative Nonfiction*, Spring 2012. Copyright © 2012 by Colleen Kinder. Reprinted by permission of Creative Nonfiction and the author.

"Summerland" by Peter Jon Lindberg. First published in *Travel + Leisure*, August 2012. Copyright © 2012 by Peter Jon Lindberg. Reprinted by permission of the author.

"Dentists Without Borders" by David Sedaris. First published in *The New Yorker*, April 2, 2012. Copyright © 2012 by David Sedaris. Reprinted by permission of the author.

"The Paid Piper" by Grant Stoddard. First published in *T Magazine*, November 12, 2012. Copyright © 2012 by the *New York Times*. All rights reserved. Used by permission and protected by the copyright laws of the United States. The printing, copying, redistribution, or retransmission of this content without express written permission is prohibited.

"A Prison, a Paradise" by John Jeremiah Sullivan. First published in the *New York Times Magazine*, September 23, 2012. Copyright © 2012 by the *New York Times*. All rights reserved. Used by permission and protected by the copyright laws of the United States. The printing, copying, redistribution, or retransmission of this content without express written permission is prohibited.

"Tea and Kidnapping" by Sarah A. Topol. First published in *The Atlantic*, October 2012. Copyright © 2012 by Sarah A. Topol. Reprinted by permission of Sarah A. Topol.

"The Year I Didn't" by Daniel Tyx. First published in *Gulf Coast*, Volume 25, No. 1. Copyright © 2012 by Daniel Tyx. Reprinted by permission of Daniel Tyx.

"Confessions of a Packing Maximalist" by Lynn Yaeger. First published in *Travel + Leisure*, September 2012. Copyright © 2012 by Lynn Yaeger. Reprinted by permission of Lynn Yaeger.

Contents

Foreword

WHEN I THINK about travel writing, I often think about photographer Henri Cartier-Bresson. A few years ago, I tried to write a critical essay about the Museum of Modern Art's huge retrospective on Cartier-Bresson. But over and over again, I failed.

At first, I thought I'd been swayed by a number of esteemed art critics, most of whom seemed disappointed by the exhibition. The show was deemed "almost unenduringly majestic" by *The New Yorker*'s Peter Schjeldahl, who gave this stern assessment of what he called Cartier-Bresson's "platitudinous" work: "richly satisfies the eye and the mind, while numbing the heart." This was seconded by the *New York Times*' Holland Cotter, who claimed that Cartier-Bresson's "ideas and emotions are diffuse" and that "surprisingly little tension builds" in the exhibition. Both critics also trotted out tired old comparisons to the work of Robert Frank, a detractor of Cartier-Bresson's who once unjustly said of the older photographer, "He traveled all over the world, and you never felt he was moved by something that was happening other than the beauty of it, or just the composition."

Soon enough, I started to feel angry about the general critical appraisal of the show, especially a certain loaded, snobbish question I'd seen raised numerous times: should we consider Cartier-Bresson's photography "art," or is it *just* (and here I imagine a critic crinkling his nose as if holding a dirty diaper) "journalism"? This stuffy and frankly out-of-touch notion was most clearly expressed by Cotter: "Are we talking about an impassable line that separates photojournalism (Cartier-Bresson) from art (Frank)?" (To Cotter's credit, he answered no.)

But I was still confused, still unable to write about Cartier-Bresson, still unable to articulate why I was so frustrated by this supposed "impassable line" between journalism and art. I returned to MoMA for a second viewing, and then it hit me: I was taking everything about Cartier-Bresson—the articles, even the exhibition itself—way too personally.

It hit me as I approached the mural-sized world maps that greet museum-goers at the show's entrance, with dotted lines tracing Cartier-Bresson's famous journeys over several decades. Ringing in my ears was Schjeldahl's snarky take: "This suggests a novel measurement of artistic worth: mileage. It seems relevant only to the glamour quotient—a cult, practically—of Cartier-Bresson's persona, pointing up what seems to me most resistible in his work."

Ouch, I thought. But mainly because I was flashing on my own career as a travel writer, one that began almost two decades ago when I gave up on writing a novel. I've always harbored deep fears that I passed, miles ago, over that "impassable" line from art to journalism, never to return.

But that, of course, is about me. And compared to Cartier-Bresson, I am a very tiny talent—a hack really, just like all the critics who write about him, as well as most artists who try to emulate him. Cartier-Bresson was a giant. And clearly he never worried at all about whether he was making art, photojournalism, or something else entirely. And this is why I love him.

I can't remember a time when Cartier-Bresson's images did not exist in my mind, suggesting an older, more authentic, more beautiful world. I knew those fishermen mending nets in Nazaré, Portugal, before I'd ever seen them myself (and snapped my own inferior version of the same photo). I'd met those old men picnicking in Sardinia before I ever traveled to Sardinia myself and tried in vain to similarly capture them in words. The French boar hunters I followed into the forest had already somehow existed, in my imagination, because of Cartier-Bresson. When I was a teenager growing up in an average American suburb, Cartier-Bresson's photo provided a particular vision of Old Europe that is permanently etched in my mind, even if it doesn't exist in the world anymore.

Yes, I know it seems almost quaint these days. "Many of Cartier-

Bresson's pictures could have been made centuries ago, if he and photography had existed then," reads the MoMA gallery text. The curators, seeming to anticipate the critical response, note that "his keen attention to particulars redeems the strain of romantic nostalgia in his work."

Pico Iyer, in a 2010 essay titled "The Photographer and the Philosopher," aptly described the travel writer like this: "A travel writer is, to some degree, Cartier-Bresson roaming around the global or local neighborhood with a book of theology in his hand." When I was young and beginning my own wanderings, that book of theology was, for me, written by lyrical correspondents like Iyer himself. In Iyer's classic essay "Why We Travel" (collected in the very first edition of *The Best American Travel Writing*), he lays out a sort of traveler's catechism: he travels in search of "subtler beauties"; he seeks "an innocent eye that can return me to a more innocent self"; he calls all the great travel books "love stories" and says "all good trips are, like love, about being carried out of yourself and deposited in the midst of terror and wonder." When Iyer writes, "Travel is the best way we have of rescuing the humanity of places, and saving them from abstraction and ideology," he may as well be describing the work of Cartier-Bresson.

With his tendency toward lyricism, Iyer has faced critical complaints similar to those made against Cartier-Bresson, such as this dismissive judgment from the *Times Sunday Book Review* about his book *Sun After Dark:* "Iyer too often relies on overblown figures of speech and pretty pastiches in lieu of solid observation or reporting."

This is no surprise. As soon as artists (or is it journalists?) start talking about things like "the humanity of places," critics uncomfortably reach for adjectives such as *platitudinous* and *melodramatic*. Likewise, whenever an artist (or is it a journalist?) nakedly sets out to capture beauty in this way, what always comes forth is that nagging question—Frank's question of Cartier-Bresson—of whether beauty is enough, or whether something *other than the beauty of it* also needs to be happening.

So I guess this is why I have failed, and will continue to fail, to write in any critical fashion about Cartier-Bresson. The couple on the train in Romania. The young boys gathered in a sunny square in Madrid. The family having a picnic on the riverbank. I can't

imagine my life without images such as these. For me, like so much
of the travel writing I love, the beauty simply has to be enough.

The stories included here are, as always, selected from among
hundreds of pieces in hundreds of diverse publications—from
mainstream and specialty magazines to Sunday newspaper travel
sections to literary journals to travel websites. I've done my best to
be fair and representative, and in my opinion the best travel stories from 2012 were forwarded to guest editor Elizabeth Gilbert,
who made our final selections.

I now begin anew by reading the hundreds of stories published
in 2013. As I have for 14 years, I am asking editors and writers to
submit the best of whatever it is they define as travel writing. These
submissions must be nonfiction, published in the United States during the 2013 calendar year. They must not be reprints or excerpts
from published books. They must include the author's name, date
of publication, and publication name, and they must be tear sheets,
the complete publication, or a clear photocopy of the piece as it
originally appeared. I must receive all submissions by January 1,
2014, in order to ensure full consideration for the next collection.

Further, publications that want to make certain their contribu-
tions will be considered for the next edition should make sure to
include this anthology on their subscription list. Submissions or
subscriptions should be sent to Jason Wilson, Drexel University,
3210 Cherry Street, 2nd floor, Philadelphia, PA 19104.

Working with Elizabeth Gilbert has been something I've been
hoping to do for many, many years. I believe we approached Liz at
least five years in a row, but her busy writing and travel schedule
never managed to mesh with the anthology's until now. It was well
worth the wait. What makes this collection special is that Liz was
committed to reading the slush pile without bylines. The direct
result is the inclusion of wonderful pieces from several smaller
journals—such as *Gulf Coast, Creative Nonfiction,* and *Legal Studies
Forum*—that have never before appeared in the anthology, alongside the usual suspects. This year's is an outstanding collection,
and I hope you enjoy it.

Finally, I am grateful to Nicole Angeloro, Timothy Mudie, and
Mary Sydnor for their help on this, our 14th edition of *The Best
American Travel Writing.*

JASON WILSON

Introduction

HERE ARE TWO facts I learned long ago about travel writing:

1. There is no story in the world so marvelous that it cannot be told boringly.
2. There is no story in the world so boring that it cannot be told marvelously.

To prove the first point, I will provide you with an example from my own personal and painful experience. Long ago, back when Bill Clinton was president and the earth was new, I worked as a writer at *GQ* magazine. It was a great job. This was still in the days before the Internet undid the magazine business—back when editors of the big glossies could still afford to send writers on long, expensive trips in order to write long, expensive stories about long, expensive subjects. Thus, my editors very expensively sent me a long way off to New Zealand to write about an obsessed scientist who was hunting for the fabled giant squid in the very deepest and most unexplored trenches of the Pacific Ocean. (This was way before there was any video footage of the giant squid to be found on the Internet, such as one can easily find today. Back then, nobody had ever yet seen one of these magnificent creatures alive.)

I was in my 20s and had a tendency toward lazy shortcuts, and probably this is why I decided—in advance of even boarding the plane to New Zealand—that this story was basically going to write itself. Really, all I had to do was sort of show up, and everything would clearly fall into place, right? Because look at the elements: Mysterious sea creature! Obsessed scientist! Unexplored crevices in the deepest trenches of the ocean! I wouldn't even have to phone this one in; I could just sort of *mumble* it in, without even bothering to pick up the phone. So I went to New Zealand, and I had a great time. I drank a lot of beer and hung out with sailors and took a day off to go snorkeling with dolphins just for my own pleasure. Then I came home and wrote the story of the giant squid in about two days—*BAM*, done. Nailed it! Easy peasy. What's next? Where's my next plane ticket?

But my editor (the indomitable Ilena Silverman, who now presides over writers at the *New York Times Magazine*) didn't love the story. She found the story to be, as they maddeningly and constantly say in the magazine business, "not yet there." She gave me some thoughtful and careful advice for how to get the piece there, and I dutifully plugged in her ideas and returned the story to her a few days later. She still didn't like it. She asked me to rewrite it again. I rewrote it. I took two weeks this time. But she still didn't like it. She didn't like my next rewrite either. Nor the next. Nor the next.

Now, Ilena Silverman is not an editor who wastes people's time, so I knew she wasn't messing with me on this. She was earnestly searching for ways to help me make this story come alive, but even she seemed uncertain as to precisely what magic was missing from my prose. By now, even I could not deny that my story was leaden, and only getting heavier with each pass. Ilena was confounded by it; I was confounded by it. We trudged ahead, though it felt like we were trudging backward.

I wrote 11 painfully executed drafts of that goddamn giant squid story—which was supposed to be the easiest thing I'd ever written—and I still wasn't getting any closer to it. Finally, after the 11th draft, my intelligent and gracious editor, who had always delivered her criticisms in the most articulate and gentle manner imaginable, became exasperated. She cracked. I had broken her spirit. She called me up one day and said simply, "Why don't you try writing this story once more, Liz. Only this time, why don't you see if you can figure out a way to make it . . . *not so boring.*"

There it was, the dreadful proof: I was the journalist who had just written (11 times in a row!) a completely boring story about a mysterious sea creature, an obsessed scientist, and unexplored crevices in the deepest trenches of the ocean. And the reason my writing was boring was that I was still laboring under the grave misconception that the story itself was *automatically interesting*—in other words, that the story didn't really need me.

Wrong.

No story is automatically interesting; only the telling makes it so. Every narrative needs a fully engaged narrator. And it was only when I charged myself at last with my proper mandate as a writer (*to make things interesting*) that my giant squid article at last drew sputtering breath and came to life. For my kind editors had not sent me to the other side of the planet to drink beer and hang out with sailors; they had sent me there to infuse marvel into a potentially fascinating tale that only I would be lucky enough to witness with my own eyes. And once I regained hold of that sense of astonishment—once I inhabited that rightful feeling of *You aren't going to believe what I just saw!*—everything lit up at last.

Which brings me to my second point—that there is no story so boring that it cannot, over time, with the right amount of love and passion and work, be told marvelously.

The travel stories I've selected for this anthology are the ones that I believe were told the most marvelously in 2012—by which I mean, quite literally, told with the biggest sense of marvel by writers who took the most personal responsibility for infusing wonderment into their tales. Some of these stories find their authors flinging themselves into mad acts of danger and some do not, but every piece contains awe in strong enough doses to render the reader enchanted, delighted, compelled, or forever unsettled.

I read a lot of travel stories in order to select these 19. I sat on a beach under an umbrella during a long and quiet vacation of my own, with stacks of magazine articles in a big brown shopping bag next to me. I pulled the stories out of the bag randomly, one after another, like an endless succession of salty or sweet snacks. I had a vague idea of what I was looking for (to be transported), but I had no way of anticipating what would transport me. I was pretty sure I didn't want any service articles ("How to Do Barcelona in Three Days!"), nor was I looking for any ideas for my own future trips. I don't read great travel writing to say, at the conclusion, "I want to go there!" I read great travel writing to feel, at the conclusion, *I have now been there.*

I wanted, by the end of my reading, to know all these places deep in my own bones.

Among the articles that I rejected were tales of extraordinary daring, gorgeous adventure, exotic locations, and impossible situations—but boring. Sometimes I was surprised by how boring the writing about such interesting places could be. I wondered, Do these people not have editors who make them write a dozen drafts so that they get it done properly?

What surprised me more, though, was when I found fascination in subjects that I might otherwise have thought to be dull, or even spent. To my mind, one of the most remarkable pieces in here is Daniel Tyx's story about *not* traveling—a faithful recounting of the year in which he *didn't* walk the U.S.-Mexico border, as he had once quite seriously planned to do. (This was during a time in American literary history when, as Tyx says, "everyone seemed to be doing something with their year, then writing about it"—a tactic with which I am somewhat familiar.) Tyx writes about the epiphanies he *didn't* have because of not taking that long trip (the loneliness he *didn't* conquer; the landscapes he *didn't* witness; the cultural exchanges he *didn't* enjoy). He ponders with real feeling and seriousness the question of what we become when we let such a journey pass us by. What happens when we choose, instead, to live a quieter year, with more domestic revelations, full of "the satisfactions and preoccupations of daily life"? This psychologically honest account was somehow heaps more interesting and suspenseful to me than a macho article about the most dangerous ski trail in the world, or whatever. I would not have imagined that this could be true—that the act of *not* traveling could make for such a good travelogue—but Daniel Tyx did it.

In fact, it was humbling for me to read many of these pieces, because they kept messing with my assumptions about what constitutes an interesting story and what does not. There are magnificent articles in this collection that I would never have assigned if I were a magazine editor. If, for instance, John Jeremiah Sullivan had come to me and said, "I want to write a long feature article about my trip to Cuba to visit my wife's family," I would have said, "Dude, nice try, but there's no way I'm paying for your trip to Cuba to visit your wife's family!" Because nobody needs to read another article about an American visiting Cuba! Seriously! I would probably have told Sullivan to go write about the most dangerous ski trail in the world instead. And I would have been dead wrong, because *everyone* needs to read John Jeremiah Sullivan's story about his trip to Cuba to visit his wife's family. It is so good, so trenchant, so quivering with human life and love and the real familial consequences of insane political theatrics that I placed it very first in this collection—right at the front of the book—just to make sure nobody skips it.

Here's another story that would never have existed if I were a magazine editor: Kevin Chroust's recounting of the time he ran with the bulls in Pamplona. Here's what I would have said if I were his writing boss: "Kevin, does the world really need to be subjected to another story about reckless young men running with those tiresome bulls in Pamplona? In fact, do we really need another story at all involving bulls and Spain and manhood in any manner whatsoever? No, Kevin. No, we do not."

Well, as it turns out, Yes, Kevin. Yes, we do. But we only need this story when it's told with such bare, vibrating honesty. There is not a trace of machismo in this piece, only a near-tearful longing for the most intense possible act of self-revolution. Until reading Chroust's story, I never really understood why a young man might need to run with the bulls in Pamplona (honestly, I've never even really understood why people need to ride motorcycles or get on roller coasters), but now—thanks to this vivid explosion of writing—I get it. I get why there are times in life when people need to put themselves "in arbitrary danger" in order to burst through to the other side, to some white-hot experience of purification more radiant than anything that mere safety could ever provide.

Still, though, I think the most dangerous story in this collection is Colleen Kinder's essay "Blot Out"—about her experiences walking through the streets of Cairo as a woman, both covered and uncovered. The risks that she took on the day she describes here are staggering in their audacity. An older woman—knowing more of men's potential savagery and infused with a more ingrained sense of self-protection—probably would not have done what she did. I myself would rather run with the bulls every afternoon for a month than expose myself to the potential of such true and vicious physical violence. And yet the ending is so victorious! A victory over violation! A victory over the absurd and the oppressive, both!

Speaking of which, I put some absurd stuff in here, too, just for fun. Travel should be just as much about light delights as about dark daring, and I've included some simple and charming tales, perfectly told. Lynn Yaeger's account of how much she packs when she travels—and why—is a messy, crazed amuse-bouche in the midst of these heavier meals.

I also want to stress that I read all these articles without their bylines attached. I know a lot of writers personally, and I didn't want to be swayed in my decision making by either my affinity or my distaste for anybody. (I was more afraid of committing an act of revenge than an act of nepotism.) My curiosity over authorship drove me nuts during the process, but in the end I was glad that I read everything blind, for it turns out that I am now madly in love with some writers I'd never heard of before—like the brave and stalwart Judy Copeland, who strikes me as the most sensible person you could ever meet, but who also took herself all the way to Papua New Guinea because of a dream she had about a red line appearing on a map of the world.

For the most part, I was completely surprised and delighted to find out who had written these pieces (though in some cases I was not surprised at all; you don't really need a byline that says "by David Sedaris" to know that something was written by David Sedaris). For the longest time, I could not figure out why I loved so much the little essay called "A Farewell to Yarns," until it was revealed that, of course, the great Ian Frazier had written it. That would explain how a piece of writing could be so simple and yet so simply wonderful—because it was in the hands of a storyteller who, after so many years at his craft, really knows his business.

There are some stories in this anthology that I felt just needed to be next to each other—the way total strangers meet on a train and somehow make each other's journeys more interesting. "The Pippiest Place on Earth" is, in its own right, a fantastic exploration of a Charles Dickens theme park, but it takes on a far deeper meaning after you've read "Dreaming of El Dorado"—which is *truly* Dickensian. I put "Bombing Sarajevo" right next to "Vietnam's Bowl of Secrets" because both of them are incredibly heartening stories about places that were, not very long ago, the very worst places in the world. Yet the cheerful "Vietnam's Bowl of Secrets" then bizarrely runs right into the disturbing "Babu on the Bad Road," but only because of this one strange link: Both stories are about the fetishistic search for a magical and mysterious fluid.

Other stories in here are, by necessity, solitary travelers. "The

Wild Dogs of Istanbul" is like nothing else in this assemblage—written in such a strange and dreamy voice that it felt to me like an Italo Calvino short story, curiously translated from some lost, obscure language. I was also charmed by Peter Jon Lindberg's essay about the pleasures of routine family holidays; its sense of quiet satisfaction is a small island of serenity in this collection of far rougher and hungrier tales. "Caliph of the Tricksters" stands alone in my mind, too; it is the only story I have ever read that features a man whose job is to lick clean the bloody eyeballs of wounded roosters during illegal Afghani cockfights. I did not know that this was a profession. I feel that my world is richer now that I do. I also feel like this piece of information spares me a trip to Afghanistan to find out about blood-licking cockers for myself.

I elected to close this collection with Rich Cohen's grand "Pirate City"—a story that I stumbled upon last summer in the *Paris Review,* and which so seduced me that I completely lost track of myself, and of time, while I was reading it. It is not merely a carefully researched history of the origins of New Orleans; it is also a wild tale about pirates and prostitutes and duplicity and British men-of-war and alligators and escaped slaves and Spanish conquistadors. Why, there is so much true-life action-adventure in this narrative, you'd almost think the story could have written itself!

But I know better.

Nothing in here wrote itself. Nothing ever can.

I salute, therefore, all the writers who made these wide and disparate acts of transportation and transformation come to life for our shock, amusement, and betterment. I salute the editors who made the writers work harder than they probably wanted to. I salute the world that keeps proving, year after year, that there is always more to be discovered—one secret noodle at a time, one benevolent kidnapper at a time, one rooster's bloody eyeball at a time.

Enjoy this journey. I promise you will not be bored.

ELIZABETH GILBERT

The Best American
Travel Writing 2013

JOHN JEREMIAH SULLIVAN

A Prison, a Paradise

FROM *The New York Times Magazine*

ON THE PLANE, something odd but also vaguely magical-seeming happened: namely, nobody knew what time it was. Right before we landed, the flight attendant made an announcement, in English and Spanish, that although daylight-saving time recently went into effect in the States, the island didn't observe that custom. As a result, we had caught up—our time had passed into sync with Cuban time. You will not need to change your watches. Then, moments later, she came on again and apologized. She had been wrong, she said. The time in Cuba was different. She didn't specify how many hours ahead. At that point, people around us looked at one another. How could the airline not know what time it is where we're going? Another flight attendant, hurrying down the aisle, said loudly, "I just talked to some actual Cubans, in the back, and they say it'll be the same time." That settled it: we would be landing in ignorance. We knew our phones weren't going to work because they were tied to a U.S. company that didn't operate on the island.

The six-year-old sat between us, looking back and forth at our faces. "Is something wrong?" she asked.

"No," my wife, Mariana, said, "just funny." But to me she did the eyebrows up and down.

"What?" I said.

"Nothing," she said, "just—into the zone."

Mi esposa travels to Cuba every so many years, to do movie-related research (she's a film-studies professor) and to visit her mother's family, a dwindling number of which, as death and emigration have surpassed the birthrate, still live in the same small inland town, a dusty, colonial-looking agricultural town, not a place anyone's heard of. To them, even after half a century, it's the *querencia,* an untranslatable Spanish word that means something like "the place where you are your most authentic self." They won't go on about Cuba around you in a magic-realist way. Nor do they dream of trying to reclaim their land when the Castros die. Destiny settled their branch of the family not in Florida, where, if you're Cuban American, your nostalgia and anger (and sense of community) are continually stoked, but in Carolina del Norte, where nobody cares. They tend to be fairly laid-back about politics. But their memories stitch helplessly back to and through that town over generations, back to the ur-ancestors who came from a small village in the Canary Islands.

My wife's 91-year-old Cuban grandmother, who lives with us much of the time, once drew for me on top of a white cake box a map of their hometown. It started out like something you would make to give someone directions but ended up as detailed in places as a highway atlas. More so, really, because it was personally annotated. Here is the corner where my father have the bodega. Here is the alley where the old man used to walk his grandson, in a white suit, and we always say, "Let's go to watch it," because he have his pocket full of stones, and when the boy runs, the old man throw and hit him in the legs. She was remembering back through Castro and Batista, back through all of that, into the time of Machado, even back through him into her parents' time, the years of mustachioed Gómez in his black frock coat. The night I met her, 18 years ago, she cooked me Turkish-delight-level black beans with Spanish olives, and flan in a coffee can. She said: "Mira, Yon, at this time"—she meant the early '40s—"they make a census, all the teacher go to have a census in Cuba. We see places nobody know the name. I ride a small horse. One night there is a storm—we pass the storm under a *palma.* In one house is *un enano.* You know what is? A dwarf. He say, 'I count half!'" Her stories are like that. You actually want them to go longer. This is no small thing for me, as my life has evolved by unforeseen paths such that I see more of this *abuelita* than of any other human being. Neither of us ever leaves the house, and during the day it's the two of us. Those could be some paw-chewingly long hours in the kitchen, if she

were talking to me about religion or something. Mostly she calls
people in Miami and watches Univision at the same time, waiting
for my wife and daughters to get home, after which she perks up.

Because my wife and her family have living relatives in Cuba,
they can get a humanitarian exception that lets you fly direct from
Miami. The legal loopholes combining to make that possible must
fill hard drives. But you can in fact go that way, if you obtain one
of these exceptions or are immediate family with someone who
does. I first tagged along 12 years ago. It's hands down the strangest way to travel to Cuba, which you might not expect, because
technically it's the simplest. But the airport bureaucracy in Miami
was so heavy, at least back then, you had to show up the night before and stay in an airport hotel so you could wake up early and
spend the day in a series of bewildering lines, getting things signed
or stamped. That first time, the tedium was alleviated by a little
cluster of Miami relatives who followed us to and through each
line, standing slightly off to the side. I spoke hardly any Spanish
then. My wife told me they were giving her all sorts of warnings
about Havana and messages for various people in their town. Now
and then one of them would rub my arm and smile warmly at me,
gestures that I took to mean, "Words aren't necessary to express
the mutual understanding of familial connection that we now pos-
sess," but that when I think about it now, would have been identi-
cal to those signaling, "You, simpleton."

One line was for having your luggage wrapped in plastic. A
couple of muscly Latin guys in shorts were waiting there. They
lifted each suitcase or bag onto a little spinning platform, turned
it blazingly fast to seal it in industrial-strength shrink-wrap from a
roll that looked like it held a landfill's worth, and charged you for
it. Their spinning was so energetic, it doubled as a feat of strength.
Everyone watched. The reasons behind the plastic were not laid
out. Later in the waiting area, a woman told us it was to discourage
quick-fingered Cuban bag handlers on the other side. They took
not gold and money, which few people were foolish enough to
pack, but toothpaste and shampoo, necessities. This year, however,
the plastic wrap was optional.

There were other post-Bush differences in the direct-to-Cuba
zone. The lines had grown fewer and shorter. Most noticeable,
the Cubans on our flight—a mixture of Cuban Americans and
returning Cuban nationals who had been in Florida or D.C. on vi-

sas of their own (some people do move back and forth)—weren't
carrying as much stuff. The crowd cast a fairly normal profile.
Last time, people had multiple pairs of shoes tied around their
necks by the laces. Thick gorgets of reading glasses. Men wearing 10 hats, several pairs of pants, everybody's pockets bulging.
Everybody wearing fanny packs. The rule was, if you could get it
onto your body, you could bring it aboard. At least five people carried giant stuffed animals and other large toys. That's one of the
things in the Cuban American community, in which going back is
generally frowned upon—but if it's to meet your *nieto* for the first
time . . .

None of that, though, is what makes the Miami-to-Havana
flights strange. It's that this most obvious route, more than any
of the much longer workarounds by which American citizens can
get to the island, lets you feel most fully the truth of Cuba's sheer
proximity. It's one of those flights in which, almost as soon as you
reach your maximum altitude, you begin your descent, and within
minutes you're looking down on a diorama of palm trees growing incongruously in green fields, and within seconds you hit the
ground and everyone bursts into applause. The country you land
in is too unlike your own to have been reached that quickly, all but
instantaneously, and is after all, you recall, on hostile terms with
your own. As if you've passed through a warp. "Why are they clap-
ping?" the six-year-old asked.

I explained that it was special, coming here. Some of these people, when they left Cuba, might have thought they would never see
it again. Some had been hearing about it all their lives and were
seeing it for the first time.

"Also, they like to clap and yell," my wife said.

The six-year-old did her philosopher face, gazing out the
window. She gets a little dimple on her forehead when the big
thoughts are brewing. "Now I'm here," she said.

"Yes, you are."

"And I'm Cuban," she said.

"You are part Cuban, that's true."

"You're not any Cuban," she said, not meanly, just sort of mar-
veling.

She looks like me, pale with blue eyes and light brown hair and
freckles. Yet she has largely been raised day to day by intense, dark-
eyed Cuban American women, and their blood is in her, and the

history of their family, with all of its drama and all of its issues, has exerted an incalculable influence on who and what she is. At some point in her life, she'll have to figure out what all of that means to her; the whole story and the way she looks will be part of its strangeness. For me it was all behind glass. I felt the sudden separation between us, between the relative depths of what this trip would mean to us, many years on. One of those moments of generational wooziness that come with having kids, like realizing there's a part of their lives you won't see.

We landed under searingly vivid skies, something like what the blue tablet from a packet of Easter dye lets off. The land right around the airport is farmed; we saw a man plowing with oxen. The fertility of Cuba is the thing you can't put into words. I've never stood on a piece of ground as throbbingly, even pornographically, generative. Throw a used battery into a divot, and it will put out shoots—that's how it feels. You could smell it, in the smoky, slightly putrid smell of turned fields. More and more, as we drove, that odor mingled with the smell of the sea.

This was the first time I was in post-Fidel Cuba. It was funny to think that not long ago, there were smart people who doubted that such a thing could exist, i.e., who believed that with the fall of Fidel would come the fall of communism on the island. But Fidel didn't fall. He did fall, physically—on the tape that gets shown over and over in Miami, of him coming down the ramp after giving that speech in 2004 and tumbling and breaking his knee—but his leadership didn't. He executed one of the most brilliantly engineered successions in history, a succession that was at the same time a self-entrenchment. First, he faked his own death in a way: serious intestinal operation, he might not make it. Raul is brought in as "acting president." A year and a half later, Castro mostly recovered. But Raul is officially named president, with Castro's approval. It was almost as if, "Is Fidel still . . . ?" Amazing. So now they rule together, with Raul out front, but everyone understanding that Fidel retains massive authority. Not to say that Raul doesn't wield power—he has always had plenty—but it's a partnership of some kind. What comes after is as much of a mystery as ever.

Our relationship with them seems just as uncertain. Barack Obama was going to open things up, and he did tinker with the rules regarding travel, but now they say that when you try to follow these rules, you get caught up in all kinds of forms and red tape. He eased the restrictions on remittances, so more money is making it back to the island, and that may have made the biggest difference so far. Boats with medical and other relief supplies have recently left Miami, sailing straight to the island, which hasn't happened in decades. These humanitarian shipments can, according to the *Miami Herald,* include pretty much anything a Cuban American family wants to send to its relatives: Barbie dolls, electronics, sugary cereal. In many cases, you have a situation in which the family is first wiring money over, then shipping the goods. The money is used on the other side to pay the various fees associated with getting the stuff. So it's as if you're reaching over and rebuying the merchandise for your relatives. The money, needless to say, goes to the government. Still, capitalism is making small inroads. And Raul has taken baby steps toward us: Cubans can own their own cars, operate their own businesses, own property. That's all new. For obvious reasons it's not an immediate possibility for a vast majority of the people, and it could be taken away tomorrow morning by decree, but it matters.

Otherwise, our attitude toward Cuba feels very wait and see, as what we're waiting to see grows less and less clear. We've learned to live with it, like when the doctor says, "What you have could kill you, but not before you die a natural death." Earlier this year Obama said to a Spanish newspaper: "No authoritarian regime will last forever. The day will come in which the Cuban people will be free." Not, notice, no dictator can live forever, but no "authoritarian regime." But how long can one last? Two hundred years?

Perhaps a second term will be different. All presidents, if they want to mess with our Cuban relations at even the microscopic level, find themselves up against the Florida community, and those are large, powerful, and arguably insane forces.

My wife's people got out in the early 1960s, so they've been in the States for half a century. Lax regulations, strict regulations. It's all a oneness. They take, I suppose, a Cuban view, that matters on the island are perpetually and in some way inherently screwed up and have been forever.

There was a moment in the taxi, a little nothing exchange but so densely underlayered with meaning that if you could pass it through an extracting machine, you would understand a lot about how it is between Cubans and Cuban Americans. The driver, a guy

who said he grew up in Havana, told a tiny lie, or a half lie. The
fact that you can't even say whether it was a lie or not is significant.
My wife had asked him to explain for me the way it works with
Cuba's two separate currencies, CUPs and CUCs, Cuban pesos and
convertible pesos (also called *chavitos* or simply dollars). When I
was last there, we didn't use either of these, though both existed.
We paid for everything in actual, green U.S. dollars. That's what
people wanted. There were stores in which you could pay in only
dollars. But in 2004, Castro decided—partly as a gesture of contempt for the U.S. embargo—that he would abolish the use of
U.S. dollars on the island and enforce the use of CUCs, pegged to
the U.S. dollar but distinct from it. This coexisted alongside the
original currency, which would remain pegged to the spirit of the
revolution. For obvious reasons, the actual Cuban peso is worth
much less than the other, dollar-equivalent Cuban peso, something on the order of 25 to 1. But the driver said simply, "No, they
are equal."

"Really?" my wife said. "No . . . that can't be."

He insisted that there was no difference between the relative
values of the currencies. They were the same.

He knew that this was wrong. He probably could have told you
the exchange rates from that morning. But he also knew that it
had a rightness in it. For official accounting purposes, the two currencies are considered equivalent. Their respective values might
fluctuate on a given day, of course, but it couldn't be said that the
CUP was *worth less* than the CUC. That's partly what he meant. He
also meant that if you're going to fly to Cuba from Miami and rub
it in my face that our money is worth one twenty-fifth of yours,
I'm gonna feed you some hilarious communist math and see how
you like it. Cubans call it *la doble moral.* Meaning, different situations call forth different ethical codes. He wasn't being decep-
tive. He was saying what my wife forced him to say. She had been
a bit breezy, it seemed, in mentioning the unevenness between
the currencies, which is the kind of absurdity her family would
laugh at affectionately in the kitchen. But they don't have to suffer it anymore. And he was partly reminding her of that, fencing
her off from a conversation in which Cubans would joke together
about the notion that the CUP and the CUC had even the slightest
connection to each other. That was for them, that laughter. So, a
very complex statement, that not-quite-lie. After it, he was totally

friendly and dropped us at one of the Cuban-owned tourist hotels on the edge of Havana.

People walking by on the street didn't seem as skinny. That was the most instantly perceptible difference, if you were seeing Raul's Cuba for the first time. They weren't sickly looking before, but under Fidel you noticed more the way men's shirts flapped about them and the knobbiness of women's knees. Now people were filling out their clothes. The island's overall dietary level had apparently gone up a tick. (One possible factor involved was an increase in the amount of food coming over from the United States. Unknown to most people, we do sell a lot of agricultural products to Cuba, second only in value to Brazil. Under a law that Bill Clinton squeaked through on his way out, Cuba purchases food and medicine from us on a cash basis, meaning, bizarrely, that a lot of the chicken in the *arroz con pollo* consumed on the island by Canadian tourists is raised in the Midwest—the embargo/blockade has always been messy when you lean in close.)

The idea was to spend some days traveling around, before going to see family. Once you see them, it gets emotional, and after that, sightseeing feels wrong somehow.

The ladies wanted to visit the Havana aquarium before it closed for the day—my wife went there when she was younger—so they took off. The hostility of the hotel workers was to be experienced. I started making up reasons to approach them, just to provoke it and make sure I hadn't imagined it. My reflex during an odd social interaction is to assume fault, and this can create its own distortion, making it hard to see what the other person is doing, but no, these people were being fantastically unfriendly. It was one of the big, newly built Gaviota hotels—Gaviota is the quasi-official Cuban tourist organization (financed in part by transnational investment but controlled by a prominent Cuban general). Loosely speaking, these men and women worked for the government. It's not that they were incompetent or mean; they just had zero motivation to be nice to tourists or in a hurry to do anything for them, and for me, after years immersed in a may-I-pour-you-more-sweet-tea culture, the contrast held a fascination. In a way it was refreshing to see people so emphatically not kowtowing to rich white tourists, even if that was you, but of course this feeling was not to be trusted: you liked their unfriendliness because they seemed more authentically anticapitalist that way. Especially wild was a woman about my age at the main reception desk, who evidently had to handle all the complaints about the *wee-fee* service in the lobby. She looked at you dead level and half-smiling when you approached as if in her mind she were already pushing in the blade. At the desk, they sold little scratch cards, with passwords on them, that looked like lottery tickets and in hindsight had much else in common with lottery tickets. But there were no cards that day. "They are in the city," she said—and in my mind I saw them being unloaded from small boats at night—"but we don't have them here." I was advised to try the hotel next door, a few minutes' walk—another, equally massive, equally generically pan-Latin-style Gaviota hotel. Would a card I bought there work here? "I hope so," she said, still doing that smile. "But," I said, "we made reservations at this hotel specifically because you advertised the *wee-fee* service." A total lie. We didn't need it. I wanted to see if she would crack. She shook her head so slowly with exaggeratedly sincere sorrow, like a long-suffering teacher forced to tell her most obnoxious pupil he had failed. "I understand," she murmured, and went back to work.

Partly what had been clashing were our respective ideas about the role of an individual in solving a crisis. In the United States, we all go around so empowered-feeling all the time, and when you travel you feel it, a sense of hypertrophy, the thing that makes us look like giant babies to the Europeans. Bring us our soda refills or we'll get them ourselves! The sheer notion that I thought she herself could *do* anything about the *wee-fee*, about getting the cards here faster, was probably genuinely amusing to her. Did I not think she wanted the *wee-fee* fixed? Did I think she actually liked standing there answering the exact same question from a never-ending line of childishly outraged foreigners?

At the neighboring hotel, they did have cards. But their *wee-fee* was down. "It's not working?" I asked the man. "It's working," he said, "but not right now." The whole island's Internet runs through three unpredictable satellites, although I had read that a cable of some kind was recently installed. If so, it did not get routed to these hotels. Which was lucky in the end—it accelerated the technological molting that had to happen and left you feeling more present. In the basement, near the business center (where a woman took delight in telling travelers from all lands that they could not do various simple-sounding things on the computer consoles), I noticed a small postcard that showed a picture of Fidel, and the caption read in Spanish, "In the history of U.S. intelligence, no greater amount of money and resources have been put toward bringing down a single man than have been spent to get Fidel." And below that, *"El mérito es estar vivo."* Roughly, "The victory lies in staying alive."

I kept seeing small groups of Asian men get on and off the elevators. That was new. Ten years ago the only Asian faces you might have seen were in Chinatown—there is one in Havana, Barrio Chino, several square blocks of ostensibly Chinese restaurants and faded signs with lanterns and pagodas on them, a neighborhood left behind by thousands of Chinese agricultural workers who arrived in the 19th century, and where very occasionally you might still see Asian features. These guys—all men, I saw no women—seemed dressed as inconspicuously as possible, loose-fitting light blue jeans and generic polo shirts and sunglasses. The bartender told me that they were here to do business. China was doing *"bastante de negocios"* in Cuba these days, including in oil, he said. At that moment a Chinese-made exploratory rig sat about 30 miles off the northern coast. We would be able to see it, he said, driving along the main highway. Cuba has lately been partnering with foreign petroleum companies to explore prospective undersea oil fields. A major discovery would be a main line to economic independence, that most long-elusive goal of the revolution. So far, though, the wells have come up dry or disappointing.

Cuba's involvement with China has been intensifying for more than a decade, as Russian influence has receded. The Chinese have built an amusement park and sold fleets of buses. They have been granted use—if our intelligence can be trusted—of a large signals-intelligence base on the outskirts of Havana near the airport, a giant electronic ear horn right off our shores, the price we pay for renouncing any involvement with a country so close. There is the sheer geopolitical weirdness of Guantánamo's being there, too: the Chinese and the Americans operating on the same island, off the coast of Florida. Guantánamo was supposed to be gone. It's holding on like the Castros.

The empty midafternoon lobby was vast and square-tiled and full of the drone of floor waxing, and the six-year-old spilled into it laughing, her mother racewalking behind her, trying to catch her. They saw me at the bar and ran over. "We have to show you this,"

the six-year-old said. She was pulling on my wife's purse. Mariana
pulled out her phone and pushed play on a movie, handing it to
me. At the aquarium, a little boy had celebrated his birthday, and
his parents had gone in for the dolphin special. You put the kid
on a raft and pushed it out into the pool. Shortly thereafter, one
of the aquarium's giant 500-pound dolphins started jumping over
the kid and raft, in great looping leaps, one after the other. The
splash was considerable. The kid looked terrified, he was face forward, clutching the raft at the edges. The repeating image of the
dolphin—frozen massive and pendulous directly above him—got
better every time. The audience laughed and clapped in the concrete bleachers; you could hear it on the video. My wife was laughing so hard she had tears in her eyes. "You wouldn't see that in the
States," she said proudly.

We scanned for the Chinese-built oil platform the next day, and
thought we saw something once, though it may have been a ship.
To ride along the coastal road with the windows down was sublime.
The gaps between houses kept giving you glimpses of the sea behind. There weren't many other cars, but the few that passed left
a heavy, organic smell of exhaust in the air. You could taste dino-
saurs in it. It carried that pre-catalytic-converter nostalgia. We were
driving down the spine of Cuba, into the vast green interior of the
island. Hitchhikers were scattered along the highway, as were people selling various things—garlic, strings of fish. They ran at you
as you passed, yelling and seeming to come too close to the car.

I woke up the next day to the sounds of morning pool activity. Water splashing on concrete. Insistent, unfamiliar bird song.
Sleepy murmurs of people rubbing lotion on themselves. Hotel
carts rattled by outside the double glass doors. It was about 8 A.M.
in Varadero on a warm spring day, which I'm pretty sure is literally
Utopia, in some vague historico-linguistic way: the northern shore
of Cuba, which supposedly moved Columbus to call this the most
beautiful place human eyes had ever seen. My wife has a thing
about going to Varadero when she goes to Cuba. I don't know if
she even likes it. She does it for her family. To them it would seem
insane to skip it—it was the place they most wanted to go when
they lived there—not to go, on returning, would be like taking a
trip to Keystone, South Dakota, and not going to see Mount Rush-
more.

Sitting up in my twin bed, I looked over at the queen bed—they were already gone. The massive cafeteria operation swung into motion for only a couple of hours each morning. You had to be there for the stampede. We were moving through different micro-Cubas so quickly; too quickly, really. The day before we rode horses through the jungle to see the ruins of ancient coffee plantations and the stone huts where the slaves were kept. We passed coopera-tive villages of *campesinos* in the forest and heard political speeches coming from loudspeakers, something about the new agriculture laws. The previous night, coming in on the suddenly pitch-black Cuban highways, zooming up to unlighted ROAD CLOSED signs at 60 miles an hour, swerving to miss car-killing potholes and horse-drawn wagons . . . that was already dreamlike. And now we were navigating the omelet and cereal stations, in lines of mainly Eu-ropean tourists: Germans, Italians, Central Europeans, and also Brazilians, Argentines, and Canadians. (You know when you're meeting a Canadian, because they always ask, in the same shocked tone, "How did you get into the country?" It's an opportunity to re-mind you that you can't go legally, and they can. And by extension, that they come from a more enlightened land. "You need to grow up about that stuff," one guy that I met at a nature preserve said, to which I wanted to tell him to get a large and powerful popula-tion of Cuban exiles and move them into an election-determining province of Canada and call me in the morning.)

The cook at the omelet station, when he asked where I was from and I told him, put up his fists like a boxer, as if we were about to have it out, then started laughing. He told me that he had family in the United States, in Florida. That's what everyone says. You can't understand the transnationally dysfunctional, mutually implicated relationship between Cuba and Miami, which defies all embargoes and policies of "definitive abandonment," until you realize that the line often cuts through families, almost always, in fact. People make all sorts of inner adjustments. I told the man I hated the embargo (the blockade, as they call it) and thought it was stupid, which was both true and what he wanted to hear. He gave me a manly clap-grasp. I didn't go on and say, of course, that I disliked the embargo most because it, more than anything, has kept the Castros in power for half a century, given them a ready-made Goliath for their David. Thanks to the embargo, when the Castros rail against us as an imperialist enemy, they aren't re-

ally lying. We have in effect declared ourselves the enemy of the
Cuban people and done it under the banner of their freedom,
hitting Cuba in a way that, after all, makes only the people suffer
and, far from punishing those in power, rewards them and but-
tresses their story. As for the argument that to deal with tyrants
would render our foreign policy incoherent, we deal with worse
every day—we've *armed* worse—and in countries that don't have
a deeply intimate history with ours, going back centuries. All this
because a relatively small but highly mobilized exile community
holds sway in a state that has the power to elect presidents. There
was no way to gauge how much of this the man would agree with.
We left it at mutually thinking the embargo sucked.

Out by the pool, where my wife and daughter were swimming,
I lay on a chaise in the shade, feeling paler and softer than I ever
had in my life and unlocatably depressed in the way that resorts do
so well. I read *Doctor Zhivago*, a new translation by Richard Pevear
and Larissa Volokhonsky (the husband-and-wife team who have
been retranslating the Russian classics for more than 20 years).
Zhivago isn't on the Tolstoy/Chekhov level, but there are wonderful passages, including one that I thought spoke to the gruffness
you often encounter in Cubans, the excessive suspicion of intro-
ductory small talk they sometimes demonstrate. "The fear known
as spymania," Pasternak wrote about Russia after the revolution,
"had reduced all speech to a single formal, predictable pattern.
The display of good intentions in discourse was not conducive to
conversation."

Every time I looked up from the book, there were more people
in and by the pool, as if they were surfacing out of the water, out
of the ripples. I had black sunglasses on, so after a while I propped
myself at an angle at which I could seem to read the book but really be moving my eyeballs, staring at everybody. God, the human
body! It was Speedos and bikinis, no matter the age or body type.
You would never see a poolside scene in the United States with
people showing this much skin, except at a pool where people
were there precisely to show off the perfection of their bodies. The
body not consciously sculptured through working out has become
a secret shame and grotesquery in America, but this upper-class
Euro-Latin crowd had not received that news, to my distraction.
I took in veins and cellulite, paunches and man-paps, the weird
shinglelike sagging that starts to occur on the back of the thighs,

cleavage that showed a spoiled-grape-like wrinkling, the ash-mot-
tled skin of permanently sun-torched shoulders, all of it beautiful.
All of it beautiful and tormenting. You watched an 18-year-old Ar-
gentine girl in her reproductive springtime walk past an ancient
Soviet-looking woman, her body a sculpture of blocks atop blocks,
and both of them wearing black bikinis, the furtive looks they gave
each other, full of emotions straight from the Pliocene, from the
savanna. The old men scowled from behind mirrored shades. The
young men tensed every muscle in order to seem not obsessed
with how the girls saw them, a level of self-consciousness I found
I could no longer really reenter, as if it had been a drunken state.
Everybody was stealing looks at one another, envying or disdaining
or gazing, like me. We were all inside a matrix of lust and erotic
sadness, all turning into versions of one another, or seeing our
past selves.

My wife's people come from a small town with a strange name, a
rare Spanish word that almost doesn't look Spanish when you see
it. When they lived there, the place was not considered all that far
from things, from the cities, but the decay of infrastructure, the
collapse of the trains, has left it stranded. There's simply no reason
to have heard of it.

The first time I went, before we were married, they made a big
thing of me. Yankees almost never appear in this town, unless they
are lost. I walked into a stuccoed, leafy house on a quiet street,
a house full of loud talking, hands grabbing my arms. Everyone
kissed and cried over my wife, whom they hadn't seen since she
was a teenager. They nicknamed me "Wao," because everything
they would tell me, I would say, "Wow." It seemed the appropri-
ate response. Wei-Wei, the *abuelita,* had come with us, or rather
we had gone with her—it ended up being probably the last time
she would ever go back—and she sent money ahead of our visit,
for them to buy food with. She's always sending money, but this
time she sent more, and they laid in pork and all the spices they
needed. There was a long table. All of the men were named some
version of Rafael, Rafaelito, Rafaelín. The matriarch, a shy and
tiny woman named Haydee (*eye-day*), presided with birdlike hands,
making little apologies. You didn't even have to chew the pork;
you could just sort of let it melt. They made *chicharrones de viento,*
"wind-crackers," the Cubans' witty name for a kind of poverty-in-

spired something, frisked up out of salt and flour and a little lard.
There was a bottle of Havana Club on the table—the first time I
ever saw or tasted it. Knowing only a little classroom Spanish, I
struggled to follow their phrases, the swift and expressive but mud-
mouthed Spanish spoken on the island.

After dinner, I made the mistake of saying something about a
cigar. It wasn't as if I asked for one. I probably said something
like, "I hear that your country is famous for its cigars." But they
took this as an overpolite way of asking for one, so the hunt began. The shops were closed, but the Rafaels started working on
the car. You've heard, no doubt, how in Cuba they still drive working American cars from the 1950s, but this was something else,
a Frankenstein made from the parts of about four different cars
from the '50s and one Russian car apparently from the '70s. They
got this creature going, and we started moving through the streets.
No headlights—one of them held an electric lantern out the window. It was wired to the cigarette lighter. We needed it badly.
Within a mile of leaving the town, we were in the face-close darkness of unlighted rural roads. They took me to a kind of kiosk, an
open bar in the middle of a field. I don't know what it was, really.
A kind of club. All of the men, about seven of them, were workers in the tobacco fields. They would smuggle out a cigar or two
each week, maybe defective ones, for personal use or the chance
to trade it away. Rafaelito told me, "This is the *puro puro.*"

Back at the house, half the neighborhood gathered to watch me
huff on this thing, many, I slowly realized, hoping to see me vomit. I
stood outside on a back patio, amid chicken coops. The cigar went
to my head like thunder. My knees became untrustworthy. But no
throwing up. Rafaelito had too much to drink and danced like a
crazy person. As a boy, he lost his only brother, drowned in the river.
His father, Rafael, approached me with a wagging finger, asking me
if I liked the country. Of course, I said, *bonita, linda y la gente.*

"*Sí.*" He looked a little bit like a Cuban Groucho Marx. "*Sí, te
gusta el país,*" he said. "*Pero, te gusta el sistema?*" He pulled the syl-
lables of *el sistema* out of his mouth like draws of taffy.

Now they were all gone, all the Rafaels. The two older ones
were dead from disease, and the youngest one had gone to Miami, I don't even know how. There is a kind of lottery, apparently.
Perhaps he won it. He's working as a mechanic. The house was
completely different. The ground floor was empty and quiet.

Haydee, the old woman of the house, was still there, even more ancient but seemingly unchanged. I saw her do the same thing now to the six-year-old that she did to my wife those years ago, wrap her arms around the girl and sort of refuse to leave, the way a child would. "I'm keeping her here," she said. "You, go back."

Her husband and son were gone, her grandson gone to Miami. Her other grandson, Erik, half brother of the boy who left, was still around. In fact, he was thriving. He had started a little furniture business. He was living in the house with his wife and daughter, and all had been going well. But just months before, they lost a son, an infant, to a respiratory disease. So within a short span of years, he lost his father, grandfather, and his brother (to emigration), and now his son. He was the only male in the house.

Erik's daughter, a young girl with glasses and reddish-brown hair, was as shy as her grandmother. She stayed on the edges of whatever room we were in. My daughter was at my feet, peeking through my legs at her. I could feel their intense awareness of each other, but neither would approach.

After lunch, while Erik was explaining different aspects of the furniture operation to me, my six-year-old came up and started tugging on my shirt. She was mouthing something at me. I kept saying, "Please don't interrupt, sweetheart." She said, "Give me your phone!" I excused myself from Erik for a second to give her a little lecture. I knew she was bored, I said, but this was an important day, and she needed to use her manners, not play with the phone. "Give me the phone!" she said, and ran off in a huff when I refused.

Barely 20 minutes later we went back upstairs and passed by the little girl's room. She and the six-year-old were sitting on the bed, playing on a phone. It was my wife's. The six-year-old had taught her cousin to play Angry Birds. They were smiling and leaning on each other. For the next two days they were completely inseparable and wanted to sleep in the same room. They communicated through my wife when they really needed to work something out. They will probably know each other for the rest of their lives now, because of that game.

We went out walking the streets, making the rounds to see other family members—to the old church, with its brightly painted statue of Saint Julian, where Wei-Wei was married and where they remembered her, *"la maestra,"* past the school where she taught and the corner store her father owned, where first she and then her children, my mother-in-law and her brother, grew up playing, before it was taken away—and as we strolled, I had a diminished, doubtless much-flawed version of the old woman's cake-box map in my head. I was hearing her voice-over, all the stories she told me over almost 20 years now, some of them repetitive, but with details emerging and receding.

Her memories of the revolution begin with the shortwave radio, kept in the backroom by her husband. Wei-Wei and her husband would gather with friends to listen to the transmissions that the Castro brothers and Che and Camilo Cienfuegos (the best loved of the young *comandantes,* at least by my wife's family, worshiped as a pop star by my mother-in-law, then 11) were broadcasting from the mountains, giving assurance that they were about to ride down and liberate the island. For years I assumed that the family had been listening to these speeches in fear—as a couple, they were about as solidly middle-class as could be, a teacher and a tobacco salesman, and their later experience of the revolution involved only pain and regret—but the *abuelita* surprised me one night, at the table, by saying that, on the contrary, they heard those speeches with great excitement. No one liked Batista, no one who wasn't directly benefiting from his thuggery and favoritism. The powerful charisma of the freedom fighters had percolated down into even quiet, apolitical homes.

There was a night back home, after a long meal, when for the first time after knowing her for so long, I got a bit pushy with her—asked her follow-up questions instead of just mm-hmm-ing—and she gave me a description of what it had actually been like to watch this optimism turn to fear, and something worse, what that had actually *looked* like. When the *milicianos* first came from the mountains, she said, "they come to say hello with this necklace made of pieces of wood and a gold cross." They mugged for the cameras with these crosses in their teeth. I asked why. "For you to look at. To pretend that they are Christian. That they believe in God.

"Everybody cooperate with Fidel," she said. "Everybody was happy that we had the opportunity to have all the freedom that he promise." She taught adult literacy classes at night.

Change came with the arrival of the *comites,* one house per block, appointed as the government representative for its house-holds. The rapidity with which that degenerated into spying and becoming complicit in spying had been breathtaking to watch play out in stark anthropological terms. Within months, they were tak-ing children aside at school and asking them about their parents. The parents started pulling the children out. The first nonpoliti-cal families started to flee. People betrayed their neighbors to the *comites.* A woman who lived in the neighborhood, a woman named Solita, "somebody accuse her of having fried pork in her house. And they make—she was a teacher—they make a public, *¿come se llama?, juicio?*" Trial. "Exactly. Accusing her of having pork."

My wife's grandfather had let it be known that he was against the Castros—not because he had preferred Batista; in fact, the family had some obscure connection, that I've never been able to get anyone to be forthcoming about, to one of the other revolu-tionaries in the mountains, a rival who was executed not long after the uprising—in any case it was known that the family's sympathies did not lie with the communists. "I remember one time we going to the farm," she said, "and when we was coming back, we stop in Mario's grandmother's house, and we saw my brother passing on the road very fast. We get scared. We say, 'What happened?' He says, 'The police is going to ask for, getting into your house.' And at this time we was already saving some American money to come here. And you believe or not? The first thing that I do in the house was burning the dollars. To be sure that they don't find it out."

The party came and took away the family business. They took the store. They took the car, covered in tobacco advertisements. They took "a house of birds." Not yours anymore. They took a little dog, named Mocha. They took pictures off the wall. They came in and counted the number of pictures, and took a certain percentage of them. Absurd things. They took away the family's tiny beach house in Playa del Rosario, "gave it to some fishman." But this succession of losses came to seem indistinct against what was happening outside. The picture had darkened. "So bad, so cruel all the things that they do it," she said. "The television was on all day long." She meant both that they were watching all day long and that the revolutionaries were transmitting constantly. There was "a man that the name Blanco," she said. And his trial concerned "if he abuse the farmers, if he do all these things that accuse him to do it." They found him guilty. "Then the people go to the street, singing, *'Paredon paredon paredon!' Paredon* means 'kill in front of the wall.' And then they put this in television. And you see the brain of this man jumping out. It was getting gross and gross and gross." She resigned her job, and they essentially went into hiding.

She got her two children out first, my mother-in-law and her brother, on waivers made possible by the CIA-initiated, Catholic-sponsored airlift known as Pedro Pan. The story goes that the CIA started spreading rumors on the island that the government was about to take away the children, raise them in camps. People panicked, and the planes were waiting to fly them away. The children wound up living with Catholic families all over the United States or, in this case, with an aunt in North Carolina. Eventually Wei-Wei and her husband got out, through Mexico, and joined the children. But Pedro Pan tore apart many families.

We arrived at the house of some cousins, two twins, small men now in their 50s, one with a mustache and one without, who live with their mother, whom they tend to hover about protectively. Their father died after having walked himself to the hospital, after a heart attack. Nobody had a car, nobody's phone worked. The revolution is famous around the world for its health care, but for a Cuban, that care can be hard to access, especially if you live far from one of the major cities.

The six-year-old and her cousin were sitting on the sofa, ignoring everyone. They were holding up dolls to each other in different poses, sort of: "What do you think of this? Do you approve of this?" We unloaded the presents we brought for the twins. They handed my wife a book of socialist Cuban film reviews from before the revolution, actually a rare and useful book—one of them is a from-home bookseller, and he had come across it somewhere.

As we were standing around he said, "Did you know that my brother"—the one with no mustache—"was on a game show?"

They brought forth a VHS tape and started reconfiguring the wires to make the VCR work. Soon a picture of the studio appeared, three contestants behind their buzzers. The tape had been recorded over many times. There was a constant flickering of white meteors across the image. Felipe to the far left, smiling, looking confident in a light green short-sleeved shirt. The game had to do with rhyming. They would say, "Two words: one of them describes a fruit, one describes a family member." Answer: *lima* and *prima.* Felipe didn't win, but did well enough, as I understood it, to be invited back. He looked onscreen like he was having a great time. The show had a carefree attitude, compared with something similar in the United States. The stakes were very low. You can't have games of chance or leisure games involving any amount of money, they said. It was outlawed by the revolution, as part of the purifying backlash against the mob-led casino power. So the prizes were things like a signed poster of a famous Spanish pop singer or a decorative mirror. Nobody was going to cry over losing. We congratulated Felipe on having held his own. He brought out the small metal lamp-sculpture he won.

Before we left the country, we spent a last day and night in Havana. Heaven weather. We stepped into the grand cathedral, on one of the main squares in the old part of town, and listened to a women's choir that was practicing for the pope. I saw blue-and-red signs announcing his impending visit, VIENE EL PAPA! The women and girls were dressed in their everyday clothes. They sang beautifully. I'm sure that they were the best that Cuba had.

In the evening, we stood on the Morro, the Spanish castillo across the bay from the Malecón, and looked at the city. There is a Havana—this was the second time I saw it, a confirmation—that cannot be captured in photographs, because it involves a totality of light from symphonic Caribbean clouds and the way they play on the whole city, and that appears often enough to represent one of the characteristic faces of the city. The diffused light turns all the buildings a range of pastels. Then as the sun reddens, it becomes rose-colored.

It was 9:30 by the time we got back to our hotel. Normally that would have been past the six-year-old's bedtime, but my wife had a telephone interview—meant to happen during the day, it got bumped—so she needed us out of the room for an hour.

Downstairs we sat and listened to the band do the inescapable (in Havana) "Hasta Siempre, Comandante," with its strange lyrics, "Here lies the clear/the precious transparency/of your dear presence/Comandante Che Guevara." Cats were slinking around. The people going by were of every shade, and many with striking faces. In the most Spanish faces you could see flashes of the Old World stock that supplied the island with settlers: the equine noses, the

long mouths, at times a Middle Eastern cast, features I knew from
my wife's family pictures.

On the sidewalk a young bicycle-taxi driver named Manuel approached us, a well-built kid in jean shorts and a tank top, about
19. He said he knew an ice cream place that was still open. We set
out through the night. Many of the streets were dark. It was chilly
already, and the six-year-old huddled against my side. It was one
of those moments when you know that you are where you're supposed to be. If your destiny wavered, it has at least momentarily
recovered its track. We ate our chocolate ice cream at an outdoor
bar, under a half-moon.

On the way back to the hotel, Manuel asked what I did. When I
told him I was a reporter, he said: "You'd hate it here. There is no
freedom of expression here."

He launched into a tirade against the regime. "It is basically a
prison," he said. "Everyone is afraid."

The things he said, which I had heard many times before—that
you can go to prison for nothing, that there's no opportunity, that
people are terrified to speak out—are the reason I can never quite
get with my leftie-most friends on Cuba, when they want to make
excuses for the regime. It's simply a fact that nearly every Cuban
I've ever come to know beyond a passing acquaintance, everyone
not involved with the party, will turn to you at some point and say
something along the lines of, "It is a prison here." I just heard it
from one of the men who worked for Erik, back in the hometown.
I remarked to him that storefronts on the streets looked a little bit
better, more freshly painted. It was a shallow, small-talky observation.

"No," he said, turning his head and exhaling smoke.

"You mean things haven't improved?" I said.

"There is no future," he said. "We are lost."

The six-year-old kept asking me what Manuel was saying. I was
doing my best to describe *el sistema*. Interesting trying to explain
to a child educated in a Quaker Montessori school what could possibly be wrong with everyone sharing.

We passed the museum with the *Granma*, the leisure boat that
in 1956 carried Fidel and Raul and Che and Camilo Cienfuegos
and 78 other Cuban revolutionaries from Mexico to a beach on
the island's southeast coast. The cruiser was all lighted up with

aquamarine lights, in a building made of glass. It looked underwater. Manuel stopped the bicycle-taxi and gazed on it with obvious pride.

"There's always an armed guard in front of it," he said, nodding his head toward a young man in a green uniform, who was standing with a machine gun over his shoulder.

"They're worried that someone will try to blow it up or something?" I said.

"They're worried that someone will steal it and go to Miami," he said.

There was a time Mariana took me to Cuba, and we went to a town called Remedios, in the central part of the island. It is one of the most ancient Cuban cities. The church on the main square dates from the Renaissance. When it was restored in the 1950s, the workers discovered that under the white paint on the high ceiling was a layer of pure gold. The townspeople had safeguarded it from the pirates in that manner. We stayed in the home of a man named Piloto. A friendly bicycle-taxi driver, who introduced himself as Max, told us that Piloto worked for the government and rented out his spare room only in order to spy on tourists, and that we should be careful what we said there. But all we ever got from Piloto and his wife was a nearly silent politeness and one night a superb lobster dinner. My most vivid memory of Remedios is of being taken to the house of an artist who lived there, a woodcarver. The bicycle-taxi driver told us that anyone who had "a great interest in culture" needed to visit the home of this particular artist. The next day he took us there, in the afternoon. We rode behind a row of houses that had strange paintings and animal figures hanging in their breezeways. After what seemed a long time for a bicycle-taxi ride, we arrived at the woman's place. Taking out a cigarette, Max told us to walk ahead, he would wait. At the door of a small, salmon-colored house, an old woman met us. Not the artist, it emerged. This was the artist's mother. We sat with her in a kind of narrow front parlor, where she made sweetly formal small talk for maybe 20 minutes, telling us every so often that the artist would be out soon.

At a certain moment, a woman appeared in the passageway that led from the front room into the main part of the house, a woman with rolls of fat on her limbs, like a baby, and skin covered in moles. She walked on crutches with braces on her knees. She had a beautiful natural Afro with a scarf tied around it. She was simply a visually magnificent human being. She told us the prices of her works, and we bought a little chicken carving. She said almost nothing otherwise—she had difficulty speaking—but when we stood up to leave, she lifted a hand and spoke, or rather delivered, this sentence. It was evidently the message among all others that she deemed most essential for U.S. visitors. "I know that at present there are great differences between our peoples," she said, "but in the future all will be well, because we are all the sons and daughters of Abraham Lincoln."

The Bull Passes Through

FROM *The Morning News*

DAN IS IN, Brian is out, and I suppose I am 51 percent in and 49 percent out. I am going with Dan into a walled-off, maybe 25-foot-wide street. People above us, in positions of safety, gaze down with looks of concern.

"Give me your stuff," Brian says, and Dan and I empty our pockets and hand him our sunglasses.

I keep my credit card, my driver's license, 50 euros cash, and my insurance card in the buttoned back pocket of my white linen pants. We shake hands and he pats us on the back. We don't try to convince him to reconsider because this is not the kind of thing you can fault someone for skipping. And if we convince him to do it and he gets hurt, we have to pay a doctor to fix him and a therapist to fix us.

"See you outside the stadium at the ticket window," I say, and turn and walk into one of the more famously dangerous places to be on July 7 every year.

The faces of people down here with us tell a story much more pertinent to my situation. Some look fast, well prepared, dressed almost exclusively in white with red accessories—neckerchiefs and shawls in San Fermín tradition. Some look drunk, like they haven't been to bed since this 204-hour party started 19 hours ago; many of them will be thrown out of the route by the *policía* before 8 A.M. We fall somewhere between. We are not drunk, but our white clothes are soaked in red sangria from the opening ceremonies. We went to bed early, but did not sleep well and do not feel well. If we were still 22 we'd be drunk.

Dan is very fast. I think I am probably faster than most of the people down here. But after speaking to people in this town for the past 36 hours, I've gathered speed doesn't much matter. This is not a race. No one is PR-ing today. No one is qualifying for Boston. Speed doesn't much matter because something like a dozen bulls are being released at the sound of a rocket, and they are going to catch whomever they want.

We walked the course the night we arrived in Pamplona. We are now on Day 12 of a 13-day, mostly sleepless trip to Italy and Spain. It is 7:15 A.M. on Saturday, July 7—the first day of the Running of the Bulls. Because it is the first day and it falls on a weekend this year, the route is crowded with spectators and runners. We fly home to Chicago tomorrow from Madrid, assuming there are no overnight hospital stays.

In 45 minutes, those bulls, weighing something like a thousand pounds each, are going to come charging after me and every other person on this cobblestone road who feel the need to put their life in arbitrary danger. Until then it is going to be a long wait, and I imagine an even longer five-minute run down this 848-meter stretch of narrow, enclosed road that more closely resembles the sidewalks and alleys I'm used to in the United States. This is particularly scary for me because before Thursday night, the biggest bull I'd ever seen was Bill Wennington.

It's a fact: people are going to get hurt. It happens every year. People are gored, thrown, trampled by humans, trampled by bulls. Sometimes people die, though no one has been killed running since 1995, according to Dan.* People down here with Dan and me are hugging, saying good luck in Spanish and English and Aussie English, trying to stay positive with each other, but looking at friends with faces that say something serious. According to the locals I've spoken to, most of the people who get hurt are foreigners—most of them don't know what to do.

"One last thing," I say to Dan. "Let's agree that neither of us should feel pressured to do this just because the other is. This is an individual choice. Neither of us hassled Brian and for good reason. Don't feel like you have to be here because I'm here, and

---

* Research shows Dan is not a reputable source. People have died as recently as 2009.

I'm not going to feel like I have to because you're here. We still have time to get the hell out."

Dan nods his head. I honestly don't think he has reconsidered this since we booked our trip two months ago. If he is scared, it isn't showing.

"I'm doing it," he says. "I'm here. I'm doing it. I have to."

For the last few months, I legitimized running with the bulls by telling people I played soccer in high school and am generally faster than most people. One hundred percent of the people I said this to laughed. Somehow they knew already that speed is going to be as valid as spandex on a bike 'n' brew.

A television camera is panning across our faces as we speak. I try to hide the worry. I think about my mom. I think about my family together at our cabin in the Wisconsin Northwoods, fishing, skiing, playing the Rolling Stones, safe, worried. I sat up all night in our hotel room while Dan and Brian slept last night, all of us in the same bed, and I still can't tell if I'm doing this as one last adventure before I make a serious attempt at settling down or if I'm doing this because this is what I'm turning into: a true model of self-destruction.

"In situations like this," I say, "I always get the feeling that if someone is going to get hurt, it's going to be me."

"Why's that?" Dan asks.

"I suppose because I'm always the one who gets hurt."

We've done some stupid things on this trip. In Cinque Terre we jumped off rocks into the sea at two in the morning after watching Italy beat Germany in the Euro semifinals. In Barcelona, I got robbed on the way back to our apartment at four in the morning, and we all got molested by prostitutes afterward.

We came to Pamplona on a bus Thursday and went to a bullfight. I don't agree with Hemingway. I don't know much about bullfighting, and maybe it was different in 1923, but from what I witnessed Thursday night, I think matadors are bedazzled cowards. They stack the deck like a Vegas house stacks slot odds. It is a spectacle of disingenuous sacrifice driven by tradition and profit. The bull is half-dead, tired, maimed, and there against its will. The matador is armed, which I suppose is understandable when facing a bull, but there's also a group of other matadors ready to jump in and divert the bull from a deadly attack.

But on this street right now, those advantages have flipped. We have numbers, but too many numbers—numbers that will force us into uncomfortable places we don't want to be where bulls are likely to find us. The locals told us this yesterday. One pretty Spanish girl and her grandmother spent an hour trying to talk us out of it. They, along with others back in Madrid, succeeded with Brian. The girl, Cindy, said at least 50 times in her Spanish accent, *Don't do eet,* and *Do not raan* a hundred. When I refused to give in, her grandmother, who didn't speak a word of English and hated Dan, just shook her head, grabbed my sticky, sangria-soaked cheeks with her wrinkled hands, and kissed me on the lips before she left. Before the trip, I had only gone up in age 3 years. Now I have gone up 50.

"If you could do it again, would you do anything differently?" Dan asks.

"Today or in life or on this trip?"

"Any."

I think for a quick moment about plenty of things that apply in my life and give a bland reply. "Nothing major. You?"

"I never would have gotten a dog with the ex," Dan says. "I loved that dog, but after our relationship ended, it caused us so many unnecessary problems. Don't get a dog before you get a ring."

I think about my ex as well and the things I would do differently now that might have put us on a different path, a path that wouldn't have me on a street this morning with bulls.

More people have gathered in from the bottom of the street, more people leave our area and walk farther up the road. And then a man passes out standing, angling forward without his knees buckling, and lands square on the side of his face on the street. The thud sounds like someone threw a 150-pound piece of clay from five stories up. People rush to him and call for a doctor. They turn him over. His face is covered in blood and he is unconscious. A doctor arrives and tries to wake him. Paramedics follow with a stretcher. We watch as they take him away. He will not be running with the bulls, but he will be among the injured.

We talk about our plan of action one last time. We remind each other to stay to the inside on the turns. We remind each other that the most important thing is to keep our center of gravity so we stay on our feet.

"If you lose a shoe, keep going," Dan says.

"Yeah, glass in your foot is better than being trampled—by people or bulls."

"If you fall, don't try to get up. Just cover your head and roll to the side."

"And if you see a bull on its own, try to get out."

This last point may be the most important in terms of living and dying. From what we've been told, bulls together are not as frightened as bulls alone. Bulls together tend to stay on a path, assuming they keep their footing. Frightened bulls directly charge people. If we see a bull alone, we will try to escape by climbing one of the wood fences. We climbed them yesterday. It can be done quick, but the problem now is there are so many spectators lining the street that you'd have the same success climbing them as jumping through the horizontal gaps between the beams.

"Sorry for calling you a douche in Madrid," Dan says.

"Thanks for calling me a douche in Madrid," I say. "I deserved it."

He laughs because he knows I deserved it, but I imagine he wants to clear the air in case I end up with a gore hole.

I wrote my mom an e-mail last night saying I was scared and I loved my family. I lay awake all night wondering if this was my last night of sleep—turns out that question made it impossible to sleep at all. I wondered if I would be injured to the point I wouldn't be able to have children. I thought about everything being different after today—different in a very bad way. But here I am. I know I'm being selfish. I know people are worried about me, and that comforts me, and that is selfish, too.

"I think," I say, "it's less about what I would do differently than what I want to do differently when this is over."

"How so?" Dan says.

"You know—living like this," I say, my hands open to my sangria-soaked shirt, and that's when it all comes out: "It has to end at some point. I want to try harder after this. Chill the fuck out some when we get home. I'm tired. I have been for a while. Maybe try to have a girlfriend again. Find a new job. You know—we've talked about this so many times and we just never do it."

"Yeah," he starts. "I realized that about my job when we were walking around Madrid the other day. I'm just not sure what to change that would change anything significantly. You have your writing, your book. You have something you're enthusiastic about. Me? I'm not sure."

A man comes by handing out newsletter-sized papers. From what I can make out, it is a benediction to the city's patron saint, Fermín. Fermín is the star of this show.

"See you in the stadium hopefully," I say.

"See you in the stadium," Dan says.

We smile and hug, pat each other on the back. We have done this man-hug thing a number of times in the last few years on a number of adventures, but never with such a feeling of potential harm.

The man finishes handing out the papers. People roll them up, raise them above their heads, and chant, Spanish followed by Basque:

A San Fermín pedimos, por ser nuestro patrón, nos guíe en el encierro dándonos su bendición.

Entzun arren San Fermín zu zaitugu patroi, zuzendu gure oinak entzierro hontan otoi.

VIVA SAN FERMÍN

GORA SAN FERMÍN

"There's no shame in pissing yourself in the next five minutes," a British man says behind me.

I laugh and turn.

"I was just thinking the exact same thing."

"Good luck, man," he says.

"Good—"

The rocket fires and the crowd erupts with the sound of carnage you'd expect when enemy sides charge each other, but only one of them carries weapons.

Everyone's first move is forward and two guys go down. No one knows what to do but nearly everyone is looking over their inside shoulder, shuffling their feet with uncertainty. A few people start to climb. A few others try to move forward and jam themselves under the wood fences that separate intelligence from stupidity.

People book it forward. Dan passes a few guys and I don't bother to follow him directly. A guy to my left goes down and I don't bother to look back over my outside shoulder to see if he is okay. There is no going back at any time.

I look over my inside shoulder to make sure the bulls aren't yet

coming, and then look forward to get my sense of direction on
the course figured out. I stop moving forward so quickly because I
don't want to get to the next turn in the position I currently have
in the crowd—I know I need to move right before the road goes
right—always be on the inside. The bulls come with such force,
I've been told, that they cannot turn the corners on the unforgiv-
ing cobblestone and often slip up. You do not want to be between
a sliding bull and a brick wall. But I am afraid to run across the
middle of the street. It is only a 10-foot space, but it is a 10-foot
space that will soon be occupied by the first pack of bulls.

I keep running forward—fuck—and I'm still on the left side
when the turn approaches.

Fuck I need to fucking get across.

I'm on the outside.

I look over my right shoulder, don't see any bulls but the volume is rising, and I sprint across, dodging people coming up the
middle, to the right where people are jammed along the wall. I
start to run past the crowd, then fight the first instinct to keep
passing them and jam myself into them. I throw myself into the
wall of other runners—five feet deep against the wall, moving forward slowly, but I don't get in. I think I am far enough over, but I
do not have anyone protecting me.

"Here they are!" someone yells from behind, and the faces I see
across the street look like faces I imagine in combat without any
cover. I don't see the bulls, but I know those guys do and I know
they are fucking close. I keep my back to the wall so if one comes
at me I can react as quickly as possible. But there is nowhere to
go. It is a mass of people within a mass of people within the mass
of people flooding this city. If a bull comes at me it will do what
it wants to me. I keep pushing myself on a diagonal—right and
forward—and hope the bulls take a wide turn and no one pushes
me out.

And then bulls are coming behind me, I push, I fucking push
three bulls across the front, I actually don't know how many total.

They look loud but the human noise overtakes theirs.

More bulls—fucking huge animals—in the back.

Everyone yells, people scream, duck their heads into their arms,
people dive out of the middle, people dive to my feet and scurry
forward, people dive right in front of the fucking bulls—they are
here, huge, huge bulls charging, here they are, just don't gore

me—throw me, break my arm, knock me down, just don't gore me.

The bulls come next to me, not at me, and their momentum carries them left, and they are the biggest mass of living matter I have ever seen, some black, some lighter brown. If they get scared, if something sets one of them off, it will try to kill me. There is nowhere to go. If one of them decides to charge this crowd, it could gore many. It could turn our white clothes much redder than the sangria. The horns look like they could go through me and whoever is behind me and maybe a third. Two feet to my side, a bull passes. I cringe and lock my legs. I could reach out—and it could reach in—

But it doesn't.

The bulls pass and people yell—people yell with a new sense of confidence and charge forward.

"Let's go!" someone yells.

Someone steps on my heel and my shoe nearly comes off, but I am able to reach down and fix it in stride.

We run with new hope, and I wonder if they know more will be coming. At first I was told there was one group of six, but yesterday I was told there would likely be three groups of several.

I move out of the pack and sprint for a few seconds, judging by the relative calm that I have a short period of time to cover ground before the next group comes, but I have no idea how long. I sprint—I fucking sprint like you can only sprint when you are sprinting from danger. I sprint with fucking *urgency,* and then move back to the right. I am in good position along a wall and am still moving. I feel safer than I have since I entered the road almost an hour ago, but the panic rushes right back in again when the volume climbs and I see three bulls over my left shoulder on the inside of the road.

Someone steps on my right heel. My shoe starts to come off. I grasp at it with my toes without diverting my attention and hobble forward in the crowd, keeping my weight right so no one can push me into the path of the bulls, my hands on the person in front of me. I hobble, shoe dangling, and watch the bulls pass—just don't gore me, I can handle the rest—I reach down and try to fix the shoe with my right hand, balance with my left—just fucking do it! I do it without falling.

I don't know if I will make it into the stadium at this pace. There

is one more set of bulls behind us—I don't know how many—and
I have no idea how far I've gone. Some people are yelling like all
the danger has passed, but I think there are more. People will try
to close the stadium gate when the third group is through. I have
to make a move.

I look over my inside shoulder and go.

I fucking go and see the long stretch of fence ahead of me on
the right that tells me we are close. I fucking go GO GO. I can see
it, I can see the stadium. I look over my shoulder and start turning
left with the road. I'm on the outside, but I know I'm okay because
the crowd is behind me. Then the volume rises and the middle of
the road clears. I go right naturally, I think I'm okay. I'm past the
turn and look over my left—it comes alone.

If you see one alone, escape.

I jump smack into the fence like Griffey and grab but don't go
over. I'm ready to climb in case it comes at me in this crowd—so
sparse compared to before—

I'm not going over.

If you see one alone, escape.

I'm going into that fucking stadium.

If you see one alone, escape.

I don't go over, I cringe, and it goes by.

It passes me and runs toward the stadium door and I don't know
if I should follow it but I do, I fucking sprint, I'm making it into
that stadium, that stadium is fucking mine. I pump my arms and
my legs, I pass people and pass people, I am making it into that
stadium—that fucking stadium is mine. I see one of the huge red
doors start to close and I sprint toward it. The gap of light inside is
closing, but the closer I get, the higher up in the stands I can see
oh my god a sea of white noise. I see people on the sides as the bull
passes through and is guided out the other end. There is a jam
of people at the closing door and I run right up to them. I keep
pushing forward and squeeze through the door and fucking sprint
into the tunnel. I gain speed and the stadium reveals itself—full of
screaming fans—everyone in white with their red neckerchiefs. I
feel the dirt below my feet so soft and forgiving and I am displac-
ing it all and I am in the Plaza de Toros, the motherfucking Plaza
de Toros de Pamplona. I start yelling as I run—I fucking scream
and let it out. I let it all out and it flows out of me like a release of
pressure that shouldn't build in a person. I scream and in the very

middle of the circle—I'm in a fucking bullfighting ring—I'm in the Plaza de Toros de Pamplona on July 7 and people are screaming for me and I am letting it all out, it's flowing from me. I stop in the middle and start jumping with the others. I jump and I scream and we chant and I jump, I fucking jump higher and higher and release it all. I know Dan is here with me. I can't see him but I know it. I raise my hands above my head and jump so I am facing different directions—all these people—all these people in white standing, waiting for me to get here, all these people—20,000, 25,000, a million—cheering me on.

I look up at them, they look down at me, and we let it out and release it—and it all makes sense—

This is why—

This is who I am, maybe it will change, maybe it—

Maybe there is a moderate amount of self-preservation revealed through a self-destructive—shut the fuck up and *jump!*

I'm connected to people I don't know. I jump I fucking jump. A part of a culture so foreign—immersion I've never known. Acceptance and capability—fucking whatever just jump! And I don't feel proud, I don't feel brave, and I don't feel manly or deserving or fortunate—just yell and jump and turn in the air and see the white, the cylindrical wall of white bodies enclosing me, centering me, thousands of white bodies building up and out above me in this stadium, this bullring—hear the volume and jump and yell and it flows back and forth, me to them and back again, and I feel—

I just feel—oh my oh my do I feel.

JUDY COPELAND

The Way I've Come

FROM *Legal Studies Forum*

ALONE ON THE grassy airstrip, I empty my backpack and kneel to sort my supplies for the climb up the mountain wall. I've landed in a tight little valley called Tekin, in Sandaun Province, whose massive ranges straddle Papua New Guinea's border with Indonesia. The plane, still droning faintly somewhere above the fog, will soon be gone. The grass is wet and cold under my knees.

As I sort, a crowd of men gather to watch me, murmuring in Pidgin, "Very fat woman!" and "Em fall down, true!" They are all very short, less than five feet tall, thin and wiry, wearing baseball caps and ragged T-shirts and scowling the same fierce scowls that startled me two weeks ago when I boarded the flight from Manila to Port Moresby and looked into the faces of the flight attendants. I've noticed that the expression doesn't necessarily signify anger. Some New Guineans continue to knit their brows even when they smile.

Luckily, some of the men speak English. When I ask them about the last backpacker to leave from Tekin, they aren't sure when he disappeared.

"A month ago," one says.

"No, a year," another shouts.

They talk about the ongoing police inquest, and debate what has become of him. Since people disappear all the time in the bush and there are lots of possible explanations, I don't really expect an answer. On one thing, however, the men agree: the backpacker was last seen quarreling with his guides over their pay; afterward, the guides returned to Tekin without him.

As I listen to the story, I wish I didn't have to hire a guide.

I've been a solo hiker for almost 40 years, ever since I was two. As an American missionary kid in Japan, I used to run away from home every few days just for the thrill of it. By the time I was three, my parents had grown used to policemen finding me and bringing me back. I remember clambering over our bamboo fence and whizzing through the college campus where my parents taught, heedless of which way I ran, nearly colliding with students with shaved heads and black uniforms, reaching the tall department stores of the business district 10 blocks away, then ducking into the mysterious maze of alleys behind them.

After we moved to the States when I was nine, I felt so frightened by all the warnings about kidnappers and child molesters that I stopped running away. It wasn't until I grew up and began backpacking alone in the North American wilderness that I reclaimed some of that old joy of running loose. Yet, two months ago, still haunted by a vague yearning for something lost, something missing from my life as an American lawyer, I quit my job and began island-hopping through Southeast Asia, an adventure that has brought me to Sandaun Province.

What I haven't reckoned on is the terrain. This morning, sitting next to an Australian missionary pilot in a little six-seater Cessna, I looked down and saw the Highland trails meander through wide valleys and over rolling hills until they vanished in the needle-sharp peaks that form the long spine of Papua New Guinea. We climbed up into the clouds, then swooped below them again, through passes so narrow I could almost reach out and graze my fingers along fern-covered mountainsides. From a small plane, you can see every thatched hut, every outhouse, every pathway leading to it. Here and there, peering into gaps too tight even for the Cessna, I glimpsed a deep, sunless valley. At the bottom a dim clump of little huts lay trapped, like children who'd fallen down an abandoned well.

I shouted to the pilot, Nigel, "Do the people in those valleys ever get over to the next valley to visit their neighbors?"

"No," he yelled above the roar of the engine, "they live and die on that spot."

Unlike other expatriates I'd met, Nigel didn't question my plans, just my choice of the word *walk* to describe them. "Have a look down there! Do you see anywhere to walk? Do you see any trails? You don't *walk* in Sandaun. You skid on your butt. You throw up. It takes hours to slog up one little hill, and the slogging makes you sick to your stomach. Not to mention the sinkholes. Some mountains are so close that the bush on either side grows together and hides the gaps between them. People have stepped into those sinkholes and disappeared without a trace."

Then the nose of the Cessna dropped abruptly, zeroing in on Tekin, and we dived into the fog. Amazed he could land blind in such a narrow valley, I said it just didn't seem possible.

"True," Nigel mused as we tilted into a curve, "according to the laws of science, it *isn't* possible. An airplane isn't supposed to be able to do this." He turned to beam at me: "If it weren't for the Lord, we'd probably crash."

I searched his face to see if he was joking, but he wasn't. I stared at Nigel, at the neatly ironed pilot's shirt-and-shorts with matching khaki knee-highs, at the ears jutting out at right angles from his head, and the long-toothed Bobby Kennedy grin. To look at him, I would have taken him for a scientist of some sort—a surveyor, perhaps, sent to ink in the last blank valleys on a map hanging on the solid wall of a cartographic institute—an avatar of rationality, anything but a loony who thought the Lord could hold an airplane in the sky. I knew his words were meant to cheer me, but for the first time since coming to New Guinea, I felt a shiver of real fear.

Once on the ground, I sort my supplies into two piles: things to haul up the mountainside and things to leave behind. Other than a short, unpaved motor road leading to the village of Kweptana, there's nowhere to walk out of Tekin but straight up, nothing but steep mountain walls on all sides. Nevertheless, considering that I could as easily die from flying as from climbing, I choose the mode of travel less dependent on the Lord. My climbing supplies, at least, are under my control.

My gear in tow, I wave goodbye to the men at the airstrip and head up the dirt road. Nigel suggested a climb he'd done himself—over a mountain to a village called Bimin—and he said I would need a guide for the steepest part. At least I can walk alone as far as Kweptana, and en route, I can overnight at a vacant mission house, to which Nigel has lent me a key.

The road meanders upward through well-kept gardens, high-canopied forests, and swirling mists. When occasionally I meet people walking toward Tekin, they shake my hand warmly and advise me I'm too fat to make it to Bimin, which I find oddly reassuring. Since nobody expects me to reach Bimin anyway, I reason, there'll be no shame in turning around if I lose my nerve. I smile and thank the people and walk on.

After several hours, I spot the mission house, its corrugated-iron roof shimmering like a silver spider web in the last rays of the sun. It's a steep climb down from the road, a scramble over several fences of sharp stakes built to keep pigs out of people's sweet potatoes. You can't walk anywhere in Papua New Guinea without risking impalement.

A few paces short of the padlocked door, darkness falls. Fumbling through all eight pockets of my safari suit, I chide myself for forgetting that there is no dusk on the equator—no grace period with kindly librarians announcing, "We will close in fifteen minutes," while you gather up your scattered papers. Here the lights get cut off without warning, and you'd better know where you put your flashlight and your key.

Once inside, I flick around the weak beam of my flashlight to reveal a woodstove, a rough-hewn table, cabinets, six drawers. I set about ransacking the drawers for a candle.

There's a knock at the door, and I hope it will be the caretaker, come to help me find things. Instead, it's an old peddler. Eyeing me from beneath the visor of his baseball cap, he holds out a peculiar object: a yard-long stick with a sharp-edged stone disk fastened to one end. When I ask what it is, he says in Pidgin, "An instrument for killing people." I tell him I don't think I'll be needing one.

The weapon doesn't surprise me. Until their conversion to Christianity about 10 years ago, some of the peoples of Sandaun practiced warfare and some were cannibals, so it stands to reason that they might have old weapons they want to sell. Still, after the peddler leaves and I crawl into my sleeping bag, I can't help wondering what a bumble-footed woman like me, a woman terrified of heights, is doing here. I can't help wondering if I've come to the wrong place. If I've once more lost the red line.

I left America, odd as it may seem, because of something I saw in a dream—a map of the world with a red line, like the ones in-flight magazines use to indicate air routes, advancing slowly across the Pacific Ocean toward Asia. After I woke up, too soon to see where the line would stop, I started the journey, flying from country to country—Thailand, Indonesia, the Philippines, now Papua New Guinea—but no place so far has felt quite right. I've always tried to follow my dreams, ever since age nine, when I had nobody to help me through the grief of leaving behind my first language and first culture, my first self, and changing from a Japanese into an American. My parents, American to start with, didn't notice my sadness, so I learned to rely on myself, on the banished, secret self who speaks to me through dreams.

Now I tighten the drawstring of my sleeping bag, breathing the thin cold air in the mission house, and dream in Japanese. I'm driving a jeep up a dusty mountain. It's a child-sized, toy jeep, and my two baby sisters bounce on the seat beside me. After circling round and round the mountain, we come to a high stone wall with a carved, medieval-looking gate. The air is very still. Not even a fly buzzes. Suddenly the gate swings open, revealing a jumble of square, flat buildings piled one on top of the other, staircases running from roof to roof. Then we see them. Up and down the narrow streets the elephants walk, slowly, quietly, with great dignity, careful where they plant their enormous feet.

As we drive through the gate, one of our tires goes flat. We all three start to cry, and almost immediately, several elephants come toward us, murmuring in Japanese, "There, there, please don't cry," changing our tire with their trunks. "Thank you," we say, and the elephants bow: "Don't mention it." I see their huge heads bobbing toward me and draw in a deep, contented breath, as sweet as the haylike scent of tatami floors, a delight at being small and helpless and cared for.

As the dream fades, I want to stay with it, am swept by a terrible sorrow at its slipping away.

Then I open my eyes to the dim morning light and feel ashamed at my mood of sappy nostalgia. I've had the dream before—I first dreamed it the night before I started law school in America—and though I don't remember much about my early years in Japan, they can't have been as Edenic as my unconscious paints them. Nobody's childhood is all sweetness and light. As usual, I dismiss this longing for a lost paradise as an embarrassingly transparent wish fulfillment. From my experience practicing law, I've learned to question people's motives, imagine worst-case scenarios, and mistrust any story that isn't at least somewhat dark.

*

Famished, I get up to look for some water in which to boil my rice.
I try the faucets in the kitchen and bathroom, not really expecting
them to work, and they don't. In the yard, I find empty pails, but do
not know where to fill them. If only I'd thought to ask the weapon
peddler where the closest water is. I unpack my peanut-butter-and-
crackers and inhale their tempting aroma, which reminds me that
I haven't eaten since yesterday morning. Reluctantly, I seal them
back in their plastic ziplock bag. On the mountain, I'll need high-
energy foods that don't have to be cooked. Since Kweptana is only
six miles farther, I decide to trudge on up the road rather than
lose time backtracking to the stream I crossed yesterday. Surely I'll
find water in Kweptana, if not before.

The next stretch of road switchbacks through uninhabited jungle. I meet no one. Carnivorous pitcher plants, their flowers pale
and viscous with saliva, wait in the undergrowth to gorge on un-
suspecting insects. With every step, rocks poke the balls of my feet,
making my thick-soled hiking boots feel like ballet slippers, but
there are no big obstacles to slow my progress. Aided by the blank
whiteness of the sky, I fall into a trancelike gait.

The solitude and the movement please me. I've always loved any
kind of repetitive motion—running, swimming, cycling—that I
can do while daydreaming about something else. I hated PE teachers who broke the spell by blowing their whistles at me and calling
attention to what my hands and feet were doing. That I might daydream on this climb, might momentarily forget my hands and feet
and fall to my death, strikes me as a distinct possibility. Could this
be why people are predicting I'll never reach Bimin? By American
standards, I'm not *that* fat. I think of my body as sturdy, a legacy of
tall, big-boned Appalachian forebears. I wonder, though, if something in the way I carry myself gives me that Jell-O-like, vacant look
of a body whose extremities aren't inhabited, whose occupant has
long ago abandoned the front parlors to closet herself somewhere
deep inside.

When the road comes to a small meadow ringed by casuarina
trees, I sit down on a rock to treat my feet with blister pads. Still
no sign of water. And still no one on the road. But I'm not afraid.
It dawns on me that perhaps it's danger I seek. Perhaps that's the
lure that has brought me here. No other force can counter the
inward pull of my dreams. While dream-people and dream-places
have always interested me more than the people and places I've

known in real life, Sandaun is the first place I've ever been that
feels too real to ignore. When I queued up to board the Cessna, I
had to step onto a scale and weigh myself along with my luggage.
A pound too many can make a tiny plane fall from the sky; one
too many daydreams can send a climber tumbling off a mountain.
I'm beginning to understand why my dream-map has led me on a
real trip, why it wouldn't have been the same just to stay home and
travel inside my head.

After I resume walking, I pass occasional thatched huts. And to
my surprise, six small, runny-nosed boys join me, wanting me to
follow them to the village soccer field, where people are milling
about at the halftime of a match between rival elementary schools.
A burly Highlander who stands a head taller than the surrounding
men shakes my hand heartily and introduces himself as Pius, the
headmaster of Kweptana school. The only one with shoes on, he
wears a collared shirt and new-looking shorts.

Pius is expecting me. I've walked up from Tekin so slowly that
the news about me has already reached Kweptana by grapevine.

"You arrived," he laughs, then announces in Pidgin to the crowd
that I need someone patient. "Patient," he says again. "The lady is
very fat. She needs someone to carry her backpack and lead her by
the hand." I nod. What else can I do?

After the crowd confers, they push five giggling girls in my direction, all about 10 years old. I stare at them. Their faces hidden
in their hands, all I can see are the tops of their close-cropped
Afros, their toothpick legs, their tiny, bare feet showing beneath
the ragged hems of their dresses, cloth so worn it's the same sepia
shade as the patches of flesh, a match that at first keeps me from
noticing the many tears in the fabric.

"No," I object. "Five is too many." I can't afford to hire all of
them.

"The girls live in Bimin and are returning there anyway," Pius
replies in English. "They want to share this job."

Thinking to discourage them, I offer to pay only five kina (about
five U.S. dollars) a day in wages, a mere pittance when divided five
ways, but the girls actually look pleased. The deal is struck.

Almost immediately, I begin to regret hiring them. My five new
employees, not being fully grown, are only about four feet tall. To

strap my heavy backpack onto one of those frail-looking creatures would, I fear, be child abuse.

Pius, however, laughs at my concern. "In these parts," he says, "girls learn from an early age to haul huge loads of firewood. Your pack is no heavier than the burdens these girls carry every day."

Still I worry. When I ask the girls in Pidgin where I can refill my canteen, they squeal with laughter and run off the soccer field and hide. Finally, one girl creeps back. She looks shyly at me, stifling her giggles enough to say that she is called Sipin. She has a fine-chiseled face, a high forehead, and exquisitely tiny ears. With light steps, Sipin leads me to a little waterfall.

"That's Soriben, Ana, Corin, and Dani," she says when we rejoin the others. Her companions, Sipin explains, have never been to school and don't know English or Pidgin, the national language. Sipin speaks a little Pidgin, pronouncing each syllable in a clear, flute-like voice, but her vocabulary is almost as limited as mine, a fact that doesn't augur well. The others speak only Bimin. None of the girls have any idea how old they are. And none of them, not even Soriben—the tallest girl, a gangling kid with a goofy smile—can be more than 12.

We begin walking up a succession of muddy hills. Or rather, they walk. I slip and slide. Instead of zigzagging, the trail tackles the hills head-on, up one side and down the other, as if blazed by sadistic gym teachers. As the hills steepen, the trees thin. I no longer have anything but the girls' hands to hold on to.

From a hilltop I catch a glimpse of the mountain we will have to cross tomorrow. Although the summit is hidden in mist, the part I can see looks dauntingly sheer. I recall what Nigel told me: The climb is one that mountaineers consider easy. It requires no special equipment, and there is only one spot from which a fall would surely be fatal; elsewhere, you can't plunge more than 30 feet.

I fail to find his words reassuring.

Suddenly hungry for the surer comfort of cookies, I stop Soriben. She is toting my backpack sideways, with one shoulder strap drawn across her forehead like the tumpline local women use when hauling firewood. I fish my Oreos out of the pack. When I hold out the package to offer her one first, Soriben grins widely and takes not just one cookie but the whole package. For several moments I stand frozen while she wolfs down my precious Oreos.

Then I snatch the package away and pass it on to Dani, who also seems to think I want her to have all the cookies. By the time I grab it from her and dole out two cookies each to the remaining girls, every Oreo has been devoured. I crumple the empty cellophane wrapper in my fist, not trusting my guides, feeling vexed and helpless.

From the next ridge, we can see Memnahop—a clump of five or six thatched-roofed huts clinging to the mountain about two-thirds of the way up. To reach it, we have to dip sharply into a jungly river valley and clamber up the other side. Branches, barbed vines, and succulents tear at my clothes and skin. There is no longer any trail that I can discern. Nor is there any such thing as admiring the scenery. The ground is so uneven I have to look down constantly to avoid tripping on a tree root or walking off the edge of a hidden cliff.

Once, as I follow the girls along a wet, rotten log, I decide to step off the log into what looks like underbrush, and I sink up to my knees in thin air. It happens too fast for fear. There's only time to feel shocked, my legs flailing uselessly beneath me, my wide hips momentarily catching me.

With worried yelps, Corin and Dani turn around and yank me up. Then I adjust my glasses-holder and watch the ground more carefully. After several minutes of dazed, unsteady walking, the panicky thought that I could have died in that sinkhole catches up with me. This is all because of my dream-map, I think suddenly. Though I've long ago stopped believing in the Lord that guides my missionary parents, it occurs to me that now I harbor my own mad faith. In fact, mine is madder. Am I going to get myself killed because of a red line glimpsed in a dream?

When at last I look up, I see angels hovering in the mist over the bushes just ahead. I wonder briefly if I'm already dead. I wipe the sweat off my glasses and look again, but there's no mistaking those golden halos. Closer up, the angels become babies astride their mothers' shoulders. Brown, naked babies with blond Afros. In the New Guinea mountains, often babies are born with yellow or copper hair that later turns black. Sometimes children too young to walk are taught to cling to their mothers' heads so that women will have their hands free to negotiate the steep terrain, which explains why I see the babies first, before I notice that most of the adults of Memnahop are standing in front of their houses, waiting to greet us.

Once we arrive in the village, I shake hands with everybody while the babies scream with fright at the sight of me, squeezing their mothers' heads so hard it must hurt. While some of the adults are wearing rags, others have on only penis-gourds or short grass skirts that remind me of ballerina tutus. Several men have fashioned earrings for themselves from scarab beetles, pieces of bone, or strings of safety pins. They each sport only one earring, and the lobe of that ear has been stretched until it droops almost to their shoulders. After we've all shaken hands, a man wearing the lid from a tin of sardines as an earring asks the girls a question in Bimin. Corin answers, and everyone who isn't holding a baby slaps their sides and falls over with laughter. They laugh with more abandon than any people I've ever met, literally rolling around on the ground. Not in on the joke, I stand and watch self-consciously, like a newcomer at a dance.

"Yaieee!" shrieks a teenage boy in English, laughing so hard that tears roll down his cheeks. "He asked if you are man or woman!"

"What did Corin say?"

"She said you are woman!" He doubles over with mirth again.

After the boy gets control of himself, he tells me his name is Phillip. He explains that the idea of wearing clothes is still something of a novelty in Memnahop, and since the villagers have never seen a woman in trousers before, they think I look hilarious. Though up to now I've felt rather proud of my safari suit, one I designed myself with pockets in all the right places, even a kangaroo pouch, now I see myself as I probably seem: a giant cross-dressing marsupial. I smile at the man with the sardine can dangling from his ear. We are both fashion victims of our cultures.

The girls arrange for me to spend the night in the home of one of their relatives, a wooden-framed, bamboo-walled house built on stilts. I have to climb a little ladder to enter, but once inside, I see about 10 people seated on a floor of wooden planks, eating roasted sweet potatoes. When I see how everyone helps themselves to the sweet potatoes, which lie in a big heap next to the cooking fire, I realize that my custom of passing the Oreos around must have seemed puzzling to my guides.

We eat dinner, and afterward the family starts swapping jokes and yarns in Bimin. Though I don't understand their words, I like the warmth of the fire and their company. It makes me want to tell a story, too, so I get my photo book of California out of my backpack and shine my flashlight on each picture. Every time I turn a page, the father whoops with joy, until I turn to a photo of a two-story building with a woman in the foreground. Now everyone murmurs excitedly.

"They want to know why in your country the people are bigger than the houses," Phillip translates.

"She isn't bigger," I say, wondering how I can explain perspective. "She's only closer to us than the house."

"She *is* bigger," Phillip insists, pointing to the plain evidence on the page.

"The house looks small because it's far away. Have you noticed how things get smaller when you move away from them?"

Phillip looks unconvinced, but he translates my explanation. The family stares at me in stony silence. One man squints at me as if I have the Mark of the Beast emblazoned on my forehead.

"Suppose you tell a friend goodbye and you watch him leave the village," I try again as 10 pairs of eyes watch me suspiciously. "Doesn't he get smaller and smaller as he walks away?"

More silence. Then a distinct muttering. "Why are you not telling the truth?" Phillip asks quietly.

In the narrow, jungly valleys of Sandaun, maybe no one ever gets the chance to see far into the distance. Thinking this, I give in: "Tell them that in my country we have people of different sizes. This woman is a giant standing in front of a little person's house."

My hosts look relieved that I've stopped lying.

"Do you know John?" asks Phillip. John, I've heard, is an American anthropologist who came to Bimin 10 years ago and has since left. As we're both Americans, no one can understand why I don't know John. Now the father begins to compare us. "John is fat, but you are fatter," Phillip translates. "At the dangerous place on the way to Bimin, he almost fell, but the Lord saved him. Yaiiee! We will pray hard to the Lord not to let you fall tomorrow."

I try not to think how large a role the Lord might be expected to play in all this.

"John speaks Bimin and you don't," the father continues. "John used to sing for us. Can you sing?"

For an instant, I hate John. I've never been able to carry a tune, and no way am I going to sing. Then just as suddenly I feel ashamed of myself. I seem to be reverting to an infantile sibling rivalry.

To satisfy my hosts, I sing a Japanese nursery rhyme that involves more chanting than singing and has lots of hand motions to draw attention away from my voice. Soon everyone is waving their hands over their heads and exclaiming with me in Japanese, "Uh-oh! The turtle is falling down!" Then I remember that the Japanese word for "turtle" is pronounced almost the same as the one for "the Lord," and that many a missionary has perplexed his Japanese congregation with long, impassioned sermons on "Our Savior the Turtle." I can't help wishing I'd picked a luckier song.

When I start to nod off, I'm shown into a room barely large enough to hold the family's bows and arrows and spears, propped against a wall, and a stained, child-sized mattress that smells of urine. How did they get a mattress up here? Did the mother carry it with a tumpline? I consider covering it with my rain poncho so I won't have to lie directly on it, but decide this might be impolite.

Instead, I sit down and unzip my backpack, unsealing the ziplock bag that holds my peanut-butter-and-crackers, the one food I don't want to share. I'll need all the energy I can muster to cross the mountain tomorrow.

As I quietly chew my snack, I listen to the people in the next room talking and laughing. I'm reminded of lying in bed at my grandparents' farmhouse in West Virginia, listening to the voices of grownups telling stories around the woodstove. My sisters and I didn't know our grandparents, our aunts and uncles and cousins. We'd been raised in Japan. Although we understood English, the Appalachian cadences rising and falling in the next room sounded to us like the language of a foreign tribe. Yet it somehow comforted us that there were grownups talking around the fire. We didn't hear the words, just the reassuring rhythm of their voices.

When I sweep the crumbs of my subversive peanut butter snack into a gap between the floor planks, a pig below the house squeals with delight, but the voices next door don't pause. Thank goodness, no one suspects.

Curling up into a fetal position, I fall asleep to the voices of my hosts, mingled with the soft sound of rain on thatch, until I'm back in the toy jeep with my sisters. We descend into a wooded valley where pythons and tigers fly at us, but we know they won't really bite because it's a magic forest. Then we're no longer in the jeep but climbing a stone staircase up into the sky. Somewhere in the ascent, my sisters vanish, and I turn into an adult. At the top, I see the white columns of an American courthouse, but before going inside, I pause on the steps to look down at the way I've come. A woman lawyer in a white powdered wig comes and stands beside me.

More to myself than to her, I say, "I've come very far. All the way from the Kingdom of the Elephants through the Valley of the Enchanted Forest."

"What are you talking about?" she demands, raising an eyebrow in disbelief as a cloud bank moves in to obscure the view.

I point indignantly to the ground below, outlining my very path with my finger, but she doesn't think there's anything there but clouds. The more she doubts my story, the more I believe it, until I'm shouting in her face, "I know the way I've come!"

The next morning, on taking my leave of Memnahop, I offer money to my host father, who refuses adamantly, then I press a can of sardines on the mother. Both she and her husband smile goodbye, still furrowing their brows.

As a cuckoo-dove coos overhead, the girls and I thread through dripping shrubs and disappear into a dark, muddy montane forest behind the village. The rain has just stopped, and cool morning mists are rising. Nigel warned me not to attempt the mountain if the ground is wet. What could he have meant? Even in the dry season, it rains at least once a day. I doubt that there ever comes a day when the ground isn't wet.

Termite mounds and tall, pale pink orchids rise from the forest floor. In the thick underbrush, long vines lie among the rotting leaves, coiled like snakes, ignoring the girls and springing up to slash my legs and trip me. I become totally absorbed in watching my feet. Whenever I fall, all five girls turn and stare in disbelief, exclaiming *"Sori!"* and then seeing that I'm not hurt, dissolve into giggles.

My guides haven't brought any drinking water for themselves. Perhaps they assumed that my little canteen would hold enough for six, for soon after we leave Memnahop, Sipin begins to complain to me in Pidgin that they're thirsty.

I remember Nigel's advice: "Don't shortchange yourself on water. Believe me, your guides can function on little or no water—they're used to it—but if you run out of water, you won't make it to Bimin." After what happened to my Oreos, I'm afraid to risk the girls' draining my canteen. So I don't offer to share. Still, I feel guilty. How could my guides have guessed I would want the canteen all to myself? Probably they had no way of imagining how much fluid a big, sweating American would need. Likewise, I fear, they probably have no idea how firm a foothold I'm going to need to bear my weight in the dangerous place.

After we've walked steadily uphill for an hour, we reach the spot where the mountain rises abruptly before us, an almost vertical wall of foliage. The sight of it makes my heart race with fear. *"Mi kisim wind fustaim"* (I'll rest awhile), I announce, and sit down on a fallen log. Ana, the smallest and most ebullient of the five, starts to scale the mountain, grasping exposed tree roots and outcroppings of rock, gliding from handhold to handhold with the lightness of a butterfly, but Sipin calls her back. With a wry smile, Ana sits down and speaks animatedly in her soprano voice, while the others laugh.

I've come to the wrong place, I think, looking up at the cliff face. I don't belong here. I should have gone to the steppes of Tibet, to those vast, open solitudes where lamas march for days and nights without stopping, their minds drawn inward, their gaze fixed far off into space, their hands absently clutching their magic daggers, their steps springy and rhythmic. Since I've rarely been present in my body for longer than a few minutes at a time, what the heck am I doing at the base of this cliff?

To quiet my heart, I look away from the cliff into the woods we've come from, thinking of last night's dream and following it like a winding forest path, following it into memories of an enchanted childhood.

I'm four years old, standing in the middle of an intersection in Fukuoka, Japan. Buses and bicycles rush past. I don't know where I am, but I'm not afraid, just tired and thirsty and ready to be found. Confident it will work, I sit down on the curb, my chin in my hands, and sob. I can't tell if I'm managing real tears or if my cheeks are just sweaty—it's one of those hot, muggy days when you can see steam rising from the pavement—but anyway, two men in business suits stop to ask what's the matter. In minutes, I'm sitting atop a police station desk, surrounded by smiling men in gold-buttoned uniforms who ply me with sodas and sweet-bean pastries. I won't talk. Though the police chief, his voice gentle, almost motherly, is reading me a list of all the foreigners in Fukuoka, pausing after each name, I make no response. He's already been over the list twice, but I pretend not to recognize my daddy's name so I can stay lost a little longer. Whenever the fun seems about to end, I thrust forward my lower lip and let it quiver, which sends one of the junior officers running to buy more sweets.

Maybe I didn't imagine it. Even though it seems unbelievable to the American I've become, a lawyer who can't see past her little cloud of "rationality," maybe I really do come from a children's paradise. Maybe I did grow up in a place where I could trust any stranger on the street to bear me safely home. I think of Takeo Doi, the Japanese psychiatrist who said in his *Anatomy of Dependence* that his society values *amae*, the passive, trusting love a child has for adults, rather than the self-reliance prized by Americans. I recall his theory of how a stunted *amae* can block a person's spiritual growth, and now I wonder if there may be something to it.

Ana starts up the mountain first. Corin goes next, looking over her shoulder and motioning me to follow. My body tenses. I reach up and clutch a small spur of rock. Lifting my foot to the nearest tree root, so high it feels like stepping into the cab of a semi, I pull myself up. I take a second giant step. A third. This root snaps. I tumble about 10 feet, hands grabbing at branches too thin to hold me.

"*Soh-oh-oh-oh-ree,*" sing the girls in unison.

For a minute or two, I lie where I've fallen, rocks digging into my back. Then I rise unsteadily to my feet, breathing hard. I feel as though a cold fear is rushing into my chest like sudden gulps of Arctic air.

After the girls huddle and regroup, we start again. This time Sipin climbs just ahead of me to point out the best roots and rocks, instructing in Pidgin, "Put hand here" and "Put foot there," while Corin hovers beside me to tap my hands if they try to stray from the correct placement and Ana and Dani follow to supervise my feet; Soriben carries my backpack. Last night's rainfall has left the handholds and footholds slick, some of them covered with a red lichen that crumbles when touched, others crawling with ants.

So this is "bushwhacking," I think. That word has always conjured up to me images of a solitary Jungle Jane slashing her way through the bush single-handedly. But on this trip, I seem to be growing more and more helpless. What's happening? It's as if my five little guides have subtly changed and become older than me. Come to think of it, maybe bushwhacking really is about asking for help. Considering that most jungles already have people living in them, what's the point of going it alone? To avoid having to share my supplies, perhaps. Or to avoid saying thank you. I try to think back to when in my Americanization the emotion of gratitude became linked with shame. It was not always so.

At every ledge, I stop to *kisim wind*, not wanting to risk exhaustion, which might cause me to lose my grip and fall. Since I can't understand Sipin well enough to be sure how far the next resting place is, I treat each one as if it's my last chance. To pass the time while I sit and pant, the girls kill frogs with a slingshot and laugh as Ana sings and tells stories, her arms akimbo, her face alternating between deadpan and imp. She never misses an opportunity to crawl out on a tree limb overhanging a precipice and hang from her knees, just to make me gasp with alarm. Always in motion, often impatient to go, Ana has to be restrained by the others until I catch my breath.

As we climb higher, lowland shrubs give way to rhododendrons with brilliant red star-shaped flowers. Because of the perpetual shadow cast by the bushes and ferns that grow horizontally out of the mountainside, everything stays wet, even after the sun rises to midmorning strength. My leather boots feel unsteady on the slippery rocks and roots. The girls, however, never slip; the toes of their bare feet splay out to grip the tenuous footholds with the assurance of fingers. Scampering up and down the mountain wall like spiders, my guides dance around me on that nearly vertical face to position themselves where they can help. Although none of them have worked for a foreigner before, they sense what I need. To them, I must seem like an overgrown baby who has to be taught how to crawl. Below me, Dani and Ana, the tiniest of the five, sometimes catch my feet to stop them from sliding, and it startles me to feel my weight held so firmly in their delicate hands. I begin to think of my guides as possessed of superhuman strength.

We come to a very broad ledge where we sit and look back at green mountains, one after another. Above the mountains lies a thin ribbon of white sky, and above that, deep violet is turning to black. I try not to think what this might mean. A solitary casuarina tree clings to the cliffside just below where we sit, its flat-topped shape like a candelabra without the candles, reminding me of the squat, typhoon-twisted pines of Fukuoka. I gulp some water and offer Sipin my canteen, letting the girls finish it.

We resume our climb with Sipin just above me, looking down and pointing toward the next foothold like a beckoning angel in a William Blake drawing. I keep my eyes on Sipin's face. It is calm but intent. I feel oddly detached, as though my slow progress up the slick mountainside is a minor part in some allegorical drama. Step by step, root by root, handhold by handhold, I seem to be ascending a dream-staircase, stairs so real they fuse with the mountain. "Put hand here," Sipin says, and my hand closes over the next tree root before she finishes her sentence. "Put foot there," she says, and my foot is already reaching for the next knob of rock. Somehow I've adjusted to the girls' rhythm, or they to mine, all six of us climbing in slow motion like legs of a single spider. To my surprise, I no longer want to be anywhere other than where I am at this very moment.

I forget to be afraid. It isn't that I've conquered my fear; I simply believe in my guides. In their own element, these five little girls, who seemed shy and awkward on the school ground yesterday, now seem so wise and self-possessed, so infallible, that I obey them without fear or question. Perhaps I'm learning, as if for the first time, what it means to trust and follow.

At the top, I pause for a few breaths of damp, icy air, my muscles trembling with relief, my feet balanced uncertainly on a narrow ridge of earth. I look down, but all I see is white. We're inside a cloud. Yet I am certain of the way I've come.

Blot Out

FROM *Creative Nonfiction*

O Prophet! Tell thy wives and thy daughters and the women of
the believers to draw their cloaks close round them [when they
go abroad]. That will be better, so that they may be recognized
and not annoyed.
    —Quran 33:59

YOU CAN PRETEND you're in a tunnel. You can make believe
you have on blinders. You can stare 100 yards in the distance at
a random point. You can walk with urgency or purpose. You can
look prickly or preoccupied. You can wear an iPod. You can make
a cell phone call. You can fake a cell phone call. You can write a
text message to no one.

These are the ways foreign women get down the street in Cairo.
These are the tricks they share, the ways they teach me to "beige
out," as one woman put it, to fog up the glasses, whenever outside.
Outside is the sphere of Egyptian men. Men run markets, crowd
alleys, fill every subway car but the very middle one, marked by a
huddle of headscarves. Females are scarce on Cairo's streets, and
those who do appear seem hurried, like mice suddenly exposed in
the middle of a room, rushing for cover.

I'm a journalist, here for just one month. The only thing I have
to do inside is write about what I see outside. In short: I can't coop
myself up in Cairo. My very first day, unsure of Egypt's codes, I
played it safe and tied a silk pink scarf around my face. In the
mirror, I looked like a little girl dressed up as the Virgin Mary.
Covered, I felt safe but no less overwhelmed. On too many streets,

mine was the lone headscarf weaving through tight teams of men. Their stony gazes felt like scorn.

I ditched the headscarf once I met American women living in Cairo. Covering my head wasn't necessary, they laughed. People knew I wasn't Muslim. I was obviously a Western woman, and, yes, that meant unvirginal here, and, sure, that aroused disapproval—all of which I should get over, quickly, and just focus on getting down the street.

I get down Suleiman Gohar Street by staring hard at middle distance. Sometimes, I practice the Arabic words for "left" and "right"—*shmal, yamin*—to the rhythm of my footfalls. And sometimes, in the blur of my peripheral vision, I catch sight of a black ghost—an Egyptian woman draped from head to toe in dark fabric—and I wonder what it's like under there, dressed in *niqab*.

The *niqab* is a headdress that covers not just the hair, but the face, ears, and neck. Paired with a long black tunic, the *niqab* leaves nothing exposed. A narrow, tight-threaded grille covers the eyes. The woman underneath can see out, but no one can see in.

Controversial in the West, the *niqab* was banned in France, seen as a means of repressing Muslim women—"a walking jail," said one French politician. That was my first read on the *niqab;* I felt sorry for the women in that brutally hot costume, imagining possessive husbands and overbearing fathers. But the Western objection to the *niqab* presumes that being seen is a freedom women desire. After walking alone as a blond, nonvirginal, youngish woman in the streets of Africa's most densely populated city, where almost everyone is a boy or a man, and looking, visibility is the last thing I desire. The *niqab* begins to tempt me like a secret passageway—a way to be outside without actually being seen. At the end of a month in Cairo, nothing sounds more liberating than erasing myself from this place.

"I've always wanted to do that," says Maryanne, a horse rancher who raised two children in Cairo, when I ask her to venture out in *niqab* with me. Years ago, she had this idea herself—she and every American woman in Cairo, it seems. I proposition teachers and journalists and a belly dancer from Los Angeles, and discover it's a common fantasy; a few women have already done it. "You feel like you're getting away with something you shouldn't get away with," says Abby, a foreign correspondent. Egyptian women, I hear, have their own history of mischief in *niqab*. Women cheat on exams in *niqab;* women cheat on husbands in *niqab;* some prostitutes go to work in *niqab*.

Kate is the only person who tries to talk me out of my plan. The editor of *Egypt Today* and an American whose expertise is Muslim culture, Kate is worth listening to. She argues that even women in *niqab* get harassed, treated like meat, ass-grabbed. That's not the point, I tell Kate. I just want a break, I say, a break from being so seen. I want to hold Cairo in my gaze.

There's a place in this city where I long to do the looking. Every Friday, there's an outdoor market—a teeming antique, junk, and exotic animal market. In guidebook write-ups, there's usually a warning for Western women (e.g., "be accompanied by male friends in order to feel more at ease"). This is where I want to pass invisibly, I tell Kate. At the great Egyptian *souq*.

"But you don't speak Arabic," Kate says. She's worried someone will try to converse with me and that my silence will give me away.

I consider Kate's point on my routine walk down Suleiman Gohar Street, where I'm heckled on average once a block. Erase the color of my skin and hair, screen the green from my eyes, hide my face, cover my neck, cloak my shoulders, wrap my arms, bury my chest and waist and hips, shroud my knees and calves and ankles, let the fabric fall straight down to the roofs of my plain black shoes, and it's hard to imagine what a man in the street would have to say.

Tori is the one who says yes. A young yoga instructor with flaxen hair and deep dimples, Tori has more reason than most to blot herself out of Cairo; she looks like California. I once rode the subway with Tori and watched tendrils of attention wind around the pole she gripped while looking only at me. The "I'm on a mission" walk: that's how Tori gets down the street.

To hide under *niqab*, we must first find one. We try Ataba, a shopping complex that's Vegas-bright on a Tuesday night. There's no clarity at Ataba on what's a street, what's a store, what's a lot, what's a place where cars won't hit you. Finally, we find a dingy mall where a man on the third floor sells the full getup. I watch this man's face closely as Tori tries it on, receding under layers of

jet-black fabric. He's not amused. He's not bothered. He just wants
to make a sale.

The sale is made, and we head to the subway, passing a woman
in *niqab* who's sound asleep on the ground by her tarp of fruit.
"Look at that," I say, pointing like a kid. I can't help it; the idea
of feeling relaxed enough to fall asleep outside in this furious
city—even when cocooned inside all those layers—is just unfath-
omable to me. But we don't have to fathom. We have the material.
We can get under there ourselves.

Tori presses down the camera's shutter, but nothing happens. The
camera refuses: SUBJECT IS TOO DARK. I am the subject, and I am
too dark. I am darkness with a slit for eyes. Only when we leave Tori's dim bedroom and stand in the kitchen will my camera cooperate. I still can't tell whether the person in my photos is Tori or me.

The *niqab* has one too many layers. There's the priestly tunic
and then a ninja-like veil that fastens right above the ears, covered
by another veil with an eye screen. Our worst-case scenario—that
the *niqab* will slip off in a crowded, male, outdoor scene—feels
quite likely now that we're in costume. If I don't grip a handful
of my long tunic, it's going to trip me. Plus, my vision is confined
now—a forward tunnel, subtly dimmed. Though I do notice Tori
slip a water bottle under her cloak.

"I have this fainting problem," she says.

Tori and I are headed to Cairo's largest outdoor market, and
she thinks maybe I should know that my companion will slip out
of consciousness if she gets too parched. I decide against telling
Tori that I, too, have a fainting problem. Mine is a new fainting
problem: All that doctors can tell me is that anticipating stress and
pain may trigger it. Fear is another trigger. I fear fainting. Fear of
fainting recently made me faint. I try not to think about triggers
and fears as Tori and I step outside. We pass from her dim living
room into an entryway, where the slam of an upstairs door and
heavy footsteps send Tori rushing like a crazed ninja down the
staircase. She leaves me on the landing, grasping for a fistful of
fabric and the courage to move quickly in *niqab*.

Mahmoud, my driver, has been waiting outside. He's actually the
driver of an American woman who assured me, jotting down his

number, "There's nothing wrong with hiring a babysitter." I dislike being babysat, both as a traveler and as a woman, but Tori and I agree that a jam-packed subway car is not the place to go in our loose-fitting disguises.

I tried to warn Mahmoud, who speaks taxi English, before I disappeared inside Tori's apartment that I would not look the same when I came back out. I would be in *niqab;* I would be bringing another woman, also in *niqab.* Did Mahmoud understand he would soon no longer see me? I didn't think so.

It's no small relief, then, when Tori and I come down the street, clutching each other like grannies, to see Mahmoud watching. I lift my hand to wave, and he does the same. Tori and I climb, without a word, into his back seat.

How is Cairo so quiet today? Fridays are always subdued, but never like this. You could hear a scarf hit the ground in Cairo today.

"Esmee Tori," my friend introduces herself in a breathy whisper. "My name is Tori."

I would love to know how all this unfolds in the mind of our driver-babysitter. Is he drawing, in his imagination, a face to match the voice of the new presence in his car? Thankfully, there's no sign that we've spooked Mahmoud. On the contrary, he's on our side, telling Tori in Arabic that we forgot gloves. Women in *niqab* wear black gloves. All we can do is bunch up our sleeves now. I look over at Tori. There's only one thing to look at: her eye screen. Tori's eyelashes have poked right through the mesh.

The hardest thing is not speaking. I keep wanting to say things to Tori while we walk down a street crowded with goats and men about to shear them. But talking is the surest way to expose ourselves, so we say just a few things, like "Hold my arm" and "I'm still nervous" and "I feel things slipping" and "Shh," adjusting gradually to the new code of silence. We are entities that waddle and watch but do not speak. We waddle carefully and watch hard. I watch the faces of the men who pass and seem focused on goats alone. I watch them tug the ears of goats that bleat as if they know it's shearing day. Everything about this feels precarious. I feel things slipping—and by "things," I mean veils, both of them, neither of which I can fix now, because the car is far behind us and

Mahmoud has opted to stay there. Still, I'm so tempted to say one last thing aloud to the entity floating beside me like a steady boat: "Nobody sees us."

What they see, all they see, is *niqab*. They see *niqab* move; they see it has a twin; they see caution, codependence. There's nothing more, though, to take from our image. Onlookers quit looking. Passersby pass right by. They beige out, resume daydreams or scan the air for other things, things with color or curves or noses. I watch it happen over and over through my eye slit, scrutinizing the gaze of every person we walk by. And no matter how many people look bored of us, no matter how many eyes gloss over, I'm paranoid about the look that somehow gets in. I'm reading every face, ready for a mouth to open, a finger to point. Instead, the first gasp comes from inside my veil when Tori and I pass a full-length mirror in the furniture mart and neither one of us appears.

It's easy to fall into reverie when you're not speaking, when you're staring through a slit, when you're dividing focus between your feet (*step with care, step with Tori, do not step on the hem*) and your head (*stay, veils; stay, veils; slide a little slower if you cannot stay*), plodding and plodding, past the aisle of toilets, the doves in cages, the Qurans on tables, bikes on train tracks, cassettes on dirt, heaping mountains of defunct remote controls. This *souq* lies on the edge of a cemetery, under the shadow of a raised highway. The market will go up in flames mere months from now, a fire sparked by a car accident; within a year, the entire city will be ablaze in political protest. But no one this Friday morning knows any of this. Today is about trade. You can buy hawks here. You can buy hedgehogs here. You can buy 1970s exercise bikes here. There's a man who swallows shards of glass, another who sells busted keyboards. It all blends together like a long and lovely hallucination, a market I dreamed up, letting boundaries blur, as dreamers do, letting the *souq* be two things at once, as things in dreams—behind the curtain of closed eyes—can be: squalid and splendid, treasure and trash.

If Tori speaks up, it's only to comment on the breeze. Tori loves breeze. When a rare gust of air makes it under her *niqab*, she thanks it aloud. If I speak up, it's to wish there were some way to take photos. My clunky camera—impossible to wield under *niqab*—is in the car, and this place is my photographic wonderland: antique mart meets junkyard meets unregulated zoo. The clashes are incredible. The clashes are so Cairo. And my photographer fantasy—invisibility—is all but granted here. I'm free to stare, to focus, ogle, dawdle—tortured to have all those new powers but not my camera.

Powerless to capture the *souq,* I ask it questions. I ask this *souq* the same question I ask all public places in Cairo: where have you hidden the women? And because there are things that qualify as girly here—pink berets and floral perfumes—I feel more entitled than usual to ask my stubborn, Western question. A grizzly looking man walks by with a rack of little girl dresses slung over his shoulder, and I let the clash—lace against stubble—amuse me. And over by the table of ladies' underwear, a few male buyers stand perfectly still, riddled with indecision (what color? what size? good lord, what cut?). I stare at their unmoving profiles and want to freeze them, right there, in a perpetual puzzle involving women's underpants, until they agree wives should be let out of homes.

There's a place, a kind of vortex at the Friday *souq,* where six different mud paths intersect. Bird vendors meet jean sellers meet spice men meet fish delivery boys meet two blond imposters under *niqab,* who sooner or later, like it or not, must enter the vortex. It's impossible to know how trafficked the vortex is until you're down in it—yes, "down," for the vortex is a dip. We—all of us—converge with the push of gravity. A Tweety Bird blanket hangs high over the fray, too high for anyone to grab. Right when my foot has found the outer banks of the dip and I am climbing out, a hand finds my ass and squeezes hard. I wriggle, shove ahead, and nearly take Tori down.

It's the first time anyone's groped me in Cairo. Kate was right. Men don't need a figure or face to treat a woman like meat. Someone with imagination pushed right through the *niqab.* We exploit our anonymity at this *souq,* and so does some guy's hand.

Back on level ground, it becomes clear that someone's following us. Tori veers us down an alley toward the cemetery, hoping to lose the stubble-cheeked man, but he keeps up, asking in Arabic, over and over, "What are you doing here?" In a whisper that she hopes hides her accent, Tori says, "Leave us alone." I don't speak Arabic. I just sweat. My *niqab* is gaining sweat weight. Tori leads us deeper into the City of the Dead, a maze of mausoleums, until finally the accuser falls away. Again: Kate was right. There were reasons not to do this. The man was ready to yank Tori's *niqab* right off.

Nothing, though, can spoil this *souq* for me. Not the sweaty fabric, not my fury at men, not my indignation on behalf of women, not a veil slipping, not an ass grabbed, not even a stranger who wants us shamed. There are places that feel like the answer to the question of why we travel in the first place, why we bother to trespass, crossing the lines that look like fences. This place is one of my few.

We're leaving, reaching the homestretch. We see Mahmoud looking straight at us, bless him, as if he's been scanning the edge of the market for twin black blobs ever since he lost sight of Tori and me hours ago. Still, Tori can't wait to reach the finish line to say aloud what she enjoyed most about wearing the *niqab*. I think of the other American women who wear blinders, who beige out, who stare at a random point 100 yards away. I'm sure they would all nod, as I do, when Tori says the best part was looking strangers square in the eye.

We collapse into the back seat of Mahmoud's car with a tremendous ruckus. We phew and sigh and breathe air like people who just crawled out of graves. We yank down veils and suck down water, making the transformation back to Westerner, back to blond and green-eyed, with a quick yank.

I watch Mahmoud watch Tori become Tori in the mirror; I catch him smile as he sees for the first time the dimpled cheeks that match the little voice. Tori later tells me how strange this was—not because she caught our babysitter peeping but because she wanted to introduce herself all over again, *"Esmee Tori."*

Mahmoud is ready to drive off, but I can't yet. I cannot leave without taking pictures. Tori, knowing I need a companion, offers to come. And so we head back into the *souq* without coverage, straight into what, at our approach, now sounds like a motel room full of male athletes who've just located the porn channel. I take Tori's hand. It's perfectly normal for people of the same gender to hold hands in Egypt, and I appreciate that fact in this moment because I need this hand. I need this hand like I might someday need a cane. Cairo is excellent at reminding me I cannot make it alone, and never more so than now: in the bright light and open air with my friend, who looks as bare as I feel, with the shadows of men like a forest just ahead.

My fingers interlock with Tori's; our knuckles can't get any closer. Many things are yelled at us. "Big dick" is yelled at us. "Sex" is yelled at us. And so is a question: "Are you lovers?" Which I find interesting. Someone in this jungle of hecklers has noticed how tightly we're holding hands. He sees something in those interlocked fingers, and rightly so. If there's a place with the power to change my sexual orientation, would it not look like this? If there were a moment when I swore off men and partnered instead with my own kind, wouldn't it be now, as I walk back naked into the Friday *souq*?

Some men stare; others hiss. Gangly boys trail us and bleat the word *sex*. But because none of that happened, just moments ago, because the contrast is so stark, so ludicrous, I want to taunt back: "We were just here, fools!" If there were a way to gloat, how I'd gloat. I'd yank a veil out of my pocket, wave it overhead like a crazy lady, and let every ogler know, "You just looked right through me."

But it's my turn to look right through people. I pretend I see no ruckus, no fury, no storm. I scan the fields of junk and, before anyone can chase us away, shoot, shoot, shoot. A half-hour into this reverie, the reverie of looking through not veil but lens, I realize I have no idea whether the boys trailing Tori and me, flinging dirty words and sticking their fingers into my photos, are the same boys who began doing so 30 minutes back. That's when I realize I've beiged back out.

I once read that camels have an extra eyelid. It's a translucent cap that keeps out grains of sand. There are many reasons camels survive in the desert. They have special pads on their feet and humps of sustenance to go days without food. The way they weather sandstorms, though, moving through the desert at its most furious, is this secret lid that slides right down over the open eye.

DANIEL TYX

The Year I Didn't

FROM *Gulf Coast*

THE YEAR I didn't walk 1,900 miles along the U.S.-Mexico border, I purchased a detail map of the border states and northern Mexico at the Circle K in McAllen. In my mind's eye, the Pacific Ocean glistened crystalline blue when I finally arrived in Tijuana along Monument Road, sun-cracked and solitude-wizened.

I debated whether to travel with a dog or a donkey. I liked the image of the latter better, for the sake of the book jacket, but there were logistical problems. How does one transport a pack animal across a transnational frontier?

I quit my job at the International Museum of Art and Science (slogan: *At IMAS, hay más*), an eclectic amalgamation of amateurish rock and insect collections and Mexican folk art bequeathed by civic-minded Oaxacan tourists. Like me, the museum couldn't figure out what it was supposed to be about, or perhaps was convinced that it could be more than one thing at a time.

Two camps: those who thought I was crazy, and those who wanted to know the details of my route, which I preferred to leave to chance or my imagination. In either case, everyone wanted to know: why was I walking?

The year I didn't walk 1,900 miles along the U.S.-Mexico border, the truth was that everyone seemed to be doing something with their year, then writing about it. There was the man who lived without electricity in Brooklyn, the woman who didn't take out the trash, the two separate guys—one a believer and one an agnostic—who lived like Jesus would.

The truth was that I dreamed of writing a travelogue that would forever alter the dynamic of the American conversation about immigration and the border. I wanted a conversation piece for life, something to bust out at parties when, as usual, I couldn't for the life of me think of something halfway intelligent to say. More than that, I wanted a story to tell myself about my life, one with a page-turning plot and a clear beginning, middle, and end.

The truth was, why not? I was already there, my girlfriend, Laura, and I having been deployed at the same time as the U.S. National Guard as part of a teaching corps that, ironically, favored a military lexicon. She had quickly become a star educator; I had even more quickly become a devastated dropout with halfhearted suicidal impulses and a dead-end job at a dead-end museum. Her previous boyfriend had moved on from her to Harvard, and the recurring thought haunted me: Was I her rebound? His unaccomplished, ham-fisted doppelganger?

The truth was that I'd thought up the idea and told the first person I saw, in the hopes that my public declaration of intent would shame me into doing something significant with my life. That person happened to be Laura, who'd recently hazarded to mention that she was thinking about marriage. Things snowballed from there.

The year I didn't walk 1,900 miles along the U.S.-Mexico border, I bought a new pair of hiking boots and stomped around the neighborhood with my '70s-era external frame Kelty backpack, wearing two pairs of socks. I carried plenty of water and tried to avoid the roving packs of Chihuahuas that bared their teeth like four-legged piranhas.

I went to the library at the University of Texas–Pan American and checked out a stack of books on the border that I found, for reasons not well understood, totally unreadable. I left them splayed open around my bedroom floor, and my cat, Che, who bit my girlfriend's toes at night out of either jealousy or boredom, slept on the pages.

Laura offered to take care of the cat while I was gone. She asked me not to leave, but said she understood if I did. Both gestures struck me as pure demonstrations of true love, though I doubted if she understood an impulse that I myself did not truly comprehend.

Of all of the adventures in my life that I have not undertaken, this one was the most fully realized.

The year I didn't walk 1,900 miles along the U.S.-Mexico border, I began to question the purpose of my trip:

Why was everyone so gung-ho about doing something exotic or noteworthy with their year?

Why couldn't they write about a year of failure, a year of discontented employment, a year of metaphysical paralysis, a year of resisting love for the sake of preserving an idealized vision of their future selves, a year of getting up every morning to feed an FIV-positive cat picked up outside Che's Restaurant in Rio Grande City, one-eyed and hairless, who howls and howls at night because he wants to go outside but can't because he'll infect the neighborhood?

What were all these people trying to prove with their years of doing something? More precisely, what was I trying to prove?

Was I on a journey to discover something, or did I already know what I was going to discover?

The year I didn't walk 1,900 miles along the U.S.-Mexico border, the sun beat hot on the white sands of the Yuma Desert. Jaguarundis lapped up water from the Rio Grande, green jays flitted from branch to branch of craggy mesquites, cacti hoarded water in thick-walled cisterns, men and women left behind soda bottles and torn underwear hanging from bulrushes at the river's edge. Trucks on longer-than-long hauls spewed thick plumes of black smoke into the cloudless sky, while children ate Whataburger hamburgers and sipped from giant vessels of Coca-Cola a hundred steps from the razor wire encasing the International Bridge. On days when the farmers burned cane, the whole world seemed as though it were on fire.

Six years later, when I heard the story on the radio about the reporter from *Esquire* who was walking 1,900 miles along the U.S.-Mexico border, I was standing on a countertop in McAllen painting yellow along the kitchen ceiling. Laura was on the floor in the adjacent office, unpacking boxes and keeping an eye on the baby. We had just moved back after a three-year graduate school sojourn in Indiana. Always prone to taking metaphors too literally,

I was convinced that borders were a place that both divided and unified, and that in order to be made whole again, one had to return to the place of initial rupture. Laura had her own reasons for wanting to return, but both of us had agreed that on the border, somehow everything felt more alive. I had feared that this sensation was rooted in nostalgia, but upon returning was relieved to discover that the remembered past still held true.

I wasn't listening, but the interviewer's question penetrated my wandering consciousness: *Why? Why walk the border?*

The reporter was doing it backward, Tijuana to Brownsville, traveling with a baby stroller and an iPhone. He had GPS and a solar-powered Kindle. Though perfectly aware of the presence of envy, I found myself judging his techi-ness: no donkey, no dog.

I climbed down from the counter and crouched, froglike, next to the radio with its staticky reception. Next to me, Laura filed the documents of our life together, her legs stretched out in front of her so that her body formed a three-dimensional Y. The reporter remarked about the difficulty of sealing off such a long border in such inhospitable terrain. My son, his posture mirroring that of his mother, glanced up, then continued ripping the pile of discarded papers in front of him. The reporter described the long stretches of nothingness as "a learning experience."

My son, past ready for his midafternoon nap, began crying. I loaded him into the stroller, and we headed out into the hundred-degree heat of late April in South Texas.

I thought of the reporter with his own modified jogging stroller, the deserts of loneliness he must be traversing—Kindle or not—that I had once coveted for myself. I thought of the circuitous path that had led me away from the border and back again, into marriage and parenthood and homeownership and the trappings of—if not the complete conviction in—a settled existence. I thought of my new job teaching community college students for whom the border was not something exotic or even particularly noteworthy, but a fact of life, its absurdities and fucked-up politics and violence and juxtapositions not so much a story to tell as a backdrop against which the satisfactions and preoccupations of daily life were set.

Arriving home again after a lap around the block, the oppressive heat having drawn my son into a gratified stupor, I thought about whether he, in his grown-up years, would take the measure of his father based on the things that I had done or the things that I hadn't, and which was better, or worse. I scooped him up from the stroller, carried him over my shoulder up the front stairs, and crossed the creaky floorboards of the living room and the hallway until I arrived at the nursery, freshly painted treehouse green. Having reached no certain conclusions, I lifted him over the lip of the crib and laid him down, as gently and carefully as I knew how.

SARAH A. TOPOL

Tea and Kidnapping

FROM *The Atlantic*

MY HOST, THE 37-year-old Bedouin tribal leader Sheikh Ahmed Hashem, had served me so many glasses of sweet tea that I had lost count. It was a hot afternoon in early July, and we were sitting on the floor of his compound in Wadi Feiran, a remote village deep within Egypt's Sinai Peninsula. A single electrical cable connects the settlement's squat cement houses; a single road runs through the surrounding mountains to the outside world. Everything felt unhurried, including Hashem's explanation, via a translator, of his people's complaints against the Egyptian government. But when I asked why the local Bedouin had started kidnapping tourists, he was quick to correct me: "It isn't kidnapping. It is a *tourist safari.*"

The sheikh's brother Mohammed, a wiry drug runner, nodded vigorously: "Tourists come to Egypt and pay for this kind of experience," he said, beaming. "Now they are getting the same thing for free!"

During the Egyptian revolution last year, the country's beleaguered security services mostly pulled out of the Sinai, the triangular peninsula that lies between mainland Egypt to the west and Israel to the east. Drug running and weapons smuggling spiked; in the northern half of the peninsula, shootouts between Islamic militants and the police became routine; the gas pipeline connecting Egypt and Israel was repeatedly bombed. In recent months, the security vacuum has emboldened a handful of Bedouin in the southern half of the peninsula to lobby for the release of jailed kinsmen via a novel tactic: kidnapping foreign tourists and using them as bargaining chips. Between February and early July, Bed-

ouin tribesmen took three pairs of Americans, three South Ko-
reans, a pair of Brazilians, and a Singaporean on "safaris" lasting
between a few hours and several days.

Egypt's Bedouin, historically nomadic Arab tribespeople who
have lived in the Sinai for centuries, harbor a number of griev-
ances against the government. After Israel returned the peninsula
to Egypt in 1982, following a 15-year occupation, the Egyptian
government accused the Bedouin of collaborating with the Jewish
state; the Bedouin have since been rejected from military service
and most government jobs. The Bedouin complain that the state's
notoriously brutal security services deal particularly harshly with
them today, imprisoning hundreds of their kinsmen without trial.
Bedouin villages have little in the way of infrastructure, health
care, or schools compared with the rest of the country. And although the Sinai's Red Sea coast is dotted with high-end hotels,
tribesmen complain that tourist cash does nothing to improve
their lives, as tourism outfits won't hire them.

The recent rash of kidnappings is well timed to mortify the
Egyptian government. The country's economy is already in free
fall, and beach tourism is a key source of foreign currency. So the
government has worked to secure the release of each batch of kidnapped tourists as quickly as possible. But a strange thing has happened: some of those freed tourists have described their captivity
in surprisingly glowing terms.

"All of this is an unforgettable memory," Norma Supe, a 63-
year-old nurse from California who was kidnapped in February,
told the Associated Press. She called her captors kind and polite.
Supe was kidnapped with another member of her tour group,
66-year-old Patti Esperanza, on a road near Saint Catherine's, the
sixth-century monastery at the foot of Mount Sinai. Their guide,
Hisham Zaki, volunteered to go along as a translator. As Zaki later
recalled, Esperanza demanded that one of her kidnappers stop
smoking: "I told her, 'Are you joking? You are kidnapped!'" But
the Bedouin kidnapper cooperated, throwing his cigarette out the
car window. At one point, Esperanza recounted, the kidnappers
stopped to prepare coffee for the women, but upon learning that
Esperanza does not drink coffee, they made her tea.

When I had finished my own tea, Hashem agreed to take me to
the area where Esperanza and Supe had been held. We got in his
truck and drove for about an hour before parking along a stretch

of sand at the base of the mountains. Once brush was gathered
for a fire and water was set to boil, we sat down on the ground,
and Hashem introduced me to Attwa, who he said had kidnapped
the Californian women. (Attwa did not provide his last name, but
a source in the Egyptian security services confirmed his involvement.) Attwa lives in a shack nearby and, like most Bedouin in the
area, makes a meager living smuggling drugs. He has tried in vain
to find other work, he said, but is proud that he has so far managed to keep his children out of the drug trade.

Attwa rolled a joint as he began telling me the story of the safari. In late January, he explained, he got word that one of his
sons had been killed and two other sons jailed following an al-
tercation with the police. Ten days later, hoping to bargain for
their release, Attwa and a friend armed themselves and drove toward Saint Catherine's. Taking Supe and Esperanza from a tour
bus proved surprisingly easy, Attwa said. "I used their translator to
make them calm, so they wouldn't fear anything. I explained that I
needed to deliver a message to the government and this is the only
way I would be heard." He added that he'd packed bread, cheese,
and juice for his captives. What would he have done if they had
become hysterical? Attwa said he would have left them, but they
didn't cry, so he brought them here.

Hashem told me that the Bedouin take only a few tourists at a
time because caring for larger groups could quickly get expensive.
"When [a Bedouin] kidnaps some people, he must be responsible for their hospitality when he takes them around on the safari
trip—their food, drinks, toilets, and their sleep. If he treats them
badly, he will be held accountable," Hashem said, referring to the
tribal justice system.

The Bedouin seem to know they are walking a fine line. Too
many safaris, and more repression might follow. Too few safaris,
and their demands might continue to be ignored. A few hours after Attwa captured the American women, he told me, the Egyptian
government promised to release his sons, and he surrendered his
hostages. But here we were, five months later, and his sons were
still incarcerated.

Shortly after my tea with Attwa, two more Americans and their
guide were taken hostage. At first, this safari seemed different.
The kidnapper, a 32-year-old truck driver, threatened to hold the
hostages until his uncle (who he said had been arrested after re-

fusing to bribe the police) was freed from prison. Four days later, however, he released them, unharmed. "We were treated just like they treat their own," the hostages' translator told a reporter. The kidnapper explained that in addition to the customary tea and coffee, he had served his guests roast lamb, a dish usually reserved for special occasions. He said his uncle remained in prison.

GRANT STODDARD

The Paid Piper

FROM *T Magazine*

A FRIEND TOLD me: "If you're looking to make some money on the side, you should try Gidsy.com, it's totally up your alley." Because it seems lately that no occupation is anywhere near my alley, I checked out this funny-named startup (*gids* is the Dutch word for "guide") in the hope that my friend was right. Started in November 2011, the website is a Berlin-based outfit that enables travelers and other novelty seekers to find activities organized by what it refers to as "real people." Via Gidsy, genuine humanoids like you and me can monetize our expertise, creativity, access, skills, or local knowledge by turning them into tours and activities offered for a price (and advertised through social networks that the site seamlessly integrates). Have access to a hot-air-balloon ride over Luxor's temples at sunrise? Know how to make buttons in your Berlin apartment? Chances are someone will pay to join you. Each activity organizer sets his or her own price, and Gidsy takes 10 percent—a tribute that will eventually trickle up to the coffers of Ashton Kutcher, one of the firm's principal investors. It's no coincidence that Kutcher would put money into Gidsy; it's a logical extension of sites like Airbnb (also in Kutcher's portfolio of investments) that aim to democratize travel knowledge and capitalize on the Internet's DIY spirit. A social media vacation, then, might involve consulting TripAdvisor to find a deal on flights, Airbnb for a place to stay, and Gidsy for stuff to do while you're in town.

I decide that my tours will combine two or more aspects of my life and interests, excluding the amusing but impractical coupling of "5k Run Plus Guitar Lesson." Within a couple of hours, people browsing Gidsy are offered "Scorsese's Downtown Manhattan Tour," in which I take movie fans to various locations featured in three of the director's films; "A Running Tour of Manhattan," wherein I whisk a huffing, puffing group along Hudson River Park, alerting them to points of interest; "A Historical Walking Tour of Occupied New York," filled with mildly insightful musings on the British administration of New York City from 1776 to 1783; and a "Manhattan Kayak Tour," in which I fuse the tedium of barely memorized factoids about the Hudson River with the exhilaration of possibly drowning in poison.

Eventually, I get a bite. Edial Dekker, a 28-year-old Dutchman living in Berlin, expresses a good deal of interest in my kayaking tour and politely asks if I can schedule one during his visit to New York in October. I'm not especially surprised to discover that Dekker is, in fact, the company's cofounder. Without disclosing that I would be writing about the experience, I tell Dekker that the Hudson River is too cold in October, and he inquires whether there might be some other way I can amuse him and his brother, Floris, who is also a Gidsy cofounder (along with a third partner, Philipp Wassibauer), on their trip. But based on the current low level of interest in my offerings, my career as a guide might be over by then.

With few takers, I begin tweeting about my capers and describing them on Facebook with instructions for my people to retweet and repost. Still no takers. So I slash my prices and add more tours. On Gidsy, if an activity doesn't enlist the minimum number of people set by the organizer within 24 hours of its start time, it's automatically canceled. One by one, I receive automated e-mails telling me that what I have to offer has failed to capture anyone's imagination and that my event is being called off due to barely contained lack of interest.

The Occupied New York and Scorsese walking tours are the first to be nixed, followed by the running tour. I decide to post another activity, something that's quintessentially me and that I don't have to cram for: scavenging food. You see, earlier in my writing career I had to become creative in how I housed, clothed, and fed myself. I started by recovering bags of discarded, barely stale bagels and soon discovered that there were luxury food items being given away all over town. In a short while, I had amassed a wealth of knowledge on the best spots and the best times for grazing. Thankfully, it's been a while since I've depended on free food for sustenance. So I spend a day scouring my old haunts to see if the pickings are still plentiful. Though we live in financially trying times, the volume of food being thrown out is greater than ever. I hurry home and write a post.

"Free food samples are designed to guilt-trip people into making a purchase. But hold your nerve and you could eat the equivalent of a three-course meal, absolutely free! I'll take you on a tour of New York City's best free-food locations. Over a 2–3 hour span, I guarantee to fill you to your bursting point with delectable morsels, gratis!"

After several tweets, retweets, posts, and reposts, I get nine takers, and we set a meeting time, 6 P.M. on Thursday in Chelsea. I focus on that neighborhood because it promises the highest concentration and greatest diversity of free food. Not only is Chelsea Market the gourmet freeloader's one-stop shop, it's also near the Thursday-night art-gallery openings, which are generally stocked with free wine and nibbles.

Before we set out, I quickly give the group—now down to six—a few pointers on boldness and tell them they'll get extra credit for going back for seconds. I hand them all ziplock sandwich bags and tell them not to let being full stand in the way of collecting samples that can be saved (even frozen!) for later.

We begin at Wrapido, a Middle Eastern joint on Eighth Avenue. Here, a tray of bite-sized falafel chunks are placed on a pedestal on the sidewalk. After five minutes of conspicuous loitering while we wait for a fresh batch, the group descends upon the tray like a swarm of locusts as flabbergasted cooks peer through the window. Then we hoof it to Chelsea Market, where I know about a wine tasting at Chelsea Wine Vault that is on until seven. We bum-rush the woman from Stark Thirst—a winery in Sonoma County—and each have a splash of a crisp, clean unoaked Chardonnay. One of the group even wants to buy a bottle, but I remind her that spending money is anathema to the ethos of the tour. (Later, however, someone else breaks the rule by buying a crunchy cheddar from Vermont that we tasted at Lucy's Whey.)

After sampling a dozen types of infused olive oil at the Filling Station, we check into L'Arte del Gelato, where I demonstrate to the group how not to be cowed by eye rolling. When it comes to

ice cream, the usual custom is "two tries then buy." Despite a salvo
of tsking I make it to five unchallenged tries. But the rest of the
group can't handle the contempt, which is just as well because being upstaged by newbie moochers would be shameful.

We're already 10 minutes behind schedule when we unexpectedly pass several food carts on the High Line that have started
the process of calling it a night. The hipster pedant running the
Northern Spy Food Co. cart tells me that it wouldn't be "food safe"
to give me the items he's in the process of throwing away because
they contain dairy. "You have nothing without dairy?" I ask. Be-
grudgingly he hands me two large hot biscuits. "They've been in
the oven awhile," he says. "They might not be great." But oh, they
are! The seven of us tear at the biscuits like a pack of wolves pulling apart a rabbit. One of my group simply asked the guys from
another truck if we could sample their cooking before they shut
off their grill. The two chefs make three types of miniature tacos
for us, which we all agree are exquisite.

We have to eat our tacos on the hoof lest the food and wine at
the galleries be ransacked. At the hpgrp Gallery on 20th Street,
I'm elated to see 10 bottles of red and white wine and three people ready to distribute it. "We ran out of cups," one says apologeti-
cally. "We just sent out for more," another says. These people are
trying to give us wine but can't and it's maddening! We descend
on what's left of the crudités and potato chips, slipping some oily
macadamia nuts into our ziplock bags, then cut our losses and
head to Pace Gallery on 25th Street, where waiters offer us water. "No wine?" I ask. "All out," says one. So I herd the gang to a
couple of more galleries where our indifference to the art raises
a few eyebrows but where the food tables are groaning with wine,
champagne, pita triangles, feta-stuffed olives, and chocolate wafer
straws. Both places are on upper floors, which confirms my theory
that upstairs galleries are much less likely to have their food and
wine offerings scoured by opportunists. You can take that tidbit to
the bank.

A few days later, I get back in touch with Edial Dekker to let
him know that I am a writer and that I enjoyed being a guerrilla
tour guide enough to reprise the role when he and his brother are
in town. He tells me that Gidsy was born after he and his brother
had trouble organizing a group to venture into the German countryside to pick mushrooms and then make a mushroom risotto.

"So we thought there was a market opportunity and we started thinking about how to connect people with experiences with a social component," he says. They started with a cooking class, followed by a seminar on how to create a startup. It was their pals at the popular app SoundCloud who mentioned them to Ashton Kutcher, who, says Dekker, "was just totally behind the idea. He immediately got that we were bringing people together." Dekker hopes that eventually Gidsy will become a common tool for anyone looking for fun—or educational or silly or random—stuff to do and fun people to do it with. "You don't have to be traveling," he says. "Meeting people doing interesting things in the city you live in is like traveling on a whole other level."

Dentists Without Borders

FROM *The New Yorker*

ONE THING THAT puzzled me during the American health-care debate was all the talk about socialized medicine and how ineffective it's supposed to be. The Canadian plan was likened to genocide, but even worse were the ones in Europe, where patients languished on filthy cots, waiting for aspirin to be invented. I don't know where these people get their ideas, but my experiences in France, where I've lived off and on for the past 13 years, have all been good. A house call in Paris will run you around $50. I was tempted to arrange one the last time I had a kidney stone, but waiting even 10 minutes seemed out of the question, so instead I took the subway to the nearest hospital. In the center of town, where we're lucky enough to have an apartment, most of my needs are within arm's reach. There's a pharmacy right around the corner, and two blocks further is the office of my physician, Dr. Médioni. Twice I've called on a Saturday morning, and, after answering the phone himself, he has told me to come on over. These visits, too, cost around $50. The last time I went, I had a red thunderbolt bisecting my left eyeball.

The doctor looked at it for a moment, and then took a seat behind his desk. "I wouldn't worry about it if I were you," he said. "A thing like that, it should be gone in a day or two."

"Well, where did it come from?" I asked. "How did I get it?"

"How do we get most things?" he answered.

"We buy them?"

The time before that, I was lying in bed and found a lump on my right side, just below my rib cage. It was like a deviled egg tucked beneath my skin. Cancer, I thought. A phone call and 20 minutes later, I was stretched out on the examining table with my shirt raised.

"Oh, that's nothing," the doctor said. "A little fatty tumor. Dogs get them all the time."

I thought of other things dogs have that I don't want: Dewclaws, for example. Hookworms. "Can I have it removed?"

"I guess you could, but why would you want to?"

He made me feel vain and frivolous for even thinking about it. "You're right," I told him. "I'll just pull my bathing suit up a little higher."

When I asked if the tumor would get any bigger, the doctor gave it a gentle squeeze. "Bigger? Sure, probably."

"Will it get a *lot* bigger?"

"No."

"Why not?" I asked.

And he said, sounding suddenly weary, "I don't know. Why don't trees touch the sky?"

Médioni works from an apartment on the third floor of a handsome 19th-century building, and, on leaving, I always think, Wait a minute. Did I see a diploma on his wall? Could Doctor possibly be the man's first name? He's not indifferent. It's just that I expect a little something more than "It'll go away." The thunderbolt cleared up, just as he said it would, and I've since met dozens of people who have fatty tumors and get along just fine. Maybe, being American, I want bigger names for things. I also expect a bit more gravity. "I've run some tests," I'd like to hear, "and discovered that what you have is called a bilateral ganglial abasement, or, in layman's terms, a cartoidal rupture of the venal septrumus. Dogs get these things all the time, and most often they die. That's why I'd like us to proceed with the utmost caution."

For my $50, I want to leave the doctor's office in tears, but instead I walk out feeling like a hypochondriac, which is one of the few things I'm actually not. If my French physician is a little disappointing, my French periodontist more than makes up for it. I have nothing but good things to say about Dr. Guig, who, gumwise, has really brought me back from the abyss. Twice in the course of our decade-long relationship he's performed surgical interventions. Then, last year, he removed four of my lower incisors, drilled down into my jawbone, and cemented in place two posts. First, though, he sat me down and explained the procedure, using lots of big words that allowed me to feel tragic and important. "I'm going to perform the surgery at nine o'clock on Tuesday morning, and it should take, at most, three hours," he said—all of this, as usual, in French. "At six that evening, you'll go to the dentist for your temporary implants, but still I'd like you to block out that entire day."

When I got home, I asked my boyfriend, Hugh, "Where did he think I was going to go with four missing teeth?"

I see Dr. Guig for surgery and consultations, but the regular, twice-a-year deep cleanings are performed by his associate, a woman named Dr. Barras. What she does in my mouth is unspeakable, and, because it causes me to sweat, I've taken to bringing a second set of clothes, and changing in the bathroom before I leave for home. "Oh, Monsieur Sedaris," she chuckles. "You are such a child."

A year ago, I arrived and announced that, since my previous visit, I'd been flossing every night. I thought this might elicit some praise—"How dedicated you are, how disciplined!"—but instead she said, "Oh, there's no need."

It was the same when I complained about all the gaps between my teeth. "I had braces when I was young, but maybe I need them again," I told her. An American dentist would have referred me to an orthodontist, but, to Dr. Barras, I was being hysterical. "You have what we in France call 'good-time teeth,'" she said. "Why on earth would you want to change them?"

"Um, because I can floss with the sash to my bathrobe?"

"Hey," she said. "Enough with the flossing. You have better ways to spend your evenings."

I guess that's where the good times come in.

Dr. Barras has a sick mother and a long-haired cat named Andy. As I lie there sweating with my trap wide open, she runs her electric hook under my gum line, and catches me up on her life since my last visit. I always leave with a mouthful of blood, yet I always look forward to my next appointment. She and Dr. Guig are *my* people, completely independent of Hugh, and though it's a stretch to label them friends, I think they'd miss me if I died of a fatty tumor.

*

Something similar is happening with my dentist, Dr. Granat. He didn't fabricate my implants—that was the work of a prosthodontist—but he took the molds and made certain that the teeth fit. This was done during five visits in the winter of 2011. Once a week, I'd show up at the office and climb into his reclining chair. Then I'd sink back with my mouth open. *"Ça va?"* he'd ask every five minutes or so, meaning "All right?" And I'd release a little tone. Like a doorbell. *"E-um."*

Implants come in two stages. The first teeth that get screwed in, the temporaries, are blocky, and the color is off. The second ones are more refined, and are somehow dyed or painted to match their neighbors. My four false incisors are connected to form a single unit, and were secured in place with an actual screwdriver. Because the teeth affect one's bite, the positioning has to be exact, so my dentist would put them in and then remove them to make minor adjustments. Put them in, take them out. Over and over. All the pain was behind me by this point, and so I just lay there, trying to be a good patient.

Dr. Granat keeps a small, muted television mounted near the ceiling, and each time I come it is tuned to the French travel channel. Voyage, it's called. Once, I watched a group of mountain people decorate a yak. They didn't string lights on it, but everything else seemed fair game: ribbons, bells, silver sheaths for the tips of its horns.

"Ça va?"

"E-um."

Another week, we were somewhere in Africa, where a family of five dug into the ground and unearthed what looked to be a burrow full of mice. Dr. Granat's assistant came into the room to ask a question, and when I looked back at the screen the mice had been skinned and placed, kebab-like, on sharp sticks. Then came another distraction, and when I looked up again the family in Africa were grilling the mice over a campfire, and eating them with their fingers.

"Ça va?" Dr. Granat asked, and I raised my hand, international dental sign language for "There is something vital I need to communicate." He removed his screwdriver from my mouth, and I pointed to the screen. *"Ils ont mangé des souris en brochette,"* I told him, meaning "They have eaten some mice on skewers."

He looked up at the little TV. *"Ah, oui?"*

A regular viewer of the travel channel, Dr. Granat is surprised by nothing. He's seen it all, and is quite the traveler himself. As is Dr. Guig. Dr. Barras hasn't gone anywhere exciting lately, but, what with her mother, how can she? With all these dental professionals in my life, you'd think I'd look less like a jack-o'-lantern. You'd think I could bite into an ear of corn, or at least tear meat from a chicken bone, but that won't happen for another few years, not until we tackle my two front teeth and the wobbly second incisors that flank them. "But after that's done I'll still need to come regularly, won't I?" I said to Dr. Guig, almost panicked. "My gum disease isn't cured, is it?"

I've gone from avoiding dentists and periodontists to practically stalking them, not in some quest for a Hollywood smile but because I enjoy their company. I'm happy in their waiting rooms, the coffee tables heaped with *Gala* and *Madame Figaro*. I like their mumbled French, spoken from behind Tyvek masks. None of them ever call me David, no matter how often I invite them to. Rather, I'm Monsieur Sedaris, not my father but the smaller, Continental model. Monsieur Sedaris with the four lower implants. Monsieur Sedaris with the good-time teeth, sweating so fiercely he leaves the office two kilos lighter. That's me, pointing to the bathroom and asking the receptionist if I may use the sandbox, me traipsing down the stairs in a fresh set of clothes, my smile bittersweet and drearied with blood, counting the days until I can come back, and return myself to this curious, socialized care.

LYNN YAEGER

Confessions of a Packing Maximalist

FROM *Travel + Leisure*

WHEN MRS. CHARLOTTE Drake Martinez Cardeza of Philadelphia settled into Suite B51–55 on the *Titanic*, she had with her 14 trunks, 4 suitcases, and 3 crates of baggage containing, among other items, 70 dresses, 38 feather boas, 10 fur coats, and 91 pairs of gloves. We know this because Mrs. Cardeza, who survived on Lifeboat 3, filed a staggering 18-page, single-spaced insurance claim against the White Star Line, seeking recompense for that lost ermine-trimmed coat and those vanished veils and parasols.

There's a reason Mrs. Cardeza needed all that stuff: fashionable women of her day were forever changing outfits—putting on and taking off different ensembles for dining, dancing, and shopping, even donning elaborate tea gowns, which never actually saw sunlight but were worn just for sitting around the parlor.

As fate would have it, I, too, have complicated wardrobe requirements when I hit the road. And it's not only because I frequently travel to Europe to cover the biannual fashion shows, where my colleagues appear to switch garments as often as an Edwardian matron (How do they manage it? Do they FedEx Goyard steamer trunks to the Hôtel de Crillon? Sneak off to Le Bon Marché to replenish hotel armoires daily?) but also because my personal style could hardly be called minimalist—and, in fact, depends heavily on puffy frocks and layered petticoats. My taste is fiercely nonconformist (well, as fierce as you can be when you are prancing around in a pink sequined dirndl and a scarlet velvet cloak).

I am sure that Mrs. Cardeza had a packing system, and I also have a carefully plotted routine, honed over decades of trial and error. First, rest assured that I do not have anything in common with those braggarts who spend 6 months in 12 capitals with two pairs of black pants and one T-shirt, insisting that they can do magic tricks with scarves. In fact, my situation is quite the opposite: I frequently don't have the right things with me no matter how much I bring, whether I'm going to the flea market in Tangiers or a nightclub in Moscow.

My predicament is exacerbated by the fact that whenever I check a bag, I am convinced it will not appear unmolested on the other side of the world, so am reluctant to fill it with anything more valuable than shampoo and skivvies. Let me be clear: I consider my wardrobe more a collection of irreplaceable artworks than a bunch of things to wear. That my luggage has never failed to arrive in no way allays this fear—in fact, it only reinforces my conviction that the odds are against me, that the next trip will be the one with the baggage disaster.

Since my carry-on must do the heavy lifting, I have been forced to employ strategies that can be more than a little embarrassing. Summer or winter, you will see me in my heaviest clothes, waddling up to the security gate in something like, say, a Dries Van Noten smock over two skirts and a vintage petticoat, in an attempt to smuggle a few more garments onto the plane. This explosion of fabric inevitably results in my being forced to submit to a series of humiliating and invasive security-related procedures, since, let's face it, there could be an entire arsenal stashed under my ensemble.

Can there be a less elegant way to begin a journey than planting your Fogal-clad feet on two filthy yellow rubber footprints, waiting for a total stranger to stick her hands up your dress and dust you down with a powdery substance? No matter! I just smile when the words "Female alert!" ring out from the TSA agent at the x-ray machine as I approach. To forestall this body search, I have been known to visit the ladies' room, peel off a few layers of clothing, stuff them into the largest conveyance that could possibly pass as a piece of "hand luggage," and hope that this now-diminished costume will get me waved through. Alas, this only works half the time. "Thank you for keeping us safe!" I cry when the guard realizes there is nothing under my dress—except maybe another dress.

At least now I am rushing to the ladies' pain-free. For years I insisted on toting a battered Louis Vuitton duffel, convinced that

this bag made me look like Sara Murphy circa 1920, heading off
to the Riviera, even when I nearly dislocated my shoulder carrying it. So I moved on to what seems in retrospect to be an insane solution, though it made perfect sense to me at the time—I
bought the duffel its own collapsible metal cart, secured it under
a crosshatch of bungee cords, and dragged the whole monstrosity
through the airport. Of course, I had to collapse the contraption
at the door of the plane and tug both it and the 100-pound duffel
down the aisle, rolling over people's toes as I fought my way to the
depths of coach.

"Get wheels!" my mom pleaded for years. "Look how cute the
flight attendants look with their little rolling suitcases!" But every
time I considered this solution, I heard the words of a stylish photographer friend echoing in my brain. "You can't have wheels," he
said in a low, disgusted whisper. "It's a terrible gesture when you
are pulling it!" Terrible gesture or not, I did eventually concede,
and the result has been life-changing. I am now the poster child
for the rabid cult of Rimowa, an ingenious brand that relies on
some kind of advanced technology (or maybe just four wheels?)
that enables me to glide through the airport as if I am walking
a shiny, cherry-red greyhound. And it's not just the ease of motion—these things also have flat tops where you can stack expand-
able Longchamp totes (another remarkable baggage innovation)
that allow you to transport all those fashion items you found so
irresistible when you tried them on in foreign fitting rooms and
now will never wear again. But that's another story.

If I had more time, I could travel by boat, which would solve
my problem. You can bring an almost endless number of cases on-
board, making you look like you just stepped out of a Fred Astaire
movie as you fidget on the buffet line. In fact, Cunard offers a
White Star shipping service that will fly your luggage from home
to the ship—as many pieces as you like!—so long as they will fit
in your stateroom. Appealing as this notion may be, it is alas of
limited usefulness: I usually have to be somewhere in eight hours,
not eight days. And anyway, wouldn't I be consumed with worry
that my cases, torn from my hands and flying on their own to some
distant dock, would lose their way?

Annoyed friends and colleagues, stuck waiting for me on the
other side of security, have gently suggested I modify my personal
style just a little. But despite the inconvenience, I stick to my guns

(perhaps not the most felicitous turn of phrase when it comes to air travel). And just when I think I am the only lonely pilgrim dolled up in layers of tulle while my fellow travelers cavort happily in Juicy Couture, another underappreciated, overdressed stalwart will sail into view. En route to the Life Ball, in Vienna, one year, I spied the fabulously louche New York nightlife legend Amanda Lepore, poured into a curvaceous satin frock and teetering on vertiginous stilettos while twirling an enormous hatbox. And what a delightful sight she was! Though she was channeling Jayne Mansfield and my costume was closer to Minnie Mouse, we shared a complicit glance—sisters under the skin. If you listened closely over the din of the loudspeakers, you could almost hear the spirit of Mrs. Cardeza, resplendent in a lace-trimmed tea gown, cheering us on.

PETER JON LINDBERG

Summerland

FROM *Travel + Leisure*

THE PIPER CUB buzzes back into view, flying just 200 feet over the waves, its red-lettered banner unfurled behind. All afternoon it's been crisscrossing the cloudless sky. Every day, the same plane, same offer: KEN'S MAINE CLAMBAKE—$19.95. When I first started coming here, the price was $8.99. Back then I could read it without my glasses.

Each time the plane passes, the kids on the beach look up from their pails and shovels and cheer. (Today, our friends' son Silas is building a sand replica of Fenway Park.) Soon there will be Popsicles, a game of foursquare. And later, as the tide comes in, we'll round up our blankets and shuffle over the dunes to the house, to start the evening ritual: fixing Maine Route 1 cocktails, shucking corn, steaming lobsters, plucking basil from the window box, making sea-urchin pasta. After dinner we'll have a round of Bananagrams while the Sox game plays on AM radio. If it's chilly there might be a fire—though we're as likely to doze off before 10, sun-drenched and surf-pummeled as we are. In the morning the gurgle of coffee will coax us from bed at dawn, and the whole routine will begin again.

I'm not sure how it started, and I can't say when it might end, but we've been making this trip together for more than a decade, my wife, Nilou, and I and this group of friends. It's become, unexpectedly yet unchangingly, What We Do. Every August, we stuff our cars with iceboxes and inflatable rafts, sharp knives and good wine, and point our caravan northward for the annual migration to Pine Point.

There may be prettier beaches, with quainter towns beyond, some on this very Maine coast. Yet this is the one I daydream about, through drizzly Aprils and slate-gray Decembers. I wouldn't necessarily have chosen this place, given my pick of a thousand others, but years ago this place chose me, and it's lured me back every summer since, so I guess it's settled. We're together for the foreseeable future.

My friend Mark and I have known Pine Point since we were teenagers; his parents, the McAdams, own a summer cottage just upshore from our rental. It was my idea to bring the group. Until their first visit in 2001, Nilou and the rest had never been north of Boston—couldn't crack a lobster, couldn't name a single Red Sox. In the years since they've become localized, loyalized: converts to the cult of Maine.

Constancy is the most underrated of virtues, in people but also in places. You can revisit London or Tokyo every six months and find an entirely new city in place of the one you remembered, such that even your 18th trip feels like a first date. Returning to Pine Point, we find everything as we left it—as if we'd merely stepped out for a Dr Pepper in the middle of a game of paddleball, then returned, 358 days later, to resume it.

Set on a peninsula south of Portland, Pine Point is a cluster of rustic cottages and slightly grander Victorians set along a series of cul-de-sacs jutting off the main road toward the sea. At the end of each cul-de-sac is a sandy footpath that cuts through a deep ribbon of dune grass that hums with dragonflies and ripples in the breeze. And at the end of the path, where the tallgrass falls away, lies a seven-mile crescent of flat, smooth, sand-colored sand.

Our first walk of the season down that path—a barefoot trudge weighed down by sloshing coolers and salt-scarred beach chairs—may be the happiest moment of my year. That it requires a bit of effort and patience only adds to the drama. The tallgrass feels like some magical green barrier that must be breached, while the slight incline of the dune means you can hear and smell the ocean before you actually see it.

The house we rent isn't much to look at from the outside, and entirely too much to look at on the inside, what with the owners' ever-expanding collection of beach kitsch. But it's our place, and through the years that's come to mean a lot. Were I a first-time renter arriving today, I might take issue with the abundance of crab figurines, the rather lumpy beds, the rusty taps and hinges on the outdoor shower. But the shower itself? No marble-clad bathroom could compete.

Our routine is quite simple: Swim. Nap. Eat. Rinse. Repeat. The start of the week is customarily filled with discussions of all the activities we might finally get to this year: a sailboat charter in Kennebunkport; a hike up Mount Agamenticus; perhaps a jaunt up to Rockland—but really, who are we kidding? We're not going to do any of it. And when the end of the week comes, we won't regret a thing.

Instead we find more modest diversions. Long beach-blanket grocery lists are made, elaborate meal plans hatched. There is the occasional detour to Portland's Standard Baking Co. for their unspeakably good brioche. At some point we'll paddle kayaks into the nearby Scarborough Marsh, slipping through reed-walled channels while herons and ibis eye us from the banks. And should we ever tire of the quiet—or crave penny candy—we can always ride down shore to Old Orchard Beach.

On summer weekends, when 100,000 revelers descend on the place, Old Orchard officially becomes the largest community in Maine. It is also, semiofficially, the tackiest place in all of New England: a honky-tonk playground of flip-flop shops, fried-dough stands, temporary-tattoo parlors, and carnival rides that makes Ocean City, Maryland, look like the Henley Royal Regatta. Needless to say, we love it. The Grand Trunk Railroad used to run here direct from Montreal, and Old Orchard remains catnip for vacationing Québecois. The fried-dough stands also sell *poutine;* signs at the amusement park are in English and French. This provides a semblance of cultural displacement: batting cages become *cages des frappeurs;* Jet Skis become *scooters des mers;* while Skee-Ball becomes, charmingly, *le skee-ball.*

As a younger man I was flummoxed by people who returned to the same place every year. What were they afraid of? Didn't they know there was more to see? Travel, I insisted, was about the unfamiliar, the undiscovered, the passport full of stamps. I still believe that last part, if less adamantly now. What I've awoken to since is the soul-affirming joy of returning. Going back, it turns out, does not mean retreat. A ritual is not a rut.

I've also learned the difference between *traveling* and *vacationing*, two words that are often used interchangeably but mean different things. A vacation typically involves travel, but travel is not always a vacation. Sometimes it's quite the opposite—fraught with uncertainty over where to go, where to stay, what to see. Vacations are a respite from all that. For us, Maine is sweet relief.

Over time, and through the McAdams, we've come to know our neighbors. Each morning the residents of Pine Point gather on the otherwise empty beach, with their dogs and their coffee mugs, to discuss last night's humidity or Ellsbury's stand-up triple. Although we're still technically "from away"—I suppose you could call us one fifty-second local—they welcome us into their klatches, in part because we, too, are holding ceramic coffee mugs. We've also become enthusiastic patrons of the neighbors' kids' lemonade stand, a smart little dune-side palapa that they've festooned with homemade thatch. And we are on a first-name basis—we don't know their last names—with the staff at Bayley's Lobster Pound, where we have a standing order each evening for a half dozen females.

Now and then we'll spot the shambling figure we call the Clam Man, a grumbly chap with a spongy beard, leering fish eyes, a coral-like complexion, and the bearing of an insane Poseidon. He appears only at low tide, loping down the beach with a bucketful of just-harvested surf clams, their long oily tongues protruding from shells the size of Nerf footballs. The local children watch him from a distance. I spoke to him once—he answered in French, then grumbled off down the beach.

And so it goes, the same characters making their exits and entrances, the scenery and plotline seldom changing. Nilou once likened our Maine trips to rereading a favorite novel: she already knows how it will end, but getting there is still as satisfying, if not more so, since she's always picking up new shades and nuances along the way. (The Clam Man is Québecois!) And, as with a cherished book, there's no risk of disappointment—unless it rains all week, which some years it has. In that case we play a lot more Bananagrams.

Of course, things do change in Pine Point. Against a familiar backdrop one notices all sorts of quotidian adjustments, like when the snack bar gets a new sign, or the pier is painted a slightly deeper green, or coconut water makes its debut at the local grocery. These subtle shifts of the light keep us on our sandy toes, while reminding us how lucky we are to have found a place that's stayed, in most respects, pretty much the same. Our friend Michael put it best last summer: "There are few things you can rely on in this world, and thank God Maine is one of them." Every visit is a sort of homecoming.

Anyway. I'm off to pack the cooler. Maybe I'll see you on the beach.

BERND BRUNNER

The Wild Dogs of Istanbul

FROM *The Smart Set*

NO, YOU'D RATHER not cuddle with them. They seem a little too unpredictable and unkempt for that. And it's not tempting to project human characteristics on them either. But it is easy to feel sorry for some of them, who bear traces of injuries, disease, and accidents. Most resemble one another: large, with a light brown, sometimes darker coat. Some have short legs paired with unusually large bodies. Despite their scars, the wild dogs of Istanbul seem self-sufficient and untroubled, as if no one could mean them any harm. You can find them everywhere: between parked cars or, early in the morning, under the chairs in front of the Starbucks on Taksim Square. Often they just lie there and doze. Are they recovering from last night's activities? Most people don't seem bothered by them, but it's obvious that some, a little uncertain, take pains to avoid them. But they are not to be made fun of because of that.

The dogs' presence in this metropolis is not entirely without problems. Some of the animals are said to be so smart they understand traffic lights, but more often they cross streets in front of terrified drivers, keep residents awake with their barking, or even attack someone. In fact, I have myself observed an incident in my neighborhood, Tarlabaşı, where a young man was literally chased by two dogs. He fell to the ground and dragged himself into a barbershop. It was painful to watch, but it all happened so quickly that one couldn't really intervene; besides, how would one disperse the dogs without any adequate stick or tool? I don't know what exactly preceded the incident, why the dogs had attacked the man in the first place. These attacks, however, happen far less often than one might expect, considering the dogs' constant presence. No reliable count exists, but according to estimates, the dogs number about a hundred thousand. When you come to Istanbul, you will see that this doesn't sound like an exaggeration.

The dogs' position is a strange one: they are used to having people around, and even depend on them, but they don't live directly together with humans. Behavioral scientist Konrad Lorenz, who once wrote about Istanbul's stray dogs, observed that they carefully avoid loose small hens and newborn sheep—a lesson they learned in order to survive. Instead, they feed themselves in two ways. First, residents in the poorer sections of the city often put their trash bags out in front of their houses, where dogs and cats plunder them before trash trucks cart off the remaining piles in the early morning. But more and more metal trash cans are popping up, and their content is inaccessible, at least for dogs. Second, many people follow a custom (unfamiliar to Western observers) of more or less adopting a dog and regularly feeding it, without bringing it into their homes. Some people even make beds out of cardboard that become a dog's regular spot in front of the house. Animals in these relationships are not full-fledged pets, but they are not complete strays either. In any case, their uncommitted "owners" never take them for walks. This reluctance to take in the animals can't really be due to the size of the apartments; in a society where the single lifestyle is practically unknown, almost all residences are designed for families, and rarely measure less than 80 square meters. So what is the reason?

In Turkey, relationships to dogs are complex. In his novel *My Name Is Red*, Orhan Pamuk enters the mind of a dog and asks himself about the origins of mankind's enmity:

> Why do you believe that those who touch us spoil their ablutions? If your caftan brushes against our damp fur, why do you insist on washing that caftan seven times like a frenzied woman? Only tinsmiths could be responsible for the slander that a pot licked by a dog must be thrown away or retinned. Or perhaps, yes, cats . . .

Although there is no clear basis for this belief in the Quran, strict Muslims consider dogs—especially their drool—to be unclean. People don't let the animals into their homes because they could dirty the prayer rug and because, even today, little tradition exists of keeping dogs as pets. Furthermore, a common belief holds that *köpekler,* as dogs are called, prevent angels from visiting. Not all Turks share these views. In parts of Istanbul influenced by the West, all sorts of purebred dogs can be found, including traditional fighting breeds. In these cases, dogs are highly desirable status symbols, and many stores sell pet supplies. However, problems with religious neighbors disturbed by the presence of dogs can arise. "Many people want a dog, but don't know how to go about it," says Bilge Okay of the dog protection society SHKD, which works toward better treatment of the animals.

Although keeping pets in this way is a very recent development, the breeding of dogs has a long tradition in the region. One of the oldest pieces of evidence for the domestication of dogs at all comes from Çayönü—in eastern Turkey, near the border with Syria—from approximately 12,000 years ago. Well-known breeds like the Kangal, a very large shorthair, come to mind as well. Kangals were herd dogs used by Anatolian shepherds even before Islam spread throughout the region; they were associated with one of the 12 months of the year. But back to the wild dogs of Istanbul. Their presence in the city stretches far back, but their origins are the matter of legend: Do they hail from Turkmenistan? Did they arrive with the troops of the conqueror Mehmed II in the 15th century? Wherever their roots may lie, they have been an established part of the city for centuries, skulking in the shadows of the buildings.

Accounts of travelers—sometimes baffled, sometimes disconcerted or frightened—rarely fail to mention the dogs. In the 17th century, Jean de Thévenot noted that rich citizens of Istanbul bequeathed their fortunes to the city's dogs to ensure their continued presence. And his contemporary Joseph Pitton de Tournefort heard from butchers who sold meat specially intended for feeding the dogs. He also saw how the city's residents treated the animals' wounds and prepared straw mats and even small doghouses for their canine neighbors. No less an establishment than the legendary Pera Palas, the best hotel, cared for the dogs and fed them regularly. Edmondo De Amicis, an Italian traveler whose book *Constantinople* records his impressions of the city in the mid-19th century, went so far as to describe Istanbul as a "giant kennel." And Grigor Yakob Basmajean, an Orientalist born in Edirne, claimed in 1890 that no other city in the world had as many dogs as the metropolis on the Bosporus. The dogs were so omnipresent that streetcar employees had to drive them from the tracks with long sticks so the horse-drawn wagons could pass through. Passersby could often stop to watch them fighting with one another. Their howling could be heard all night; there were so many dogs that their voices blended into a constant sound "like the quaking of frogs in the distance," as one observer vividly described. It sounds like the dogs, not the authorities, set the tone. In popular shadow-puppet plays, dogs were compared to the poor.

Dealings with canines were always marked by ambivalence. Although dogs formed part of a romantic cityscape, caricatures from the Ottoman period depict them as threats to be stopped, along with cholera, crime, and women in European clothing. Again and again, attempts were made to catch them and remove them from the city. In the late 19th century, Sultan Abdülaziz decreed that the dogs should be rounded up and deported to Hayirsiz, an island of barren, steep cliffs in the Sea of Marmara. Sivriada, a tiny island to which Byzantine rulers once banished criminals, made headlines in 1911 when the governor of Istanbul released tens of thousands of dogs there. A yellowed postcard shows hundreds of dogs on the beach; their voices could be heard even at great distances. However, an earthquake that occurred shortly thereafter was taken as a sign of God's displeasure, and the dogs were brought back.

Attempts to stem the plague of dogs in the city continued, with more or less success. Their presence was always seen as a sign that the city could not impose order and guarantee the safety of residents. Cities like New York and Paris, where the problem was under control, became role models. Shortly after the revolution, Mary Mills Patrick, an American who taught at Istanbul's Woman's College, thanked the new Turkish regime for its efforts in this area; after all, a civilized city was no place for packs of dogs. But even in the decades that followed, the dogs never completely disappeared. Occasional efforts to eliminate them were seen as acts of barbarism. Until 2004, when a law to protect the animals was finally passed, meatballs laced with strychnine were not uncommon. But today such draconian measures are things of the past.

Real change will only come once new solutions for the city's trash problem are found and garbage is no longer simply placed on the curb, as it is in many neighborhoods today. Then things will be tough for the dogs. Animal protection activists today call for a concerted effort to catch the dogs, vaccinate them against rabies, sterilize them, and tag them before releasing them back into their territory. The World Health Organization also recommends this strategy. But gray areas exist in how authorities deal with the problem. Animal advocates claim that inexperienced veterinarians pack the neutered dogs into overcrowded cages, load them into trucks, and dump them in Belgrade Forest, about 10 miles northeast of the city near the Black Sea coast. There, the dogs are often attacked by wild animals or starve. "In the end, it would be better to put the animals to sleep than to release them in the unfamiliar wilderness," says Bilge Okay. "But that would be against the religious beliefs of the people operating these facilities."

Since status-conscious Turks have little interest in keeping mixed-breed dogs as pets, some of these animals make their way to Germany, where new owners adopt them. But this involves bureaucratic hurdles and high costs, especially since the dogs cannot simply be sent airfreight but must be accompanied by someone to transport and deliver them.

The city today is also full of stray cats. They have it better—nobody is out to kill them. But that's another chapter in the story of humans and animals in Istanbul.

DIMITER KENAROV

Bombing Sarajevo

FROM *Outside*

"WE'VE GOT PERMISSION to use the cannon!" says Ismar Biogradlic, the coach of Bosnia and Herzegovina's national snowboard team, with a smile. "Hurry up!"

A snowcat waits for us, orange lights flashing in the dusk. We
hoist a coiled length of hose onto the flatbed and climb up. Biogradlic, a 37-year-old man with close-cropped graying hair and a
ring in his left ear, taps the roof of the cab and yells "Go!" The
driver revs the engine, and the cat jerks forward like a tank.

After hours of negotiations, Biogradlic has finally convinced the
state officials who own Bjelašnica, a ski resort near Sarajevo and a
former Olympic venue, to let him use a snow gun. It's early February, normally the snowiest month in Bosnia's Dinaric Alps, but
Bjelašnica's trails are barely covered and entirely devoid of skiers.
This is problematic for Biogradlic. In less than a week, he is scheduled to host a slopestyle and big-air event for the Snowboard Europa Cup—a small-budget European version of the X Games—at
the resort. But Bjelašnica's management, a couple of decades and
one significant war removed from the salad days of the 1984 Sarajevo Olympics, is pinching pennies, and Biogradlic has only a few
hours with the snow gun.

As we grind up the hill, the snowcat churns up a stew of gravel
and dirt. High on the peak, the skeletal remains of rusted-out
chairlift towers that haven't operated in 20 years are silhouetted
against the evening sky. Around us, in the surrounding forests, red
signs issue a harsh warning: MINES! KEEP OFF!

At the top of the terrain park, we jump off the snowcat.

"Quickly," Biogradlic says, shoving a pickax into my hands. "Start digging a trench."

The snow gun, brought up by another cat, is set strategically over the slope. While I dig a protective trench for the hose and cables running between the hydrant and the gun, Biogradlic makes sure the connections are tight. Enes Vilić, 26, one of Bosnia's best freeskiers, meets us at the top and begins helping.

It's now dark, and the temperature has finally dropped below freezing. A slight wind picks up, bending the tops of the dark pines. It feels peaceful, until the control lights of the snow gun come to life.

"Ready?" Biogradlic yells.

"Ready!" Vilić yells back.

"Let's have some fun then," Biogradlic says. The scream of the snow gun pierces the night. In a few moments, the hose grows stiff with water, and a thick white beacon of millions of fine ice crystals shoots up into the air. It's snowing in Bosnia.

Ismar Biogradlic and Enes Vilić have a wild idea. The two men, both Bosnian Muslims, or Bosniaks, hope to revitalize their country's alpine-sports scene, which was the pride of the Balkans until the Yugoslavian civil war ripped it apart. Biogradlic has spent the past decade fostering youth snowboarding, coaching the national team and courting international events like the Europa Cup, one of the major circuits of the International Ski Federation. Vilić, meanwhile, takes a less formal approach: the 26-year-old skier leads a freewheeling, multiethnic group of snow punks called Madstyle Team.

The crew seems a bit ragtag—its members came together to get discounted lift tickets at Bjelašnica and Sarajevo's other resort, Jahorina, and can seem as dedicated to beer as to skiing. But Madstyle has recently begun to attract big sponsors for their competitions. What's more, they represent a sentiment that's palpable upon setting foot in Sarajevo: the desire of Bosnia's youth to move on from the brutal event that for years has defined their country in the eyes of the world.

"We imagine this developing—not just snowboarding and skiing, but other sports like skateboarding, rafting, rock climbing," says Vilić, who is lanky and handsome and who wears a blue bandanna around his neck at all times. "The plan is to put things on a larger, social level. It's the community that counts."

It's worth remembering that Sarajevo has had a love affair with alpine sports dating back to the Ottoman Empire. In the 19th century, bored kids would hike up the hills to do *liguranje,* a precursor to the luge. By the 1930s, when Bosnia was part of Yugoslavia, a confederation of Balkan states, the mountains filled with skiers who built lodges and jumps on 6,300-foot Mount Jahorina, about 20 miles southeast of Sarajevo. The resort got its first chairlift in 1953, and Jahorina quickly became an international ski destination, hosting the European and World Cup circuits. In 1978, the city was awarded the XIV Winter Games. To host the event, the government built Bjelašnica on the opposite side of Sarajevo in 1982.

The Games almost never happened. On the morning of February 9, 1984, a day after the opening ceremony, Sarajevo woke up buried in snow. Three feet had fallen overnight in the mountains, overwhelming the men's alpine course at Bjelašnica. The conditions were similar at Jahorina, the venue of the women's alpine events. Winds of 125 miles per hour buffeted the high peaks.

In response, 36,000 organizers and nearly every able-bodied citizen of Sarajevo threw themselves into the battle against the weather. They carried picks, shovels, and brooms and stayed warm with homebrewed rakija, a highly flammable local moonshine made from plums. They cleaned up the roads to the venues, dug out the buses from the drifts, and groomed the trails.

It worked. Some 1,400 participants from 49 nations took their shot at a medal. The IOC president at the time, Juan Antonio Samaranch, proclaimed the Sarajevo event "the best-organized Winter Games in the history of the Olympic movement."

Then came the war. Nationalistic fervor had been simmering in Yugoslavia for a long time, with each of the country's major ethnic groups—Bosniaks, Croats, and Serbs—driven by centuries-old dreams of their own pure state. In 1991, the worsening economic situation and a few radicalized politicians blew the lid off. Hostilities broke out in Croatia, and it wasn't long before Bosnia and Herzegovina went down the same road. The Bosnian Serbs, led by Radovan Karadžić, struck first. In 1992, with the whole world watching live on TV, military and paramilitary bands pil-

laged villages and laid siege to Sarajevo, shelling Muslim neighborhoods—war crimes for which Karadžić would be charged after
he was finally captured in 2008.

The Olympic venues were not spared. Bjelašnica and the surrounding villages, where Muslims and Serbs lived side by side, became the frontline of the attack. In 1993, the resort's lifts were
wrecked, the slopes mined, and the hotels torched by Bosnian Serb
forces commanded by the notorious general Ratko Mladić. The
Olympic bobsled track on Mount Trebević, above Sarajevo, became
a snipers' nest for the Serbs, who fired down on the Muslims below.
The edifice of Zetra Hall, the site of the hockey and figure-skating
events, was shelled from the hills. Its ice rink served as a makeshift
morgue, the wooden seats providing material for coffins.

When the war ended in 1995, Bosnia and Herzegovina won independence, but it was divided into two autonomous, mutually
hostile entities: the Muslim-and-Croat-dominated Federation of
Bosnia and Herzegovina, and the Serb-dominated Republika Srpska. Even the resorts became spoils of war: Bjelašnica was given
to the federation, while Serb-controlled Jahorina, which was left
largely unscathed by the conflict, joined Republika Srpska.

Only recently have the old wounds begun to heal, thanks in
part to a new generation of kids who don't hold their parents'
grudges. Vilić is one of these kids. Though his family was kicked
out of its Sarajevo home by Serb paramilitaries and had to move to
another neighborhood, his memories of the war are surprisingly
fond. "It was the best time," he says. "Everything was anarchy! We
stole gas from the cars! Of course, during shelling we would hide
in the basement."

Vilić used to be part of the National Youth Alpine Team and
won third place in an International Ski Federation race in 2003.
Still, career options for a would-be professional skier are slim in
Bosnia. These days, Vilić studies architecture in Sarajevo, works for
a ski-repair service, and spends the rest of his time in the mountains with Madstyle Team. Sometimes they go to Jahorina, sometimes to Bjelašnica.

"We don't care about who is Bosniak or Serb or Croat," he
says. "Madstyle is a few good friends who have a passion for winter
sports. That's all."

*

A stuffed hawk stares out at us from the wall with glass eyes. Biogradlic, Vilić, and I are the only customers in the only open bar in Bjelašnica. We sip hot bean soup and guzzle beer, waiting for the snow gun to do its job. Biogradlic looks nervous. His cell phone rings every few minutes: various teams for the upcoming Europa Cup calling with requests. The South Africans need help with their Bosnian visas; another team wants to change hotels.

"This year the Austrians are coming," Biogradlic says, taking a nervous swig from his bottle. "I wouldn't be worried if it were just guys from Balkan countries—we could have a few beers and talk things over. But the Austrians can be grumpy if the conditions are bad."

Biogradlic fell in love with winter as a 10-year-old kid watching the Sarajevo Games. He competed in two Olympics in luge, representing Yugoslavia in 1992 at Albertville and the newly independent Bosnia and Herzegovina in 1998 at Nagano. He couldn't compete at Lillehammer in 1994; he was busy fighting off the Serbs. During the war, he sustained gunshot wounds to his wrist and shoulder.

Biogradlic eventually dropped the luge, in part because the bobsled track on Mount Trebević was in ruins. He began snowboarding, borrowing his first board from a Greek friend, and soon opened a snowboard shop in downtown Sarajevo, in 1999. Three years later he organized the national team, which is now composed of three riders, ages 17 to 28. The members have finished in the middle of the pack in big-air and slopestyle events at Europa Cup competitions. Soon after I left, in April, they went to the Junior World Championships in Valmalenco, Italy, where they finished dead last in slopestyle.

Hanging around Biogradlic, you get the feeling that snowboarding is his life. It's difficult to get him to talk about anything else, except for his wife, Nina, and his young son.

At the bar, I ask him about his role in the war, and he clams up. "I don't want to talk about this," he replies curtly. "A lot of time has passed, and we need to move on. People should just get a snowboard or skis or whatever and enjoy the simple pleasures of life. Snowboarding is not nationalistic. Everybody can get together on the slopes. All we need is a bit more snow and investment in the sport."

Vilić chimes in loudly: "Our government is investing a lot of money into soccer, but they don't seem to care that much for snowboarding and skiing."

Indeed, funding the alpine resurgence has been a challenge. While Jahorina, which has less varied and exciting terrain, has received some $30 million in the past three years for improvements like a pair of six-seat high-speed lifts, Bjelašnica has wallowed. Organizations such as the International Rescue Committee provided $100,000 for reconstruction, but since 1997 only a fraction of the mountain has been open on a regular basis. One of the renovated lifts, a triple, runs about halfway up the slopes and then abruptly stops. A few hundred weekend warriors come regularly from Sarajevo for the challenging terrain, but there are only six usable runs. Beyond that, in the woods, the mines from the war haven't all been cleared yet.

The past few years have seen modest improvements at Bjelašnica. The resort finally bought snowmaking equipment and built a 2.6-million-gallon water reservoir. Plans are underway for a gondola that would run to the top of the roughly 6,800-foot mountain, which offers about 2,600 vertical feet of skiing. Still, investment in the resort's infrastructure pales in comparison with that going on at the base of the hill, where two new hotels and a group of slick condos have already been built—second homes for Sarajevo's nouveaux riches. The problem, Biogradlic tells me, is that the mountain is still operated by a cumbersomely bureaucratic state company. "Except for a few decent guys, the whole organization is clumsy," he says. "Just look at what we have to go through to make some snow." He sighs and gulps his beer. "Let's check out the cannon," he says. "Maybe there's enough snow already."

There's not enough snow. When I return to Bjelašnica a few mornings later, rivulets of slush and dirty snowmelt run down the terrain park. The thermometer reads 45 degrees Fahrenheit. Though the rails and boxes are still in place, the large kicker at the finish resembles a beached whale. Biogradlic and Vilić have been here all night, spreading artificial snow over the slopestyle course. Biogradlic runs up and down the terrain park, a shovel in one hand and a cell phone in the other. Vilić shapes the approach to one of the boxes, scrambling around on his knees. A few riders from Sarajevo have come to help, including Vilić's buddy Nikola Krneta, a 28-year-old Serb who is one of the founders of Madstyle and a member of the national snowboard team.

"I'm starting to believe that the lack of snow is the government's fault," says Krneta, who wears a black bandanna around his neck and a curved barbell in his left ear. He pops open a beer can. "Two more days of sun and I'll switch to writing poetry."

Just a month ago, Madstyle organized a huge jib contest, the Madstyle Games, in downtown Sarajevo. It took them more than six months to land sponsors like Toyota and Red Bull, who threw in a few thousand dollars. Madstyle invited riders from Slovenia, erected a 35-foot ramp, and littered the city with promotional posters. When the day arrived, the temperature was 54 degrees. The event took place, thanks to a giant refrigerator truck that brought hundreds of bags of snow from the mountains. But now we're *in* the mountains; there's no snow to import.

"If the temperature doesn't drop, we won't be able to make snow tonight," Biogradlic says with a sigh.

While he and Vilić debate the options, six young snowboarders show up. They are far too fair-skinned to be Bosnian.

"Hey, what's up?" calls out a teenager in a San Jose Sharks sweatshirt. "I'm Matt from Idaho. My friends and I were at a Bible camp in Switzerland and decided to come here—teach snowboarding and help out."

"Yes. We prayed to God, and he told us to come here," says another kid, who looks to be about 18. He has blue eyes, freckles, and a wispy blond beard.

The Bosnians—who, it would be fair to say, have seen it all—are stunned. The Evangelical boarders are here with a local adventure group called Nova Zora (New Dawn) run by an American guy from Georgia, Merle "Tomas" Jones. One of the boarders has a smiling Jesus on her helmet.

"All right," Biogradlic tells them. "Go to the big kicker and start clearing out the dirt and larger stones."

In a few minutes, the Evangelicals are scrambling over the muddy hump, stones flying in all directions. Soon their bright jackets are covered in dirt. One by one, they sit down on the side.

Biogradlic looks at them and shakes his head. "I think it's time to call it quits," he says, pulling out his cell phone. The Europa Cup at Bjelašnica will be postponed.

Two days later, on a warm Saturday afternoon in Sarajevo, street-cars covered in ads for soda and bubble gum trundle along the city's main boulevard, Zmaja od Bosne, once known as Sniper Alley. Except for a few pockmarked facades left unrepaired for lack of money, there are no visible reminders of violence. A new skyscraper, the Avaz Twist Tower, rises over the minarets of the old town. A dump truck crawls its way toward Sarajevo's downtown skate park. Seeing it, a girl in a black hoodie yells, "The snow is coming!"

The truck humps over the curb and stops in the middle of the park. A crowd of about 30 skiers and snowboarders awaits. Vilić and Krneta are here, along with some friends from Madstyle Team. So are the jibbers for Jesus. Biogradlic, beat from the week's efforts, stayed home.

Vilić and Krneta had suggested the idea: if we can't have a Europa Cup, let's bring a truckload of snow to the skate park in Sarajevo and have our own jib session. Sublime is blasting from Krneta's parked Audi, the four doors wide open, the hatchback full of beer.

"You have to make the best of the worst, dude," says Matt Gencarella, the evangelist from Idaho, sipping from a can of Sarajevsko beer. He has *BFC/DFL* tattooed on his wrist. It means Boarders for Christ/Down for Life.

"The sports I do, I do for God," he declares.

"Funny, I've never been in a mosque or a church," Vilić says, grinning wide.

The truck unloads the snow to cheers. A couple of guys pick up shovels and begin covering the approach ramp with powder and preparing the landing. Some snow is put aside for a makeshift beer cooler. In 20 minutes, everything is ready. Waiting patiently on top of the ramp, snowboarders and skiers drop in one by one, sliding down the flat box at the end. The snow is wet, and there's hardly any speed on the approach, but Vilić, Krneta, and the others manage a few stylish tricks—nose presses, lip slides, blunt slides. Beers are downed quickly and often. The skiers talk about girlfriends and boyfriends, jobs, Jesus Christ, marijuana farming. Now Dubioza Kolektiv, the hottest reggae-rock band in Bosnia, thumps from the stereo. When dark descends over the city, people pull their cars up and shine their headlights on the ramp. The party goes on. Then, one by one, the minarets on the hills come to life for evening prayer.

"This is absolutely the worst winter I can remember," says Krneta, popping another beer. "But I love it anyway."

DAVID FARLEY

Vietnam's Bowl of Secrets

FROM *Afar*

"BA LE . . . ?" I said to a shirtless man, who halted me from going any farther down the narrow lane. He simply pointed, his long fingernail directing me the opposite way. I was on the back streets of Hoi An, a prettied-up UNESCO-protected town on the central coast of Vietnam. I had ventured into this neighborhood, clearly not a place many tourists wander, in the hope of finding a well. The Ba Le well was actually listed in my guidebook, which I'd accidentally donated to the seat pocket of the airplane earlier that morning.

As I reversed course and proceeded deeper into the neighborhood, the buzz of scooters grew fainter with each step, replaced by the incongruent sounds that poured out of open doors and tangled in the open air—American B-grade movie dialogue and Vietnamese pop music. A few turns later, there I was, staring at the square-shaped, concrete Ba Le well, one of its sides abutting the wall of an old building. Two men were using a bucket, tied to a rope, to fish out water and then pour it into huge plastic containers on a bicycle fashioned into a cart. They ignored my presence as I looked down the well: splotches of Day-Glo-green moss clung to the bricks, and a billowy image of myself looked back at me from 10 feet below.

Until relatively recently, Hoi An's 80 or so wells, centuries old, were the town's main sources of drinking water. The town now has a modern system for running water, but many residents still make the pilgrimage to Ba Le. The well is thought to have been built in the 10th century by the Cham people, a native population whose empire flourished in central Vietnam until the 15th century. As the story goes, there's something special about the water from the Ba Le well. An entire mythology has accrued around it. Some say the water is medicinal; others claim the well has some mystical connection to fairies.

But finding the well was only the first step of my quest in Hoi An. My main motivation for traveling 10,000 miles from New York was to eat one particular dish identified with this town, a dish supposedly made exclusively with Ba Le water.

In 2012, most major cosmopolitan cities offer nearly every cuisine, including Vietnamese. One Vietnamese specialty you'll almost never find, though—not in Little Saigon in Southern California nor even in the real Saigon in southern Vietnam—is *cao lau* (pronounced "cow laow"). According to tradition, this pork-a-licious, herb-scented noodle dish has an umbilical attachment to Hoi An. The uniquely textured noodles must be made with local ingredients—specifically, water from the Ba Le well and ash from a certain tree that grows on the Cham Islands, some 13 miles off the coast of Hoi An. But not many people know how to make cao lau noodles. One family has, for generations, had a monopoly on making the six-inch-long rectangular rice noodles that look like a thicker, shorter version of fettuccine. And its members have never told anyone the recipe. For these reasons, cao lau is one of the few dishes in the world that has largely escaped the giant sponge we call globalization. You can't take cao lau out of Hoi An, nor can you take the Hoi An out of cao lau. It's the ultimate example of culinary terroir.

I had tried cao lau for the first time a year earlier, when I visited Hoi An after eating my way around the rest of Vietnam. It was a revelation, or a series of them: the snap of crisp aromatic sprouts, basil, and coriander; the sublime unctuous quality of thinly sliced salty pork; the crunch of flat, square croutons (made from the same ingredients as the noodles); the silky, smoky broth, spiked with Chinese five-spice seasoning; and at the heart of the experience, the rice noodles, thick and chewy with a coarse texture on the outside and a slightly starchy taste. I'd never had a dish like cao lau in Vietnam. Its flavors and composition were completely unlike pho, the noodle dish most people associate with the country. I thought, This can't be Vietnamese.

After my first visit to Hoi An, I did a little research. It seems no one really knows where cao lau came from. The prevailing origin tale is that Japanese traders brought it with them when they set up shop in Hoi An in the 16th and 17th centuries. The most famous Japanese remnant in town is the stout wooden bridge that crosses a small canal and connects the two major streets of the old quarter. Other versions of the dish's genesis story claim cao lau originated with the Cham. There are also tales of Chinese adventurers who turned up with the noodles in the 19th century and taught someone how to make them. The name does seem to come from the Chinese characters for "high steamer"; unlike most noodles, which are boiled, cao lau noodles are steamed.

Now, a year later, I had returned, hoping to uncover the mysteries behind a dish that seemed like an enigma wrapped in rice noodles and shrouded in slices of pork. Where did cao lau really come from? What made the noodles so magical that the dish couldn't be reproduced anywhere else? On my first afternoon back in Hoi An, the ordinary-looking Ba Le well wasn't revealing anything. I walked away even more determined to find the answers.

That evening, I was sitting in a restaurant talking to Thao, a 29-year-old Hoi An local and friend of a friend, who agreed to help me with my mission. We were at Trung Bac, a restaurant in the center of town that is famous for its cao lau, mostly because it has been serving it for so long. An engraved wooden sign states (in Vietnamese), THIS RESTAURANT HAS BEEN OPEN MORE THAN 100 YEARS.

Thao said he took me here not only because the cao lau is good but also because the owner of the restaurant was related to the cao lau noodle-making family.

"Is there anything you want to ask him?"

I figured I'd shoot for the Holy Grail right away. "Yes. Ask him if I can watch the family make noodles," I said.

Let me get one thing straight: I was not looking to steal the recipe for cao lau noodles and sell it on the culinary black market where foodies and chefs linger down dark alleyways, waiting for a guy to open up his trench coat to reveal contraband recipes for sale. I'm just a food-loving traveler obsessed with unraveling weird mysteries.

Moments later, Tran Tan Man, the owner of Trung Bac, stood at our table. Thao introduced me and explained that I was in town to learn about cao lau. Then he popped the question about meeting Tran's extended family to find out how the noodle was made. "Absolutely not," Tran said, shaking his head from side to side. "No one watches!" And then he ran off to greet a gaggle of tourists that had just streamed in.

"He's right," Thao said. "No one watches. I don't think they have ever let anyone from outside the family watch them."

A couple of decades ago no tourist groups traipsed into restaurants in Hoi An. In fact, the few travelers who knew about the town saw a very different Hoi An. It was a rundown backwater. There was one place to stay, the Hoi An Hotel, which was more like a boardinghouse. There were few restaurants, save for the usual makeshift eateries one finds in the alleyways of every Vietnamese town. All that began to change when Lonely Planet included Hoi An in its guidebook *Vietnam, Laos & Cambodia* in 1991 and *South-East Asia on a Shoestring* the following year. The attention quickly cemented the town's place on the backpacker's grand tour of Southeast Asia. Cheap and midrange hotels popped up in the late 1990s. And after UNESCO designated Hoi An's historical central district (Ancient Town) as a World Heritage site in 1999, posh resorts, most of them along the coast just outside town, laid out their red carpets. Western-oriented Vietnamese restaurants followed soon after.

Thanks to all those tourists (and support from UNESCO), Hoi An is no longer the ramshackle town it once was; its buildings glow with that recently refurbished shine. But the local economy has benefited in other ways as well. Thao works at the upscale Nam Hai resort, and as I went around town with him, we kept running into friends of his who were employed by Nam Hai or other resorts. "Before, young people couldn't wait to get out of here," he told me one day over coffee. "Now we all have jobs and no reason to leave."

All this development has put an indelible mark on the town. Walking through the streets, flanked by one- and two-story buildings and ornate Chinese-style temples, you are accosted by the usual "Hello" and "Buy something!" from vendors and "Where you going?" from motorbike taxi drivers. But Hoi An also has a kinder, gentler way of assaulting the visitor's senses: classical music wafts out of loudspeakers affixed to telephone poles throughout the car-free center of town (*Eine kleine Nachtmusik* is a recurring standard), while the sweet smell of incense seeps into your olfactory glands. If you factor in the upscale restaurants aimed at wealthy Westerners, the absurd number of tailor shops, and the pro-communist government slogans on banners stretching over the street, you've got one of the oddest towns in Asia. It's a place trying so hard to seem "authentic" that it becomes wildly inauthentic, like some kind of culturally dissonant theme park, collectively dreamed up by Ho Chi Minh, Karl Marx, Milton Friedman, and Wolfgang Amadeus Mozart.

One person who caught the tourist wave early is Hoi An native Trinh Diem Vy, who opened Mermaid, her first restaurant, in 1991. The place served a menu of Vietnamese staples and Hoi An specialties, including cao lau, and over time Ms. Vy, as she is known locally, built up a mini empire that now counts a handful of restaurants, a cooking school, and a new book called *Taste Vietnam*. She has become the culinary face of Hoi An.

While Thao was at work one day, I met with Ms. Vy at Morning Glory, her cooking school and restaurant, which specializes in dishes inspired by street food and old family recipes. We sat at a small table next to the kitchen. Lines of Western tourists snaked through the high-ceilinged front dining room on their way to the upstairs classroom-kitchen. Ms. Vy had a bowl of cao lau brought over to me. Because she prefers an extra dose of crispy texture, it had rice crackers among the toppings in addition to the fried noodle-dough croutons. The key to good cao lau, Ms. Vy said, is the pork, barbecued in the Chinese style called *char siu*. "This is what I call 'tourist pork,'" she said, jabbing a chopstick at a thin slice resting atop the mound of noodles and herbs. "Fatty pork is better—it just melts in your mouth—but I fear my customers won't eat it."

As for how the noodles are made, Ms. Vy said she didn't know the secret. But she told me that two branches of the same family make them, and she gave me a lead: I could find Madame Trai, the matriarch of the family, selling cao lau noodles at a stand in the central food market.

After finishing my bowl of extra-crunchy cao lau with Ms. Vy and watching more tourists flow through her restaurant, I walked to the central market. More than a few food stalls had hand-lettered signs advertising cao lau and pho. Pangs of nervousness poked at my stomach. This, I thought, could be a defining moment in my hunt for the secrets of cao lau. At the end of the lane, I came to a table with piles of brownish cao lau noodles stretched across it. A teenage girl behind the table made eye contact with me. "Madame Trai?" I asked. She nodded toward a plump sexagenarian sitting at the other end of the table. The woman looked like a rotund hen sitting on her eggs. The scowl on her face made her a forbidding presence.

"*Xin chao,*" I said, "hello" in Vietnamese.

She hardly moved, and uttered nothing.

"Do you speak English?" I asked. Madame Trai remained mute. "Cao lau," I said, pointing to the noodles on the table in front of her. "I want to know about cao lau. Can you tell me how it's made?" Just then the younger woman said something—translating, I figured—for Madame Trai.

But Trai just stared back at me. As her grimace deepened, I felt myself shrinking. Her eyes narrowed with suspicion, as if I really were a culinary secret agent who had come to Hoi An to steal the family cao lau recipe.

I walked away, ignoring the girls tugging at my arm to take me to their families' tailor shops. I felt defeated; my quest might be over.

Later that day I met up with Thao, and he took me to Thanh, a favorite place for cao lau, about a 15-minute walk from the center of town. I told Thao about my encounter with Trai at the market and how discouraged I was about my chances to get into the noodle-making family's home factory.

"I can talk to them," he said, as Ms. Thanh, the owner, put two bowls of cao lau in front of us.

As I dug in, a horrified look spread over Thao's face.

"No!" he said, glaring at the spoon in my hand. "Never use a spoon! That's for pho."

Cao lau is, in a way, the anti-pho. Broth is the star in pho, Vietnam's national dish; rare brisket, tendons, and soft noodles play supporting roles. Conversely, cao lau is short on broth; a dark shallow pool comes as a hidden surprise when you get to the bottom of the bowl. Ms. Thanh's broth was especially good. She deviates slightly from the traditional recipe, she said.

"How so?" I asked.

"It's a secret," she said, smiling wryly.

A secret. What is it, I wondered, with this town?

When Thao picked me up on his scooter the next day, he told me that maybe the greatest food mystery in this town of culinary secrets was about to be unraveled for me.

"I went to see the family that makes cao lau," he said, referring to Madame Trai's branch, "and I told them about you." He paused, waiting for a reaction, and then added, "They said yes. They are going to welcome you to their house where they make the noodles."

I put my hands on my head in disbelief. Even Thao seemed surprised.

"We have to go there early," he said. "They make it very early so it's ready for breakfast."

At five the next morning I was on the back of Thao's scooter, riding down a dirt road on the outskirts of town, past a small outdoor market, a few bars with open facades, a colorful Buddhist temple, and a wandering cow. I still had my doubts that this was going to happen. It seemed too easy.

The front of the one-story house was almost obscured by two 10-foot-high piles of wood. We hopped off the scooter and walked around the house to the back. There, in two adjacent, low-ceilinged rooms lit only by fire, where spider webs hung to eye level, four family members worked silently, each at a different step in the cao lau noodle-making process. Other than a fan on a floor stand, I saw nothing that used electricity. Fires crackled and steam rose from pots. The few machines in use—to knead dough and cut noodles—were manually operated. It felt as though I'd just stepped into a medieval workshop. I'd made it to the secret epicenter of cao lau noodle production.

Ta Ngoc Em, 54, the family patriarch, came out to greet us, brushing powder from his hands. Thao handed him a cigarette and lit it for him, as if that were part of the deal, and they exchanged a few words. Em, who had an Uncle Ho–style beard and blackened teeth, then went back to stirring a giant cauldron of bubbling dough. The cigarette dangled from his lips as he pounded a wooden stick into the dough with both hands.

"You can ask them anything you want," Thao said, fanning his right hand toward the silent workers.

I was suspicious. Why did they allow me to come here? I suppressed my skepticism. I should take advantage of my good fortune, I thought, and I began peppering Em with questions about the process.

Here's what I learned: Em had already mixed ash into the water (he burns wood to create ash only once every few months, he told me) and then sifted out the larger bits. The ash helps give the noodle its chewiness. Em pours rice into that ashy water and boils it and pounds it until he gets a huge cauldron of thick dough that he stirs and works for 45 minutes. Then he puts the hunk of dough on a broad flat basket in a huge fire-heated metal steamer for 75 minutes. The ash, the local water, and the steam all contribute to the unique character of cao lau noodles.

At the end of the steaming, Em and his brother carry the dough into the next room, where several women put it through a giant crank-operated mixer, like a preindustrial restaurant-sized KitchenAid. After the dough is kneaded, rolled flat, and brushed with peanut oil, Em's sister-in-law puts the flat sheets through a manual pasta cutter and slices them into six-inch-long threads. But that's not the end. The noodles go back into the steamer again for another 75 minutes. Finally, they're covered in banana leaves to cool off. Then they're done.

Em said his brother—that's the second branch of the family that Ms. Vy referred to—also makes cao lau noodles but in much smaller quantities. Between the two sides of the family, he said, they supply all the restaurants in Hoi An with the precious noodles. He said there's a guy just outside of Hoi An who figured out how to make them but he doesn't produce much.

When I asked Em, the fourth generation of his family to make the noodles, where he thought cao lau originally came from, he shrugged and said, "China?" That's how his family became the sole producers of the noodles, he explained. Someone from China taught his great-grandfather the recipe, and the family has kept it a closely guarded secret ever since.

How, I asked, do they transport the water from the Ba Le well in the center of town out to this house? Em stood up, took the cigarette from his mouth, and leaned against a pole. "We stopped doing that during my father's time," he said. "We dug our own well here"—he nodded to his right, toward the side of the house, where chickens were scratching in the dirt—"and it had properties similar to the Ba Le well."

The main component, he said, was alum, a chemical compound that has been known to have medicinal and preservative properties (and is sometimes used in baking powders).

"What about the wood," I asked, "the wood from the Cham Islands?"

Em laughed, shook his head, and said, "Cham is now protected, so we get all this wood from the surrounding area. It's the same type of tree, though."

Em added, "Sure, the water and the wood are essential to make cao lau, but our family has been making cao lau noodles for so long that we have a reputation now." Translation: it's not so much about the water or the wood; it's the technique. Em has been doing this routine 364 days a year, taking a day off for the beginning of Tet, the lunar new year, since he was 12.

Just then his son turned up on a motorbike, returning from his first round of delivering noodles to various restaurants around town. Em nodded toward him and said, "He's next. At least I hope so."

"So you're not sure he'll take over your job?" I asked.

"We don't want to push him. He has a good career as a tailor in the center of town," Em said. "But if he doesn't do it, then it could mean the end of our family making cao lau noodles."

A silence fell over us for a moment. Then Em told us a story:

One day, about a year or so ago, a government official showed up and said the family had to be more open about the secret of the noodles—that if something happened to the family, there would be no one to make them. Now that Hoi An is thriving with tourism, city officials said it would be a disaster if cao lau, the city's chief culinary attraction, disappeared.

"This is why," Em said, "we decided it would be okay if you watched us make it."

Everything was starting to make sense.

"Since we're not sure what the future holds for cao lau noodles, I would teach someone how to make them," Em said, pausing before adding: "For a price." When I prompted him, he said he'd do it for 100 million dong (about $4,800). I was tempted to take him up on his offer but it felt like too much pressure to be the sole upholder of the cao lau legacy. So I passed.

Given the greater opportunities young Vietnamese have in Hoi An these days, and the laborious life of a cao lau maker, it's hard to imagine someone would want to assume the cao lau–making mantle. The irony is that Hoi An's rise as a prosperous tourist attraction is also threatening the existence of the town's most iconic dish. Cao lau's survival depended on the people I was standing with: Em, his son, and the various family members who help make cao lau noodles daily (as well as Madame Trai, who sells them at the market).

And with that, Em's son, who makes his deliveries every day before going to his tailor job, wrapped a bungee cord around the packages of freshly made noodles on the back of his scooter and rode off. I stood there with Em and Thao, watching as Em's son sped down the gravel road until we lost sight of him, and the buzz of his scooter faded away.

JESSE DUKES

Babu on the Bad Road

FROM *Virginia Quarterly Review*

> Then the angel showed me the river of the water of life, as clear
> as crystal, flowing from the throne of God.
> —Revelation 22:1

ON JANUARY 10, 1991, Ambilikile Mwasapila dreamed a cure
for AIDS. A woman appeared to him, a woman he knew to be
infected with HIV, and God sent him into the bush for a cure. It
was only a dream, and at the time, Mwasapila, a Lutheran pastor
in the remote northern Tanzanian ward of Loliondo, was not sure
what it meant. He continued to work in Wasso, an outpost town
surrounded by dry and dusty plains occupied by the cattle-herding
Masai, and earned a reputation as honest and upright, humble
and kind. In 2001, he retired from the ministry and considered
moving back to the more populous Babati, where he had lived as a
young man. But he heard the same voice, God's voice, in dreams,
telling him to stay, for there was work for him in Loliondo.

Mwasapila remained, and the voice returned many times in the
next few years, sometimes when he slept and sometimes when he
just closed his eyes. He saw a recurring vision of a multitude gathered under a ridge. He saw tents, cars, and even security guards.
In 2006, he moved to a small house in the village of Samunge, at
the base of the ridge he had envisioned. One night, he dreamed
of a ladder stretching across the sky from the west to the east, colored red as blood. The ladder stopped directly above him. Then,

in 2009, God's voice returned with specific instructions. God told him to climb into the hills to find the bark and root of the tree the local Sonjo people call *mugariga*. There was a woman in the village whispered to be HIV positive, and on May 25, he gave her a cup of liquid made from boiling the bark. Three weeks later, God's voice told him the woman was now cured. Later, doctors from the Wasso Hospital tested the woman—and she was shown to be HIV negative.

Mwasapila continued to give the cup of liquid to people with HIV/AIDS, telling them that, after seven days, God would seal the mouths of the viruses inside them. Unable to feed, the virus would die within weeks. In 2010, God told him to give the same medicine to patients with cancer, and later with diabetes, asthma, and epilepsy. In October, the word had spread so that Mwasapila had visitors nearly every day, some traveling a day or more to see him.

In November, a newspaper journalist named Charles Ngereza happened to be traveling from Lake Victoria to Arusha. In the small town of Mto wa Mbu, 200 kilometers south of Samunge on a major route, he saw crowds of people waiting for a bus to take them north, to the middle of the bush. He joined the crowd to see where they were going, met Mwasapila, and interviewed several people who claimed to have been healed by drinking the cup of liquid. The story ran in the national papers.

In January 2011, a contingent of church officials from the Evangelical Lutheran Church, Mwasapila's former employer, visited Samunge to satisfy themselves that he was not a witch doctor. They returned convinced, traveling to different congregations to bring the news of a new gift from God. More people came to drink a cup of the cure, and there was now a constant queue of vehicles in the road leading into the village.

By March, Mwasapila's earlier vision had come true. The line of cars and buses to Samunge reached over 20 kilometers on a road that was usually rarely traveled. People waited for days to see Mwasapila and drink a cup of the liquid. Tanzanians took to calling him "Babu"—meaning "Grandfather"—an appellation of respect and affection for any old man. People with chronic illnesses spent small fortunes hiring transportation and traveled for days, using whatever conveyance they could afford. Anybody who owned a car or bus could earn money packing it full of pilgrims seeking Babu's cure. Entrepreneurs brought trucks with supplies and sold them off the backs of motorcycles for three times their normal value. Travelers slept on the ground, washed in the river, and defecated in the bush. Dozens died waiting to see Mwasapila.

To many Tanzanians, Babu's medicine was a miracle, a one-step cure. To expatriate tour operators or visitors, it presented a puzzle: how could the locals believe drinking a cup of liquid once would cure a slew of diseases? To many doctors and health professionals—expats and Tanzanians—it was a terrible setback. HIV/AIDS, diabetes, and high blood pressure could all be controlled effectively with modern medicine. Years of effort had gone into developing effective medications and soliciting aid for East Africa, and years more went into convincing Tanzanian patients to submit to HIV testing and maintain the proper regimen of antiretroviral drugs (ARVs). Now many hundreds of people were abandoning ARV therapy, believing themselves cured. Some doctors, respectful of their patients' beliefs, quietly advised them to continue taking medications, no matter what they were told at Samunge. A few openly predicted disaster.

"It's just a little farther; we are almost to Digo Digo," Simon softly calls from the back of the Land Rover. It's 4 A.M. on June 29, very dark, and I'm driving over a dirt track with photographer Sarah Elliott and Simon, a Masai guide and translator. We woke up a little after midnight to travel from Ngare Sero village, hoping to make Samunge by dawn. The plan came together at the last minute, and without inquiring about the proper paperwork we gambled that if we just showed up at Samunge, I could talk my way into an interview with Mwasapila.* We are taking a route the map calls merely "Bad Road," ascending the Gregory Rift escarpment in a series of tight turns through hills and canyons. It's the same road the government plans to turn into a highway that will cross the Serengeti National Park, joining the large city of Arusha with communities on Lake Victoria.

We've already been stopped twice in the small hours, and both times, Simon has had to crawl from the back of the overstuffed car

---

* The faith healer's surname is sometimes spelled "Mwasipile" or "Masapila," sometimes in the same article. "Mwasapila" is the most common spelling and conforms to the most common pronunciation, although the *w* is quite subtle.

and argue with armed police, who used our lack of papers as an excuse to shake him down for a "fine."* After the second shake-down, the newly appeased guards made the friendly suggestion that we take an alternate route to Samunge, through a nearby vil-lage called Digo Digo. That route stays clear for emergencies and allows supplies and VIPs to enter Samunge without waiting in the queue. Unfortunately, the way is not so well-worn, and we take a wrong turn—rumbling by small settlements and farms, and sliding in sand and fording rivers before Simon finally admits we're lost.

He crawls out of his car to knock on the door of a mud house. By the light of a kerosene lantern, a woman gives him new direc-tions and, now confident, we drive for another hour, joining better roads, and enter Samunge, just as the sun rises. Samunge is stark and beautiful; the soil is a red clay and, perhaps because it's in a river valley, the vegetation seems more green and vital than the drier highlands nearby. The narrow Sanjan River flows southeast through the soda flats below, entering the alkaloid Lake Natron. Along the way, it crosses the rift where two great tectonic plates slammed together and have been pulling away from each other for the last 40 million years, forming the Great Rift highlands, volca-noes, and the African Great Lakes, and slowly revealing humanity's origins in the nearby Olduvai Gorge. Mwasapila's new Eden is less than a hundred kilometers from our most famous early ancestors.

Samunge lies at the base of a three-peaked range of hills that looks like the Southern California chaparral. Most of the houses are small, framed with sticks, and fleshed with mud. Dirt roads are lined with drab tents and makeshift tarps. The village slowly fills with people seeking medical help, brought by rickety vehicles. The whole scene strangely resembles the set for *M*A*S*H*. A dis-embodied, Swahili-speaking Radar O'Reilly shouts instructions through a tinny bullhorn somewhere. People are to gather in a half-hour to hear Babu speak.

Simon goes off to inform officials of our arrival. A crowd is form-

---

* The common word for these payments is *chai*, which, of course, literally means "tea." The same word can mean either a small bribe or a legitimate tip one might offer a waitress, driver, or bellhop. The use of *chai* could be a way for officials or police to have deniability ("I was just asking for something to drink!"), or it may reflect the attitude that rather than extorting the payee, the official is actually per-forming an extra service, helping the payee out of an administrative jam he has created by having the wrong papers or a broken taillight.

ing at a widening in the main road. People are walking from their cars parked several hundred meters away. Some look obviously un-well, limping or shuffling, helped by relatives. One woman's foot is twisted 180 degrees from her ankle. Simon returns with a bleary man in striped pajamas; he claims to be an immigration official and asks our business. I explain we are journalists who have come a long way to learn about Babu. "Do you have a permit?" he asks. This is the first I've heard of any such thing; I tell him no.

He nods and politely directs us to sit and wait at a small open-air café. A young soldier in green fatigues with a dinged-up assault rifle stands a few meters away. We begin to hear Swahili over the tinny speaker again, and Simon says it's one of Babu's assistants ex-plaining how the medicine will be dispensed. Simon has brought other Westerners here before—Americans or Europeans on safari who wished to see the faith healer. He says they usually pay a small fee and then they get to see Mwasapila. But 10 minutes later, the formerly bleary man returns wearing an immigration uniform. Now significantly more imposing, he explains that I will have to "fulfill a process" to get permission to speak to Mwasapila. I ask if I can fulfill the process on the spot. He sighs regretfully and says it's not within his power to help me. Simon pleads on my behalf, hint-ing we might pay an informal fee, but, to Simon's surprise, this has no effect. Apparently, journalists are not as welcome as tourists.

The immigration officer disappears, and Simon tells me the voice we now hear over the speaker is Mwasapila. The voice is crisp, medium-pitched, and slightly nasal, and we hear him list the diseases the medicine will cure: diabetes ("sugar," as Tanzanians say), hypertension ("blood"), cancer, tuberculosis, and HIV/AIDS. The officer returns saying I need to travel to Wasso to speak to the district administrator, who will help me obtain the proper papers. "When you walk to your car, you may just peek at Babu over there." A man in a tie standing nearby objects in Swahili, and Simon tells me not to peek at Babu after all. I obediently look away, hopeful that I will get a chance at a better look later.

Wasso is a 90-minute drive away, and the district administrator is much less patient than the immigration officer, and equally un-budgeable. I have to return to Arusha, the largest city in the north, immediately, and I may conduct no interviews. We leave at first light the next day, and after driving an hour, we spot a minivan from Kenya on the side of the road, its passengers milling around. I pull over and speak to a man who tells me he has just taken a cup of the medicine to cure his diabetes. His eyes are bright, and he says with excitement, "Already, my headache is completely gone." He says he will stop taking insulin in a week if he continues to feel better.

Another slight man with pale skin approaches the Land Rover. He says, "Excuse me," in formal English, his voice high and weak. "I have stomach cancer and diabetes." His belly is distended to the size of a watermelon, and his feet are extraordinarily swollen. "This bus is very cramped, and I very uncomfortable. May I ride in your car to Arusha?" He says his doctor told him he has a month to live, but he is now hopeful the cancer will vanish. I explain our car is full, apologize, and wish him good luck.

After several hours, we descend from the highlands to Ngare Sero on the plain, where Simon makes his home. He introduces me to a man who says his stomach ulcers and indigestion have vastly improved since he visited Samunge last February. This man heard about Mwasapila when Lutheran bishop Thomas Laizer came to his remote village in the Ngorongoro Highlands with word of a miracle cure. As we talk, the young village chairman grabs Simon's elbow. The Loliondo administrator has sent word by radio that an American journalist might come through the village, and he must not be allowed to conduct interviews. The chairman turns to me and says in English, "If you had come here first, there would be no problem, but now, we have heard the word from Loliondo." We say a hasty goodbye to Simon and make the five-hour drive back to Arusha.

In 2006, Francis Tesha tested positive for HIV. He lived in Wasso, the outpost town where Ambilikile Mwasapila had been a Lutheran pastor before his retirement. Francis was about 40, married, and had a job at a local hunting lodge partly owned by the royal family of Abu Dhabi. His employers liked him so much that they brought him with them to Abu Dhabi to work for months at a time. When they heard about his diagnosis, he was fired and sent back to Wasso. His wife died a few months later—of malaria. Their neighbors believed the shock weakened her and that she may have also had HIV, but she refused to be tested or take medication.

Francis did accept ARV therapy and took the pills every day.

He joined the HIV support group in Wasso and became its secretary. He was gregarious and well liked. In October 2010, he heard reports of a healer in Samunge who could cure HIV. Although Francis felt healthy, he figured if he killed the viruses in his body, he could be certified HIV negative, allowing him to get his old job back. On October 2, he took a bus from Wasso to Samunge, drank the liquid, and spoke with Mwasapila, who assured him that after 21 days, the virus would be gone from his body. Francis returned to Wasso in high spirits, telling his friends at the HIV support group that Babu could free them of the virus and the ARVs.

Francis stayed off the ARVs for three weeks as instructed, and then excitedly went to the hospital for an HIV test. To his dismay, he was still HIV positive, and in fact, his CD4 count had diminished.* He reluctantly began taking ARVs again, but now he felt much more vulnerable to side effects, becoming dizzy and nauseated when he took the drugs. To settle his stomach, he occasionally skipped his ARVs. In February, he was hospitalized for a secondary infection and, when he got out a few days later, started saying he no longer believed in Mwasapila's medicine. His neighbors whispered that Francis had a new girlfriend with whom he had sex with no condom. Babu had cured him, they reasoned, but he allowed himself to become reinfected.

Despite Francis Tesha's faint warnings, by February of last year, Babu was a national phenomenon, and the BBC reported 6,000 people in line at his clinic. Unlike Francis, many people returned from Loliondo with powerful testimonials. Diabetics swore their blood sugar had normalized and they could drink sodas and eat bread again. Stomach ulcers subsided, and aches and pains vanished. Newspapers reported the woman Babu treated in 2009 was confirmed HIV negative, and people excitedly related stories of cousins or neighbors who were cured of HIV/AIDS.

The Tanzanian government seemed internally conflicted about how to respond to Mwasapila. In March, the Ministry of Health

---

* The CD4 count is one of several metrics used to measure the progress of HIV. The metric is literally the number of a certain type of white blood cells per cubic millimeter of blood. A CD4 count of 500 or higher is considered normal. Counts under 500 indicate HIV infection. Counts under 200 indicate AIDS. The World Health Organization recommends ARV therapy for anybody with a CD4 below 350, but Tanzania does not provide ARVs to patients unless their CD4 is 200 or less, possibly due to a shortage of ARVs.

announced they were ordering the healer to cease his activities. At the same time, ministers from other parts of the government enthusiastically made the trip to Samunge. Dr. Salash Toure, the Arusha regional health officer, declared publicly that his hospital had tested dozens of people who claimed to be cured of HIV, and all had tested positive. However, the influential Lutheran bishop Thomas Laizer lobbied on Mwasapila's behalf, calling the liquid "a gift from God." The lines at Samunge grew.

On March 25, the government reversed course, announcing that the herbal concoction was safe to drink and that they would take no action to stop people from visiting Samunge to take the cure, but would start registering vehicles and providing basic services like first aid and toilets to the overtaxed village. The Ministry of Health appointed a team of doctors to study the effects of the liquid. In April, the government acknowledged 87 people had died while in transit to Samunge.

Kati Regan, the American managing director of Support for International Change (SIC), felt compelled to go directly to the Ministry of Health to clarify government policy toward Mwasapila. The NGO provides treatment and counseling to people with HIV, and she estimates 20 percent of their clients abandoned ARV therapy in March or April. Some of her Tanzanian colleagues told her Mwasapila's cure worked, and she had to fend off HIV patients who wanted to borrow the organization's truck to make the trip. For Regan, this was a huge setback. "You never want to see someone going off treatment, especially when you've worked for years to have it be part of their routine," she said. But Regan still refrained from offering an opinion of Mwasapila's liquid out of respect for her clients' beliefs. "I didn't want to offend someone who decided to go, and I sympathize with someone who wants a cure."

Not all health workers were as circumspect. Pat Patten was especially blunt: "I don't believe in faith healing; I think this is a deception. And I'm a Catholic priest." Patten is also a pilot and the director of Flying Medical Service. He has lived and worked in Tanzania for over 30 years. A Spiritan priest, he wears secular jeans and T-shirts while flying bush planes to remote settlements, providing regular rotating clinics, and flying emergency evacuations. "I'm open to a powerful placebo effect, but placebo effects only relieve the symptoms, never the root of the problem."

He remembers the shock of flying over Mwasapila's village in

February, looking out the window of his Cessna 206 to see a traffic jam. Now, after talking to doctors throughout the region, he is convinced Mwasapila's treatment has led to disaster. "What we're seeing is a lot of AIDS patients dying in hospitals because they've stopped taking medicine. Diabetics are now going blind, suffering kidney failure, experiencing swelling in their hands and feet, and getting diabetic sores on their extremities." He worries about an outbreak of drug-resistant tuberculosis and adds, "These are all unnecessary deaths, all of them."

And the famous story of Mwasapila's first patient, Patten claims, was a lie. He spoke to doctors familiar with the case who said the woman had never tested positive before taking Babu's cure, that she only feared she might be infected—but, Patten says, "the damage has been done."

> And the leaves of the tree are for the healing of the nations. No longer will there be any curse.
> —Revelation 22:2–3

Back in Arusha, after my first failed trip to meet Mwasapila, I spend the day in government offices, talking to clueless clerks, waiting in hallways, and pleading with bored and impatient officials. Nobody seems to know or care who can issue the proper documents to allow an interview. In the late afternoon, I find myself in an office with Jotham Ndereka, the Arusha regional information minister. I explain for about the ninth time that I need a permit to go to Loliondo to interview Mwasapila and take photographs, and he says brightly, "Yes, this is possible."

"It *is*?" I say, surprised. Ndereka explains that I need a filming permit, such as one might get to make a TV commercial, and for an extra fee, the Ministry of Information can issue one in a week. I spend the next week looking for patients with HIV who drank Mwasapila's liquid but can find nobody willing to talk to me. I do manage to talk on the phone with the Wasso Hospital administrator, Madame Josephine Kashe, who invites me to visit in person if I make the trip to Samunge.

A week later, I rent the same Land Rover, load it with supplies, and return to Jotham's office. The minister presents himself in a gray suit, smiling smugly. He hands me a handwritten "Filming Permit" signed by the national minister of information. I thank him and start to leave when he says, "Wait! If you look at the permit, you will see that your activities are to be done under the supervision of the Arusha regional information officer. This means I am to accompany you." My heart sinks. It appears the government has assigned me a ride-along censor.

"I do not think that will be possible; I have to leave today," I say.

"Today?"

"Yes, you told me the permit would be ready, so I have made arrangements that I cannot change." He leaves to make a phone call and returns five minutes later to say that everything is fine, his boss has given him permission to go with me for three days. I tell him I am planning a four-day trip, and he says that's fine, too; he'll just need me to pay a $40 per diem for his meals and lodging.*
He has me over a barrel—I need him to ensure an interview with Babu—so I ask, "How soon can you be ready?"

Two hours later, we are driving into the setting sun, five hours behind schedule, but moving at last. Jotham has changed into a Tommy Hilfiger shirt, loose jeans, black leather jacket, and baseball cap. He looks like an American executive at his son's soccer game in Connecticut. For the next four days, we will be constant companions—and frenemies. We call each other Mr. Jesse and Mr. Jotham. He will claim to help me, but apart from arranging an otherwise impossible interview he will offer mostly foot-dragging and his own unverified opinions. For my part, I will act grateful and keep my skepticism to myself. We talk about world leaders—he admires Mandela and Qaddafi—and acknowledges the latter should have stepped down while he was still popular. He admires John F. Kennedy, Richard Nixon, and Dale Carnegie. The night we drive west from Arusha, Jotham recalls the time, when he was just a boy, he saw Henry Kissinger on an official visit to Tanzania. I say, "Oh, yes, he was Nixon's secretary of state."

"Yes," Jotham says. "Also, he was with President Ford."

*

* Conventional wisdom among expatriate tour operators, researchers, and NGO workers in Tanzania holds that it's almost impossible to find a government official in his or her office, since they travel as often as possible. The government salaries are relatively low, but the per diem rate is generous, and most officials can find food and lodging for about $15 a day, pocketing the balance, which allows them to double or triple their salary. The practice may be infuriating, but it is considered aboveboard.

I once again pull into Samunge at dawn, just as Mwasapila is preparing to greet his visitors. At the widening in the road, Mwasapila's medicine station, a tall, middle-aged, balding man addresses the gathering crowd. He wears a clean shirt and tie and speaks with a high throaty voice in Swahili, using the tinny public address system. After a time, he pauses and tells the crowd they will now hear from the man they came to see. Reverend Ambilikile Mwasapila takes the microphone. He is a short, old man, with close-cropped, white hair and a round face. He greets the crowd by lifting one hand high above his head, silently waving hello. Several hundred hands rise to return the greeting.

He begins speaking in Swahili, first acknowledging he is the same Babu they've seen on TV or in the newspapers. Then he launches into a practical FAQ about the medicine itself, taking on the tone of a shift supervisor laying out the safety rules of the new machinery: *Okay, folks, there are only two size cups of medicine, child and adult. It doesn't matter how large you are: you still only get one cup.* (This draws laughter.) *If you vomit here in Samunge, they will give you another cup. If you vomit after you leave, don't worry, the medicine has already worked.*

He lists the diseases the liquid cures, but he stresses: *You're not immune, just cured. Don't engage in risky activities like unprotected sex. By all means, don't commit rape or be promiscuous. Keep your diet moderate. Don't drink any alcohol today because it may interfere with the medicine.*

After covering the practical matters, the speech becomes more theological, and Mwasapila takes on the familiar rhythm of a Baptist preacher, asking for assent every few moments. *I don't know anything about medicine. I was surprised when God called me to give you medicine. It is neither the tree nor the hand of Babu that heals. It is God who cures. He has put his power in the medicine, but he could have cured you directly. Okay?*

Yes!

There is no illness that is too tough for God. He has decided to eradicate this disease from all over the world. We associate it with Him, saying: "God has brought it; it is a punishment by God," but that is not true. It is the devil who has brought this disease. Do you hear?

Yes!

People tell me they have to take ARVs every day for HIV or pills to control diabetes, so after drinking from the cup, should we continue with our drugs? I want to be clear about God's instructions. He told me the medicine here is stronger than the drugs; it takes over from the drugs, unless you just want to be a slave of the drugs. You can keep taking those drugs like a person swallowing clay.

The entire speech lasts for about 20 minutes, after which he concludes with a short prayer. People begin shuffling to their cars, and an East Indian man from Kenya taps Mwasapila on the shoulder. He asks in English if he should continue taking his blood pressure medication, but the healer doesn't understand. The two struggle to communicate for a moment, and then Mwasapila is called away. One of his assistants, who looks about 16, overhears and tells the man in English, "You should throw it away."

Samunge transforms itself into the world's largest brew-through, serving over a hundred vehicles in roughly an hour. There are safari vehicles, Toyota HiAce minivans, Toyota Coaster minibuses, and full-sized coach buses as well as a handful of private SUVs. They pull up to Babu's station, and workers of all ages carry trays of bright plastic cups, placing them into hands stretched out from windows. One little girl drinks her cup and vomits out of the window a few seconds later. Workers quickly wash each used cup and return it to service. Mwasapila, with his head bowed, works quietly alongside his assistants, ladling the liquid into trays loaded with cups. After each vehicle is served, it turns left and uphill, looping behind Mwasapila's station, and begins the long trip back to Arusha, Kenya, or even farther-flung destinations.

An hour later, I find Mwasapila resting in a white plastic chair on a patch of red earth just a few meters from his newly built but modest block house. He has on a printed T-shirt, green pants, and pink low-top Converse All Star knockoffs. He shakes my hand and gestures for me to sit down.

A handful of people gather around to listen. Through Jotham, Mwasapila tells me his given name, Ambilikile, means "one who was called," and explains about first seeing the visions of this place, Samunge, in 1991. I press for details about his visions, and whether he actually sees God. He says he never sees God, only hears a voice. When he tells about the first woman he treated for HIV in 2009, Jotham tells me, "I would ask about the patient who has been cured of HIV, but he said that she is living far away. Maybe ask the next question."

I ask Mwasapila why he won't take his cure to Arusha, Dar es Salaam, or any other populous place so people don't have to endure hardship, spend their savings, or risk death in order to travel here. Mwasapila's answer is that it's God's choice. *If I was another healer, I might advertise and travel here and there, but God chose here, so I will do my work here. If he decides later that I should move and go to another place, then I will go.*

He tells me the medicine works by faith. To be cured, one must drink and believe. I ask if a Muslim, Jew, or Hindu would be healed as well as a Christian. *God doesn't look at the religion; he looks at the person who comes here with belief of faith. If they used the medicine, they will get better.*

As we talk, the tall bald man who earlier spoke to the crowd pulls up a chair and begins to listen intently. He says nothing at first, but begins to chime in during Jotham's translations, emphasizing or elaborating certain points. Unlike Jotham, or Mwasapila, he seems impatient with my questions and scowls at me. The effect is disturbing, and I start to get the sense that I am no longer interviewing Mwasapila but instead arguing with this unidentified man.

Finally, he asks me whether people know about Mwasapila in America, and I say there's only been one newspaper article. "I think in America we are used to putting our faith in doctors even though we are also very religious. So some people will say, 'That sounds like it can't be true.' Other people will think, 'That sounds like something I would like to see for myself.'"

The man tells me Americans should read Revelation verse 22, lines 1 through 3. "You will see what God did during Jonah's time."

"Since you have now offered something, may I have your name?" I ask. This is apparently daring and makes the small crowd titter.

He tells me it's Frederick Nisajile and that he works for the Tanganyika Christian Refugee Service, which I later learn is an NGO affiliated with the Lutheran Church. Both Frederick and Mwasapila seem intently interested in America. The healer predicts many more people will come. *God has already shown me people from Asia, Europeans, Americans. Right here is not big enough. The place to do this service is behind this mountain on the great plain.*

Frederick and Mwasapila both want to know what American doctors or drug companies would think if they heard about this cure. I joke that they probably wouldn't understand, and would instead take the plant to test in laboratories to extract and make money.* Frederick and Jotham both chuckle. Sensing my audience will end soon, I make one more attempt to ask an important question. I explain I've spoken to at least one person who believes there might be something wrong with Mwasapila's brain, causing him to hear God's voice. "And I just have to ask, respectfully, did you ever wonder, when you first heard from God, if your brain was playing a trick?"

Jotham hesitates, and then starts to translate this, but Frederick emphatically cuts him off, almost shouting, "No, no, no!"

He launches into an explanation in English that I barely understand, saying David and somebody else in the Bible heard God's voice many times, and in David's case, he spoke to an elder to verify it really was God. He claims Mwasapila heard God's voice for nearly 20 years before acting on the instructions, even writing down the date each time he heard the voice. His point seems to be Mwasapila has done his due diligence. Frederick says, "Now, forget about that. After hearing all of this, what is your comment, sir? Do you believe people can be cured through voices or this medicine?"

Surrounded by the faithful, my skepticism feels like a dirty secret. Struggling to form a polite answer, I tell Frederick that while I have heard of many people who seem to be doing much better with minor complaints or even diabetes, I am still trying to find people who have had HIV who could tell me directly what happened to them. "I do not know what to believe," I say. "I think if I were suffering I would take the medicine though."

Frederick tells me to drink a cup of the medicine right now, and I say that I will, even though I am not suffering. Frederick says that we all have many unknown problems with our body and I may be cured without knowing it. Then he tells me to swallow the entire dose; don't try to keep a small amount in my mouth to take back to a laboratory.

The audience is over, and I thank Mwasapila, who just nods and shakes my hand. Frederick walks me down the hill to the road, where plastic cups of Mwasapila's cure sit on a card table. A small crowd follows to watch the action. He presses a cup into my hand.

---

* I later learn that an herbal medicine company has done exactly this over the summer, marketing a "*mugariga* extract."

The liquid is warm and slightly bitter, with a subtle and distinctive flavor, like anise or ginseng.

Later, I speak with Madame Kashe over the phone, and, despite the bad connection, it sounds like she has found a patient for me to talk with. Jotham spends about two hours eating lunch and chatting with Frederick and a couple of policemen, while I wait impatiently in the car.

Much later, when I read the translation of my audience with Mwasapila, I will realize Jotham blatantly mistranslated a small part of the conversation. When Jotham asked about his first patient, the woman he treated for HIV in 2009, Mwasapila actually responded that she lived in Samunge and might be available to talk. This is most likely the same woman Pat Patten told me about, the woman who famously tested HIV negative but, according to Patten, had never been HIV positive. Jotham knows full well I am trying to find people who have taken Mwasapila's cure for HIV, but he says nothing as we drive toward Wasso, away from Babu's most famous patient.

In Wasso, Jotham introduces me to the district medical officer, and I interview him outside of a loud bar while PA speakers blare global hip-hop in the background. His answers are noncommittal. When I ask him if there's evidence that Mwasapila's cure works, he says that many diabetics have demonstrably better blood sugar levels after drinking the liquid. He says he knows of no cases of HIV patients testing negative after taking the cure, but he also says some have shown small improvements in their CD4 counts. "The Ministry of Health is conducting a study about this now, and you should really go to them for answers." I ask him if he can help me speak to HIV patients who went to Mwasapila, and he promises to make inquiries on my behalf. When he leaves, I have to remind him to take my contact information so he can follow up.

After the medical officer leaves, Jotham grins and says, "I do not think anybody with HIV will speak to you. These people do not like to talk about their condition. I am glad we had this conversation with the district medical officer. He is a better person for you to speak to than the hospital administrator because he is the official in charge."

"Maybe so," I say, "but I did tell Madame Kashe at the Wasso

Hospital we were coming today, and I promised to visit her. So I think we need to go there at least to say hello to be polite."

Jotham counters, "We will not have time to go tonight, I think, since we will have to find a hotel and something to eat." We check into a small guesthouse, and Jotham negotiates the price from $15 to $10 a person. A man promises we'll have hot water, which Jotham seems to really care about, and the man begins heating a barrel of water with charcoal. After an hour, the water is only tepid, and Jotham insists that we cannot go to find Madame Kashe until it's hot enough to bathe.

My mobile phone rings: it's Madame Kashe calling. "We are waiting for you here," she says. "When are you coming?" I explain we've checked into a guesthouse and are waiting for hot water to clean off the grime of nearly two days of travel.

She asks me why I went to a guesthouse. "We have hot water here. And food, and beds." It dawns on me that when Madame Kashe told me we would be welcome, she was inviting me to stay at the hospital, apparently in guest quarters.

I apologize for the misunderstanding and hand the phone to Jotham. He speaks in Swahili for a few minutes and then hands the phone back. I say, "I think we made a mistake, and I really think we should go see Madame Kashe now." Jotham surprises me by agreeing—maybe it's the promise of hot water—and we wrap up in our warmest jackets and head into the suddenly cold desert night.

Madame Kashe greets us outside what appears to be a chapel and welcomes us inside, where we find a table set with steaming food.

A tall, baby-faced young man sits in a corner, speaking softly to another man and woman, both middle-aged. The young man comes over and introduces himself as Gedeon Omari, a doctor at Wasso Hospital. Madame Kashe asks us about our trip and asks me what I think of Mwasapila. She makes it clear she is fond of the healer, but skeptical of his cure and adds, "I like how they're taking care of Babu now! He seems much more energetic. He looked wasted before." The food is delicious, and Madame Kashe invites Jotham to take a hot shower in some other part of the compound, which he gratefully accepts.

After a long meal, when I think we may be preparing to go to bed, Gedeon addresses me directly. Speaking very softly, in English, he asks me what I'm hoping to achieve. I speak slowly and match his quiet tone. "I have heard about Babu, for many weeks now. And I've talked to many people who tell me they have been cured of minor ailments. But I haven't spoken to anybody who has gone to see him for more serious conditions. Like cancer. Or HIV. So I want to talk to people who have and find out what their experience is."

Gedeon introduces the other man and woman, who have said almost nothing. He explains they are his clients; both are HIV positive, both are taking ARV therapy. Each visited Mwasapila in November 2010, months before he became famous. After drinking the medicine, they stopped ARV treatment for a matter of weeks. Their CD4 counts began to drop, so they resumed therapy. Both appear to be lucky—discontinuing ARVs can allow the virus to develop a resistance to the drugs—but both feel healthy after resuming their ARV treatment.

In the car on our way back to the guesthouse, Jotham clucks his tongue and tells me that neither patient seems to have strong faith.

The next morning, we meet Madame Kashe and Dr. Omari again, and this time I interview three patients. The first, Margaret, has type II diabetes, but her blood sugar has normalized since drinking Mwasapila's liquid last fall. She also lost over 50 kilograms. Gedeon and Madame Kashe both suggest that she continue a low-sugar, low-starch diet.

The other two patients have similar stories to the two I spoke with the night before, the difference being that they both have marginally improved CD4 counts.

Jotham watches the interview with decreasing interest from the side of the room, and when he steps out to make a phone call, I ask bluntly: "Do you know any HIV patients who went to Babu and got sick or died?" Gedeon tells me that just three weeks ago, a man from Wasso died. I ask if he was friends with either patient, and it turns out he was the secretary of their HIV-positive support group. They say he was a good man and a friend.

His name, as it turns out, was Francis Tesha.

A few days later, I speak with Francis's sister Flora over the phone and hear his full story. She tells me that shortly after Francis left the hospital in February, he was struck by another bout of opportunistic infections and left bedridden. He lost all hope. He couldn't eat and refused ARVs. He coughed constantly from tuberculosis. Flora recounts, "We brought him to the hospital on April 12, and this time, he did not get out until he died." Now Flora tries to warn people away from Mwasapila. "You can't stop someone from going to Babu, but the fact is that all of the people who went to drink the medicine regret it now. Many of them have died. I get so angry when I see somebody going there to drink that medicine."

> My people are destroyed for lack of knowledge.
>   —Hosea 4:6 (quoted in an editorial in a Kenyan paper, advising
>   people not to visit Mwasapila)

On my second-to-last day in Tanzania, I meet with Dr. Paul Kisanga at Arusha Lutheran Medical Centre. Unlike most Tanzanian hospitals, which could be movie sets for *A Farewell to Arms,* ALMC is a freshly painted steel-and-glass building, in which a director could film an episode of *House.* A large bronze plaque hangs on the wall with the names of dozens of donors, many of whom are Lutheran congregations in small towns in Minnesota.

Dr. Kisanga wears a dark, closely tailored suit, and I notice an iPad on a stand in his office. He is gracious but obviously busy. Like the Wasso district medical officer, his answers are politic. He reminds me that his hospital is part of the same Lutheran diocese as Bishop Laizer, who has enthusiastically promoted Mwasapila, and tells me, "As a medical scientist, I have no reason to think this works. However, we have a few people in the last three months with improved hypertension and blood sugars."

He tells me about a formerly diabetic patient whose blood sugar has been normal for several months. "She is the wife of one of the staff here." Kisanga makes a phone call, and a few minutes later, a white-haired man appears in a black shirt, white clerical collar, and glasses—the Desmond Tutu look. He is Reverend Gabriel Kimerei, the hospital chaplain.

Reverend Kimerei has known Ambilikile Mwasapila since 1974, when the former brick mason, not yet known as Babu, enrolled in a seminary program. Kimerei was his theology instructor. "He was a very quiet student. You wouldn't know what he was thinking, but if you asked, he always gave you the right answer."

Kimerei speaks near-perfect English; he studied theology in Iowa in the 1960s. He is an enthusiastic believer in Mwasapila's cure. "My wife has been tortured by diabetes for twelve years—swallowing the drugs every day." Kimerei's wife went to Samunge in February. When she returned, she stopped taking her oral anti-diabetics. She eats a low-sugar, low-starch diet, and, according to Kimerei, "she is doing well, she is doing very well, but she checks her blood sugar every week."

Kimerei acknowledges Mwasapila's cure doesn't work for everyone. In April, when Dr. Kisanga and other ALMC colleagues told him that some patients who abandoned medication were suffering, he proposed they take a trip to Samunge to speak to the healer. Kimerei says before their visit, the Ministry of Health tried to convince Mwasapila to instruct his visitors to keep taking their medications until they were sure they were cured. "He would not agree. He wasn't happy about that." But when Reverend Kimerei, Dr. Kisanga, and two colleagues spoke to him in April, he was swayed by his former teacher and agreed to change his instructions.

It appears as of July, Mwasapila continues to honor the letter of the agreement, telling people they may continue taking medications, even though he says it will be as effective as "swallowing clay."

According to Reverend Kimerei, there are a half dozen HIV-positive patients in the local Lutheran parish who are completely cured. His colleague, a local minister, says they have already tested HIV negative. Kimerei graciously begins making phone calls, and an hour later, he has arranged for me to meet with an HIV patient who has recently tested negative. She is going to retest tomorrow at the hospital, and I am invited to witness the test.

The next morning, Reverend Kimerei and I drive to the church to pick up a girl who looks about 16. She wears a green T-shirt and *khanga*—a skirt made from decoratively printed fabric—and she keeps her eyes to the ground. I introduce myself and she asks me, through the translator, to change her name, so I will call her Alma.

We drive back to the clinic, where a female doctor takes us to a small room. I take a seat next to a cardboard box labeled HIV PREVENTION — CONDOMS. The doctor introduces herself, saying, "I'm Lucy, or Sister Mulingi," in Swahili, and introduces another man and woman, who are apparently counselors. She asks a series of questions, which Alma answers in a soft voice.

Alma first learned she was HIV positive in 2005 but has probably had the virus from birth. Her father died in 2001, and she lives with her mother, who is also HIV positive. Twice a day, she takes ARVs issued by the clinic, and she has never stopped, even after visiting Mwasapila. Sister Mulingi asks, *Does anyone, any friends at school know about your problem?*

No.

That's good—we must help you avoid discrimination. Did you go to Samunge?

Yes, I went to Samunge in March.

After you came back from Samunge, did you take another test?

No.

But based on your belief you hope that you're healed?

Yes.

Would you like that we establish your status at this moment?

Yes.

There are two possible results. The first result could show that your blood is still infected with the HIV virus. The second one could show that there are no traces of the virus in your blood; that would mean you're cured.

If it comes out without traces of the virus I'll be very happy.

Sister Mulingi takes Alma from the room to administer the blood test. A few minutes later she calls Reverend Kimerei and me into a larger room. Alma is sitting on an examination table, and I sit next to her. Also in the room is a male doctor, the two counselors, and the translator, Jackson. Sister Mulingi stands in the middle of the room and then announces, dramatically in English, that the test results are positive. Alma still has HIV. She repeats the results in Swahili for Alma, who nods her head slowly. The male doctor explains that at this clinic, they have tested over a dozen people who have been to Samunge and all of them are still HIV positive. Reverend Kimerei furrows his brow and says, "That is strange because the volunteer I spoke to said she was tested and she was told she was negative."

I ask Alma how she feels about the test result. She answers very quietly in Swahili. *I feel just fine. I was just fine before, and I am still okay.*

*

I can't say for certain that Mwasapila's cure doesn't work. I *can* say that every account I heard about somebody being cured by Babu of HIV/AIDS turned out to be either impossible to verify or verifiably untrue.

Two doctors at separate hospitals confirmed they had multiple patients who, like Francis Tesha, went to Samunge, stopped taking ARVs, and got sick and died. Pat Patten estimates that several hundred people have died that way, and based on my small sample, his math seems conservative. Perhaps the number would be higher if Reverend Kimerei and Dr. Kisanga hadn't insisted Mwasapila allow patients to continue taking Western medicine.

On the other hand, there were numerous accounts of people claiming to be cured of stomach ulcers, aches and pains, insanity, and even diabetes. Multiple people echoed Dr. Kisanga in saying they had patients whose blood sugar had normalized after taking Mwasapila's medicine.* It is tempting to think of the hundreds of thousands who visited Samunge as dupes, but many clearly felt better after taking the cure. And while I certainly didn't find anything to support Mwasapila's claim of a cure for HIV/AIDS, it took three weeks of intense effort—and a cultural background that predisposed me toward skepticism of faith healing—to feel secure in discounting Mwasapila. Most Americans wouldn't spend three weeks investigating the widely believed claims of their respected family doctor. We trust our appointed healers, and Tanzanians trust theirs. After Alma's HIV test, Reverend Gabriel Kimerei was troubled to hear so many people continued to test HIV positive, and embarrassed to have passed on bad information.

"That embarrassment is to his credit," Pat Patten tells me over the phone. Patten considers many Tanzanian leaders to be complicit in a prolonged series of exaggerations—if not lies. In a June newspaper editorial, he wrote about the profiteering of the bus, truck, and taxi drivers, as well as the entrepreneurs and builders who found business booming because of Mwasapila. He noted that

---

* A placebo effect has never been shown to have a long-term impact on diabetes, but Dr. Tor Wager, an expert in placebo effects, wrote this to me in a private letter: "Sensory cues can generate an insulin response, but only (as far as I know) after conditioning: i.e., when you sit down to dinner, the associated cues cause insulin release. This is probably less related to conscious belief than it is to low-level learning in your brain, but nobody really knows whether beliefs in a one-time cure could affect insulin levels."

the government charges a hefty tax to all vehicles bound for Samunge, and the Lutheran Church leaders "can now claim that one of their own, not a Pentecostal, is the preeminent religious healer in the country." Many government officials had chosen to stake their reputations on Mwasapila's cure and risked embarrassment if they were shown to be wrong. "All sorts of people benefit from these lies," Patten wrote.

But the voices promoting Mwasapila seem to have fallen silent. In the months since I left Tanzania, Patten says Mwasapila's popularity has steadily declined. The Health Ministry still hasn't issued the results of their study about the liquid, and the Lutheran bishops are no longer talking about the healer. "They ought to be embarrassed and ashamed," Patten tells me, "and I think they're hoping people will just forget."

I haven't been able to reach Reverend Kimerei to ask about his wife or what he thinks now, but I have spoken to a friend—a safari driver who took three carloads of patients to Samunge in March and April. He was convinced Mwasapila's liquid worked back in the spring, but he now says 9 out of 10 Tanzanians discount Mwasapila's medicine. People may have felt better for a few weeks, he says. "But nobody who went there was cured. Not one."

SAM ANDERSON

The Pippiest Place on Earth

FROM *The New York Times Magazine*

FIVE YEARS AGO, I flew to England to see the grand opening of something improbable: an attraction called Dickens World. It promised to be an "authentic" re-creation of the London of Charles Dickens's novels, complete with soot, pickpockets, cobblestones, gas lamps, animatronic Dickens characters, and strategically placed chemical "smell pots" that would, when heated, emit odors of offal and rotting cabbage. Its centerpiece was the Great Expectations boat ride, which started in a rat-infested creek, flew over the Thames, snaked through a graveyard, and splashed into a sewer. Its staff had all been trained in Victorian accents and body language. Visitors could sit at a wooden desk and get berated by an angry Victorian schoolteacher, watch Dickensian holograms antagonize one another in a haunted house, or set their kids loose in a rainbow-colored play area called, ominously, Fagin's Den, after the filthy kidnapper from *Oliver Twist*. The park's operating budget was $124 million.

Dickens World, in other words, sounded less like a viable business than it did a mockumentary, or a George Saunders short story, or the thought experiment of a radical Marxist seeking to expose the terminal bankruptcy at the heart of consumerism. And yet it was real. Its existence raised a number of questions. Who was the park's target audience? ("Dickens-loving flume-ride enthusiasts" seems like a small, sad demographic.) Was it a homage to, or a desecration of, the legacy of Charles Dickens? Was it the reinvention of, or the cheapening of, our culture's relationship to litera-

ture? And even if it were possible to create a lavish simulacrum of
1850s London—with its typhus and cholera and clouds of toxic
corpse gas, its sewage pouring into the Thames, its average life
span of 27 years—why would anyone want to visit? ("If a late-20th-
century person were suddenly to find himself in a tavern or house
of the period," Peter Ackroyd, a Dickens biographer, has written,
"he would be literally sick—sick with the smells, sick with the food,
sick with the atmosphere around him.")

Well, despite its obvious absurdity, *I* wanted to go to Dickens
World. I love Charles Dickens. I don't mean "love" in the weak
sense, the way people love frozen yogurt or casual Friday or the
'80s. I am—like probably millions of readers spread over many
different eras—actively in love with Charles Dickens, or at least
with the version of his mind that survives in his writing. (The man
himself, as several new biographies remind us, was significantly
harder to love.) Of all the mega-canonical writers, Dickens is the
most charming. At a time of great formality in literature, he wrote
irreverently, for everybody, from the perspective of orphans and
outcasts. His best work—*Great Expectations, David Copperfield, Bleak
House*—plays the entire xylophone of a reader's value system, from
high to low; you can almost feel the oxytocin dumping, sentence
by sentence, in your brain. Taken together, his books add up to
perhaps the most distinctively *living* literary world ever created.
The chance to pay $20 to walk through a lovingly produced three-
dimensional version of that world seemed (despite some nagging
highbrow reservations) impossible to pass up.

And so I went to Dickens World. This was April 2007: the best
of times. The global economy was booming. The county of Kent,
where the park is, turned out to be the kind of verdant paradise
I'd only read about in Romantic poetry: wooded hills, chalk cliffs,
and that classically deep, soft, green English grass punctuated by
huge spreads of yellow flowers, like some bureaucratic deity had
gone over all the valleys with a giant highlighter. Even the city of
Chatham—Dickens's childhood home, which had fallen on hard
times—seemed to be coming up in the world. The city's formerly
derelict dockyards, where Dickens's father worked, and where
Dickens World was opening, were suddenly covered with cranes,
the sign of a thousand real estate projects blooming. It was a time
of investment, development, fortune, progress, joy—and Dickens
World seemed to be at the heart of it.

The only problem was that Dickens World didn't open as planned.

Shortly before I arrived in Chatham, the park's website announced (with all the sunny bluster of a Dickens politician) that it was "proud" to report that, instead of holding a ribbon-cutting ceremony as scheduled, its opening would be delayed for a month and a half. Instead of a functional attraction, I found a vaguely Dickensian construction site. The park is housed inside a big blue warehouse, and when I got there, teams of workers were filling all of its pseudo-19th-century nooks with litter and noise and tattoos and Mohawks and sexual novelty T-shirts (*Excellent Growth Potential*) and aggressive handwritten signs. (One of them, taped to a cinderblock wall, read, NICK MY TOOLS, AND I'LL PUT A CHISEL IN YOUR THROAT.) I got a tour from the park's manager, who was wearing a hardhat and a reflective vest. He told me I couldn't go on the Great Expectations boat ride because it was being repaired. (A worker later told me that it had broken down during a gala celebration the day before, forcing the local VIPs, he said, to put on big rubber boots and wade out through the water trough.) I couldn't go into the haunted house, he said, because technicians were using special welding torches that might burn out my eyes. There was a red tractor working outside a miniature version of Newgate Prison. Extension cords squiggled all over the imitation cobblestones. Everything smelled powerfully like sawdust.

It was fascinating to watch. The laborers had been hired to do basically the opposite of a typical construction job. They were building squalor—making new things look old, clean things look filthy, dry things look wet, solid things look rotten. A worker named Phil explained to me some of the park's technical aspects. The ivy was silk. The trees were polyurethane cores surrounded by sculptured plaster. The cobblestones were made from a latex mold of actual cobblestones. The moss was a mixture of sawdust, glue, and green paint—you stirred it in a bucket and flung it on the walls. The bricks were casting plaster that had been dyed pencil-eraser pink; they arrived in big rolled sheets that were bolted to the wooden buildings, in thin layers toward the top (where no one would touch it) and thick layers below—because, Phil said, kids tend to kick things. Later, professional scene painters came along to make the pink bricks look grimy, adding highlights to signify texture and smoke. The result looked so good that, when I got back to London, some of the actual Victorian-era brick and moss and ivy struck me as unrealistic.

Being at Dickens World, at the moment of its creation, felt exactly like being in an episode of *The Office*. The manager told me that, when the park advertised for 50 jobs a few months earlier, nearly 1,000 people had applied. (The job market in Chatham has been desperate since the navy pulled out of the dockyard in the early '80s.) He also told me that he and his staff narrowed the pool with *American Idol*–style auditions. "We made the applicants demonstrate customer service," he said. "What they'd do if somebody lost a child, or injured themselves. Or if there was a complaint, unfortunately. But then I said to them, 'The twist is, *you have to do it in a Victorian manner.*'"

I left Dickens World after a couple of days. As a literary experience, it had been pretty thin gruel. But like Oliver Twist, I wanted more.

What is the best way to commune with an author, other than reading his books? Stand in his childhood bedroom? Retrace the route he used to walk to work? Write his name, in his house, with his own quill pen, on a postcard of him?

Such behaviors have become staples of literary tourism, a tradition that has been around for at least a couple of centuries. A literary tour is the secular echo of a religious pilgrimage. The hope is the same as with saints' relics: that some residue of genius will survive in the physical objects an author has touched, that the secret to his mind will turn out to be hidden in the places his body passed through—the proportions of a doorway, the smell of old stone. Literature, for all its power, is an abstract transaction: a reader gives time and attention, an author gives patterns of words that call up vivid people and landscapes that—mystifyingly—are not physically there (at least beyond the level of neurons firing). It seems like a natural human response to try to plug that gap—to look for solid, real-world corollaries for those interior landscapes, whether it's walking the route of *Ulysses* on Bloomsday, stuffing a bagpipe with haggis on Burns Day, or wizard-spotting on Platform 9¾ at King's Cross station. It's the brain's attempt to anchor an abstraction, to make the spirit world and the boring world finally align. It is, in my experience, one of the cheapest forms of magic available.

In England, literary tourism took off at the end of the 18th century, just before Dickens was born. By the time his books exploded into popularity, in the 1830s, literary tourism was an established tradition. Dickens was the first author to earn what we'd think of as a mass readership, and visiting places from his fiction was a way for individual readers to make an intimate connection with a sometimes distressingly public figure. (When Dickens visited New York in 1842, Tiffany's sold copies of his bust, a barber reportedly sold scraps of his hair, and crowds followed him through the streets; in Boston, ladies with scissors tried to cut off pieces of his coat.) Dickens's work seemed to lend itself especially well to literary tourism. Its characters walked on real English streets and spoke in real English accents, so—despite all of the cartoonish exaggerations—its atmosphere felt strangely real. As G. K. Chesterton put it: "It is well to be able to realize that contact with the Dickens world is almost like a physical contact; it is like stepping suddenly into the hot smells of a greenhouse, or into the bleak smell of the sea. We know that we are there." During Dickens's lifetime, readers often visited the settings of his stories, and in the decades after his death, a number of books were published to guide Dickens readers to Dickens spots: *A Pickwickian Pilgrimage, About England with Dickens, A Week's Tramp in Dickens-Land.* By 1941, Dickens tourism was common enough for Edmund Wilson to complain that "the typical Dickens expert is an old duffer who . . . is primarily interested in proving that Mr. Pickwick stopped at a certain inn and slept in a certain bed."

Dickens himself was a literary tourist. He once spent an entire day at Sir Walter Scott's house, contemplating the dead writer's hat. He also partook, strangely enough, in Dickens tourism. (Dickens was, in many ways, the world's biggest Dickens fan.) He commissioned paintings of his characters, named his daughter after Dora in *David Copperfield,* and went out of his way to visit a pub named after *Our Mutual Friend.* It's said that a few days before he died, Dickens was seen standing in a park in Rochester, just a few miles from the future site of Dickens World, gazing wistfully at a stout brick building across the street. It was the actual house on which he modeled Miss Havisham's house in *Great Expectations.* Dickens lived, and then he died, in his own Dickens World.

Last month, a few weeks before Dickens's 200th birthday, I went back to Dickens World. It was the worst of times. In 2007, the plan was to create 200 jobs and attract 500,000 visitors a year and help reignite the region's economy. But the attraction opened just before the global economy tanked. The management company that had generated those early projections was fired for failing to deliver anything even close to them. The park reduced performers' work shifts, dropped managerial positions, and even turned off the Dickensian gas lamps. Today Dickens World survives largely as a landlord, collecting rent from the Odeon movie theater next door and the restaurants (Pizza Hut, Subway, Chimichanga) that surround it. Its marketing plan now focuses on attracting schoolchildren and retirees.

I arrived at Dickens World at noon on a gray and windy day. The most striking feature of the building's exterior is a big clock on which the numbers run counterclockwise. (I wasn't sure if this was supposed to signify some kind of mystical journey back in time or was just an installation error.) As I approached, the clock started to chime the hour, which triggered a little show: its face opened to reveal Charles Dickens sitting in a wooden rowboat along with two kids and a dog. (I have no idea.) The figures started talking, but I could hardly understand anything they were saying because of the pop music blasting from Nando's, the Portuguese chain restaurant next door, and also because the trailer for the new Muppets movie was playing on a giant screen outside the Odeon. Compared to this ambient multimedia barrage, Dickens and his crew seemed oddly lifeless. I gave up listening and went inside.

I recognized, immediately, many of the buildings I had seen in progress five years earlier: landmarks from Dickens's life and work, all scaled down and crowded together. There were rows of leaning houses with crooked chimneys, Warren's Blacking factory (where Dickens worked as a boy), and the Marshalsea prison (where his father was imprisoned for debt). It was all, still, technically impressive. But Dickens World, it quickly became clear, was an attraction very much down on its luck. This was the low season for park visitors—the numbers are highest around Christmas and over the summer—and only a smattering of families wandered around. Dickens World had been closed, during recent weeks, for its annual maintenance session, and yet things still weren't quite running smoothly. Posts were abandoned; displays were broken; animatronics failed to animate. In the schoolroom, the schoolmaster was conspicuously absent, and some of the desks' interactive touch screens were out of order. (I managed, on a functional one, to play a quiz game and earn 75 Dickens Points, although there was no indication of how the scoring worked or what the points were good for.) The gift shop was called—in blatant disregard of both Victorian spelling and the title of Dickens's novel—the Olde Curiosity Shoppe. One of the performers in the plaza was riding a unicycle, a mode of transport that wasn't invented until after Dickens's death.

The visitor experience consisted mainly of listening to recorded speeches, many of which were either dull or unintelligible. This made it the opposite of a Dickens novel, in which your experience is expertly guided, your attention constantly engaged. Dickens's genius was to unite all kinds of contradictory impulses: education and entertainment, misery and fun, violence and laughter, simplicity and sophistication. At Dickens World, these contradictions just felt contradictory. The result was sad and funny, in a way that Dickens would have loved. He was obsessed with grand plans that ended in failure, with the comic tragedy of provincial ambition. In this way, Dickens World was a perfect tribute to Charles Dickens.

For a park that markets itself to children, Dickens World was surprisingly grisly. I saw at least two severed heads, and when the performers lip-synched their way through a dramatization of *Oliver Twist* in the courtyard, it ended as the novel ends: with Bill Sikes murdering Nancy by beating her head in with a club, then being chased by a mob until he accidentally hangs himself. The violence was suggested rather than shown, but still—I flinched slightly for the kids who had been pulled in from the audience to play orphans. The gruesomeness was admirable, in a way: you wouldn't want Dickens World to exclude the darker side of things—that would be a misrepresentation. But it made me wonder, again, if the idea of this place really made sense.

I had brought a friend to the park—another Dickens enthusiast—and, with sinking hearts, we decided to try the Great Expectations boat ride. There were signs, at various points in the line, announcing that it would be a 45-minute wait from here, a 30-minute wait from there—but it was a zero-minute wait, and we walked to the end unobstructed. Instead of an attendant, we found a black chair occupied by only a walkie-talkie and a Stephen King novel. After a minute or two, someone came and put us on a boat. Halfway up a dark tunnel, the chemical smell pots engulfed us in a powerful cloud of sour mildew. It was genuinely unpleasant, and in the midst of that cloud of stench I felt something suddenly slip inside of me: two centuries of literary touristic tradition, the pressure of Dickens reverence, the absurdity of this commodified experience—all of it broke, like a fever, and what poured out of me was hysterical laughter. I laughed, in a high-pitched cackle that sounded like someone else's voice, for most of the ride. At some point the boat swiveled and shot backward down a ramp, splashing us and soaking our winter coats, and an automated camera took our picture. It caught us looking like a perfectly Dickensian pair: me in a mania of wild-eyed laughter, my friend resigned and unhappy—comedy and tragedy side by side, "in as regular alternation," as Dickens put it in *Oliver Twist,* "as the layers of red and white in a side of streaky bacon." Afterward, in the gift shop, I bought a copy of the picture, as well as a 59-page version of *Great Expectations* published by a company called Snapshot Classics. "In the time it takes to read the original," promised the book's cover, which was designed to look soiled and creased, "you can read this Snapshot Classic up to 20 times and know the story and characters off by heart."

All the Dickens World employees I talked to—the performers, the bartenders, the marketing director—were unfailingly kind and seemed to be working hard. Many of them had worked at the park since it opened (they called themselves "originals"), sticking with it even when it could no longer guarantee them regular hours. They said they felt like a family and seemed to genuinely mean it. I wanted them to succeed. But the whole project seemed doomed. None of this was their fault. It was modernity's fault, capitalism's fault, Charles Dickens's fault. I found myself fantasizing that Dickens World would be adopted by a wealthier park—maybe the Wizarding World of Harry Potter, in Orlando, Florida—and that it would manage to somehow vanquish its villains, overcome the odds, live happily ever after.

When the plan for Dickens World was announced in 2005, many people were predictably horrified. The *New York Times* wrote an editorial full of earnest handwringing ("There is a lot to fear here") over the way that Literature, this sacred receptacle of Truth, was being tainted by consumerism. But if Dickens World seems to violate certain unspoken treaties about the commercial exploitation of literature, it's worth remembering that Charles Dickens did so as well. His art was gleefully tangled with capitalism. The first printings of his novels, in their monthly installments, often had more pages of ads than they did of fiction. His stories inspired endless adaptations, extensions, and tributes, including hundreds of spinoff products: Dickens-themed hats, pens, cigars, songbooks, joke books, figurines, sheet music, ladles. Theater companies in London staged rival versions of his novels before he'd even finished writing them.

All of which is to say that paying tribute to Dickens gets very tricky very quickly. Homage and exploitation shade into each other. Dickens World is just the latest in a long line of attempts to profit by making Dickens's fictional worlds concrete. The park doesn't fail because it's too commercial—it fails because it's too reverent, and reverent about the wrong things. It treats Dickens as an institution, when what we want is what is gone, or what survives only in the texts: the energy, the aura, the spirit.

Which brings us back to religion. Dickens World sits in the center of Dickens territory, right on the river Medway—the young Dickens, confined to his attic bedroom with terrible pains in his side, might have been able to see the attraction from his window. My friend and I, looking for traces of whatever energy Dickens left behind in the actual world, made our own self-guided pilgrimage through Kent.

We drove a tiny rented Hyundai between curving hedgerows into Cooling, a country village that feels more like the absence of a village, a negative space defined by bird song and horizon and wind. We parked next to Saint James, an 800-year-old church, to which Dickens often walked, and which seemed to exist today in a pocket of such deep, eternal silence that I felt immediately alienated from my iPhone. Its graveyard contains one particularly tragic cluster of stones: 13 tiny markers, each of which represents a child killed, before Dickens's time, in a malaria epidemic. Ten of those children belonged to a single family. Dickens gave this tragedy (slightly downsized for plausibility) to Pip, who begins *Great Expectations* trying to imagine, based only on the shapes of their graves, what his parents and his five siblings were like.

Standing there, looking at these real stones that were also Pip's fictional stones, I felt a powerful confluence: the lovely loneliness of the landscape, the sadness of that family's tragedy, the old elegance of the graves (Pip thinks of them as "lozenges"), my affection for *Great Expectations* and this immediate physical connection to its author, whom I tried to imagine standing on this same spot, his body touched by these same patterns of cold wind, having some version of these same feelings. There was no parking garage, no admission fee, no gift shop, no hidden camera taking my picture. I felt pinned between worlds.

We drove deeper into the country, to Dickens's old house, Gad's Hill Place. This was the emblem of Dickens's success: as a child, he walked by it many times with his father and fantasized about someday buying it. As an adult, he came back and did. It's now a private school, and on this day it was empty and locked. We stood outside its front gate for a while, looking. My friend said, finally, that it looked exactly right: the kind of house a child would find impressive but that's not actually great—drab, slightly pompous. I just kept trying to imagine the actual human Charles Dickens walking across this lawn. I was having trouble not picturing him in black and white.

We drove to Rochester, an ancient Roman town whose castle and cathedral had been staring at each other for many centuries before Dickens was born. Dickens wanted to be buried there but was overruled, after his death, and taken to Poets' Corner in Westminster Abbey, where he remains pressed up against Thomas Hardy and Rudyard Kipling. (And so the great enemy of institutions began to be institutionalized.) In Dickens's final, unfinished novel, *The Mystery of Edwin Drood,* a character remarks that being in Rochester Cathedral was like "looking down the throat of Old Time."

For all its history, Rochester has been for years now a kind of proto–Dickens World. Many of the stores on its High Street have kitschy Dickensian signs: A Taste of Two Cities Indian restaurant, Pips grocery, Little Dorrit's Piercing Studio. Down an alley you can find Dickens's actual writing hut: a two-story chalet decorated with Swiss frippery in which Dickens wrote for the last five years of his life. It was moved, years ago, from the yard at Gad's Hill Place and is now (according to the informational banner in front of it, which also calls it "the most iconic building in British literature") about to collapse. It's being held up, inside, by steel props, and the Dickens Fellowship is hoping to raise £100,000 to fix it.

Our last stop was one of Dickens's last stops: Miss Havisham's house. My friend, who was skeptical about literary tourism when we started our trip—authors, he insisted, are just ordinary people—was suddenly in ecstasy. "Of course this is Miss Havisham's house!" he shouted. "Look at that window up top—a perfect window for peeking!" The house is open to visitors during the summer, but today it was closed. My friend was determined to see into its walled back garden, so we walked down an alley, ascended a metal staircase on the side of a church, climbed on top of the stairs' highest railing—and from there we could see down into it: Miss Havisham's garden, the Eden of the 19th-century novel, source of all desire, conflict, motion, disturbance, and growth. It was manicured now rather than overgrown, but it still seemed like the right place. Looking into it felt like looking into the nerve center not only of *Great Expectations,* or of Dickens's imagination, or of 19th-century literature—but of the entire history of the novel. And we had it all to ourselves.

We left Rochester in an ecstasy of Dickens communion, my friend exclaiming about how, in just a few hours, in one morning, he had come to understand Dickens on a totally new level. This, then, seemed to be the real Dickens World, at least for us, on that day.

MARIE ARANA

Dreaming of El Dorado

FROM *Virginia Quarterly Review*

FOR AS LONG as Senna Ochochoque can remember, she has worked to support her family. She began at four, helping prepare food that her family would hawk about town, when her father was too sick to pick rock in the gold mines. She would accompany him to market three hours away, bumping down mountain roads in a dilapidated minibus in the freezing penumbra of dawn. She'd haul bags up the slippery inclines, lug water down from the trickling glacier. To earn a few extra cents, she'd drag rocks from the maws of mineshafts, apply her tiny frame to the crushing of stones.

When she turned 10, she was hired to run one of seven public toilets that served the town's 20,000 inhabitants. There is no sewage system in La Rinconada; no water, no paved roads, no sanitation whatsoever in that wilderness of ice, rock, and gold, perched more than 18,000 feet up in the Peruvian Andes. Senna's job—from 6 in the morning to 10 at night—was to hand out tiny squares of paper, take a few cents from each customer, and muck out the fecal pits at the end of the day. When she was 12, she took a job that paid a bit more so that she could buy medicine for her dying father. Trudging the steep, fetid roads where the whorehouses and drinking establishments proliferate, she sold water trucked in from contaminated lakes.

Senna has pounded rock; she has ground it to gravel with her feet; she has teetered under heavy bags of crushed stone. But she was never lucky as a child miner; she never found even the faintest glimmer of gold. Today, with her father dead and her mother bordering on desperation, she makes fancy gelatins and sells them

to men as they come and go from the mineshafts that pock the un-
forgiving face of Mount Ananea. When she is asked why she slogs
through mud and snow for a few hours of school every day, as few
children do, she says she wants to be a poet. She is 14 years old.

Peru is booming these days. Its economy boasts one of the highest
growth rates in the world. In the past six years, its annual growth
has hovered between 6.2 and 9.8 percent, rivaling the colossal en-
gines of China and India. Peru is the world's leading producer of
silver; it is one of Latin America's most exuberant founts of gold,
copper, zinc, lead, and pewter. It is an up-and-coming producer of
natural gas. It harvests and sells more fish than any other country
on the planet, save China.

But it is the gold rush that has gripped Peru—the search for El
Dorado, that age-old fever that harks back to the time of the Inca.
More than 500 years later, it is in full frenzy again, in men's imagi-
nations as well as on front pages of newspapers.

In 2010, Peru extracted a total of 170 tons of gold from its
mountains and rain forests, the highest production of that min-
eral in all of South America. Last year, it produced somewhat less.
Every year has seen a drop in the output, which is hardly surprising since there is so little of this precious stuff left to dig out. "In
all of history," *National Geographic* reports, "only 161,000 tons of
gold have been mined, barely enough to fill two Olympic-size
swimming pools." More than half of the world's supply has been
extracted in the last 50 years. Little wonder that the price of gold
has soared in the past decade; little wonder that multinational
companies have scrambled to wrest it from remote corners of the
globe.

La Rinconada's "informal" mines alone yield as much as 10
tons a year—worth up to $460 million on the open market. Even
illegal operations are claiming a place in the boom. The irony is
that every niche of this gargantuan industry—from Tiffany's to the
mom-and-pop store—owes Osama bin Laden a debt of gratitude
for its rising profits. After the sobering events of 9/11, when fi-
nancial markets grew jittery and the dollar began to lose ground,
gold began its meteoric upward spiral. Everyone seemed to want
it, especially in the form of jewelry, and especially in countries
whose populations were clawing their way up toward the middle
class: India and China accounted for the highest demand for gold,

their surging numbers driving the prices ever skyward. One ounce of gold, which sold for $271 on September 11, 2001, now sells for $1,700, a whopping increase of 600 percent. That boom has prompted an equivalent explosion in the population crowding into La Rinconada; it is why the number of inhabitants on that icy, forbidding rock—less than 20,000 in 2007—has doubled and tripled in the course of five years.

Today there are 30,000 miners working the frozen tunnels of Mount Ananea, most of them with families, and all in the service of a buoyant global market. There is no legal oversight, no benevolent employer, no operational government, no functioning police. At least 60,000 souls have pressed into the lawless encampment, building huts on the near-vertical cant of that dizzying promontory—harboring hope that this may be the day they strike a gleaming vein, cleave open a wall to find a fist-sized nugget. They think they'll stay only as long as it takes to find one. There are just enough stories of random fortune to keep the insanity alive.

The mines at La Rinconada are called "informal," a euphemism for illegal, a status without which Peru's economy would screech to a standstill. For 40 years now, the Peruvian government has turned a blind eye to increasingly wretched conditions in this remote community, its government agents unwilling to scale the heights, brave the cold, take control. In the interim, what was once a region of crystalline lakes and leaping fish—replete with alpaca, vicuña, chinchilla—has become a Bosch-like world that beggars the imagination. The scrub is gone. The earth is turned. What you see instead, as you approach that distant glacier, is a lunar landscape, pitted with rust-pink lakes that reek of cyanide. The waterfowl that were once abundant in this corridor of the Andes are gone; no birds flap overhead, save an occasional vulture. The odor is overwhelming; it is the rank stench of the end of things: of burning, of rot, of human excrement. Even the glacial cold, the permafrost, the whipping wind, and driving snows cannot mask the smell. As you ascend the mountain, all about you are heaps of garbage, a choking ruin, and sylphlike figures picking idly through it. Closer in are huts of tin and stone, leaning out at 70-degree angles, and then the ever-present mud, the string of humanity streaming in and out of black holes that scar the cliffs. Along the precipitously winding road, flocks of women in wide skirts scrabble up inclines to scavenge rocks that spill from the mineshafts; the children they don't carry in slings—the ones who are old enough to walk—shoulder bags of rock.

A miner lucky enough to find work once he reaches this mountain inferno labors in subzero temperatures, in dank, suffocating tunnels, wielding a primitive pick. In the course of that work, he risks lung disease, toxic poisoning, asphyxiation, nerve damage. He exposes himself to glacial floods, collapsing shafts, wayward dynamite, chemical leaks. The altitude alone is punishing: at 14,000 feet a human body can experience pulmonary edema, blood clots, kidney failure; at 18,000 the injuries can be more severe. To counter them, he chews wads of coca. He carries pocketfuls of the leaf to curb his hunger, prevent exhaustion. If he lives to work another day, he celebrates by drinking himself into a stupor. The ore he extracts, grinds down, leaches with mercury, then purifies in a blazing furnace will make his boss and his boss's bosses very rich; but for the vast majority who slave in that high circle of hell, gold is as elusive as a glittering fool's paradise.

The system of *cachorreo*, used by contractors in La Rinconada and elsewhere, is akin to the Mita, the system of imposed, mandatory servitude that once enslaved Indians to the Spanish crown. Under *cachorreo*, a worker surrenders his identity card to his employer. He labors for 30 days with no pay. On the 31st day, if he is lucky, he is allowed to mine the shaft for his personal profit. But he can take only what he can carry out on his back. By the time a miner struggles out under his cargo of stones, grinds it, and coaxes the glittering dust free, he may find he has precious little for his efforts. Worse still, because he must sell his gold to the ramshackle, unregulated establishments in town, it will fetch the lowest price possible. On average, a miner in La Rinconada earns $170 a month—$5 for every day of grueling labor. On average, he has more than five mouths to feed. If he has a bad month, he will earn $30. If he does well, he will earn $1,000. In most cases, workers simply go up the hill, spend their hard-won cash on liquor and prostitutes, and count themselves lucky if they make it home without a brawl. Crime and AIDS are rampant in La Rinconada. If work doesn't kill a man, a knife or a virus will. There are few miners here who have reached 50.

It's hard to imagine, as we hover over the gleaming counters of jewelry stores in Paris or New York, or even Jakarta and Mumbai, that gold can take such a hallucinatory journey, that the process remains so medieval—that little has progressed in half a millennium of human history. Families like Senna Ochochoque's, who have spent as many as three generations under the spell of gold's promise, live in abject poverty, barely able to eke out an evening meal. The world boom in the value of gold has not translated to better lives in La Rinconada. It is the same in the gold mines of Cajamarca in northern Peru (owned by the U.S. giant Newmont Mining Corporation), or in Puerto Maldonado, where anarchic mines carve into the Amazon jungle. In Cajamarca, which has poured $7 billion of gold into the global market in the last 30 years, 74 percent of the population lives in numbing poverty. In the outlying areas of Cuzco, where Australian and U.S. companies are busily ferreting Peru's gold out into international markets, more than half of the population earns less than $35 a month. Peruvians, in other words, may perch on some of the world's most valuable mountains, but as the naturalist Alexander von Humboldt is said to have observed 200 years ago, "Peru is a beggar, sitting on a bench of gold."

Humboldt was quick to see—when he traveled Peru in the early 1800s—that the terrain just south of Lake Titicaca, where the Andes make a stately march south to Potosí, held vast reserves of gold and silver. According to him, Mount Ananea harbored a considerable store of wealth, even though its mines had lain dormant for a hundred years. History books tell us that during the 1700s the glacier atop Ananea had grown heavy with accumulated ice; eventually it collapsed the Spanish mines and flushed them with freezing water, drowning all life within. Spain tried to resuscitate their operation in 1803, but the land was too difficult to govern, its peaks too vertiginous, its cold too lacerating. The winds and snows of Ananea had done what the Inca could not: they had driven the conquistadors away. But, by then, Spain had scores of mines to satisfy its voracious lust for gold and silver. So it was that Ananea remained that mythic titan—remote, frigid, and threaded with gold.

Nevertheless, the myth had preceded Humboldt, preceded conquistadors, proliferated with the Inca, and had the force of immutable truth. According to local lore, a gold block the size of a horse's head and weighing more than 100 pounds had been found on Mount Ananea. The region's rivers were said to be strewn with glittering nuggets. Garcilaso de la Vega, a half-Inca, half-Spanish chronicler who lived in the late 1500s, wrote that precisely that stretch of Peru contained gold beyond our imagining. Chunks of coruscating rock as large as a human head—and 24-karat pure—had rolled from cracks in the Andean stone.

It isn't surprising, given the attendant mythology, that a swarm of enterprising locals, toting little more than picks and hammers, would climb those reaches again. They began to come in the 1960s. Senna Ochochoque's father arrived in 1980, a strapping young man with wildly ambitious dreams and legs sturdy enough to carry them. In La Rinconada, he met Leonor, a young woman who had been born there 15 years earlier. He built a one-room house of rock, covered it with tin, and invited her to live there with him. They proceeded to have four children, of which Senna was the third. Strangely enough, that inhospitable peak was not a bad place to be during those fateful years of the '80s and early '90s. The Shining Path, the Maoist terrorist organization intent on capsizing Peru's power structure, was slashing its way through the countryside, killing whole villages as it went.

This is where Senna's story shifts, turns, like a skein waiting to ravel. In 1998, when Senna was born, Peru was, for all its rich history, an emerging chrysalis—a nation that had swung violently between democracy and dictatorship for 174 years under the rule of nearly 100 presidents. Three years later, as the country crawled out from under its long decade of civil war—when Juan Ochochoque was still a robust, fully functional miner in La Rinconada—19 Arab terrorists who had pledged their lives to al-Qaeda flew airplanes into American landmarks and, paradoxically, Juan's future began to brighten: the value of gold began to grow. But months later, that bullish trajectory would halt altogether for Juan. The shaft in which he was working collapsed. Just as in days of yore, when the glacier had sent torrents of water down the ancient tunnels, a plummeting mass of ice now crushed the mine's delicate corridors and trapped the workers inside. Juan, who had been pounding a wall of stone, along with his six-year-old son, Jhon, who had been sweeping out the gravel, were caught in a sudden, airless black.

When father and son eventually clawed their way to freedom, they thanked the mountain god for their lives, but they soon found they hadn't escaped entirely. The boy was plagued by a sickness of the spirit the Indians call *susto:* he ducked at the slightest sound, could hardly eat or sleep; he was deeply traumatized. Juan, on the other hand, was suffering a very manifest physical deterioration. His legs ballooned to three times their normal size. His arms grew weak. His joints ached, hands shook; he could scarcely bend his knees. Before long, he began to have seizures; and then came the constant, bone-rattling cough. He couldn't walk more than a few yards, much less climb the path to the mine.

In the course of a fleeting moment, Juan Ochochoque had become a marginal citizen. He had joined the women, the children, the maimed and dispossessed—those relegated to distaff roles in a full-blooded macho society. He was too sick to do women's work: *quimbaleteo,* for instance, which requires one to stand on a boulder and rock back and forth, grinding ore with mercury; or *pallaqueo,* in which a woman crawls up a cliff, scavenging for rock that spills from the mouths of mines, stuffing anything that shines into a backbreaking rucksack. Nor could he do even the simplest work: the *chichiqueo,* which requires a woman or child to bend over crushed gravel in standing water for hours, picking through stones in hopes of finding a gold fleck. These were impossible tasks in his condition. But he had to do something: there were bills to pay, mouths to feed. In time, he decided to cook for a living. Hunched over an ethyl alcohol burner on the bare earth of his hut, he produced pot after pot of soups, spaghettis, stews, and sent his family out into the streets to sell them. At night, he drank whatever alcohol was left, to dull the pain of humiliation.

The labors of Juan's children, which until then had been sporadic and secondary, now became indispensable, primary. His wife, Leonor, and eldest daughter, Mariluz, dedicated themselves to the *pallaqueo,* scaling escarpments with hundreds of women who worked their way up like an army of ants. It is brutal, exhausting work and, in it, a body suffers a pounding battery—no less from the weight of rocks than from the relentless cold, which can dip to −4 degrees Fahrenheit. The women of La Rinconada are old by the time they are 20. Chances are they have lost their teeth. Before girlhood is out, their faces are cooked by sun, parched by wind; their hands have turned the color of cured meat; their fingers are humped and gnarled. You can feel the toll of the *pallaqueo* when you see Senna look up and cringe at the bright, blue sky. She squints at a camera flash, shades her eyes. Her black eyes have turned a milky gray.

According to the United Nations, more than 18 million children between 10 and 14 are engaged in hard labor in Latin America. Most are "informal" workers like Senna—underpaid, overworked, and grossly undercounted. More than 2 million are in Peru, which accounts for the highest ratio of child laborers in all of Latin America. To put it more plainly: one out of every four Peruvian children works regularly, and does so in physically dangerous conditions. Perhaps because of ignorance, certainly because of necessity, parents whose children work alongside them in La Rinconada find nothing wrong with this practice. They are repeating an age-old cycle. Their children accompany them to work just as they once accompanied their parents. When a young mother enters a mine with a baby strapped to her back, she does not know that the dynamite fumes and chemical vapors can do lasting damage to her infant's brain; ditto for the mother whose child pours mercury into the mix while she grinds away on the *quimbaleteo;* ditto for the father who wades into a cyanide pond side by side with his son. No government official has come around to explain the long-term effects: blindness, brain damage, nerve damage, lung disease, lumbar deterioration, intestinal failure, early death. According to the Institute of Health and Work in Peru, more than 70 percent of all children and adolescents in La Rinconada suffer chronic malnutrition; as many as 95 percent exhibit some form of nervous impairment. But even if the parents of these children were lined up and given this tragic news, they might have no choice but to keep them working anyway. How else could they afford to eat? How else to keep warm? How else to buy the tools to work another day?

Aware that to tamper with this fragile system of survival would be to undermine the poor population's ability to subsist, the Peruvian government has been slow to outlaw child labor. Peru was one of the last Latin American countries to ratify the United Nations convention that prohibited children under the age of 14 from working (ILO/UN #138). Even so, although Peru finally signed that document in May 2001, the mining boom that immediately followed made it difficult to enforce the law. To do so would mean Peru would have to pull 50,000 children from the nation's work force. And that is a very hard thing to do when business is booming and a country's growth rate is among the highest in the world.

Few places expose the dark side of the global economy more starkly than the lawless 25-acre cesspool of La Rinconada. For every gold ring that goes out into the world, 250 tons of rock must move, a toxic pound of mercury will spill into the environment, and countless lives—biological and botanical—will struggle with the consequences. It doesn't take a social scientist or a chemist to walk through that wasteland and reckon the costs.

For a girl like Senna, there is a further danger, very different from the toxins, vectors, and violence that plague her town. La Rinconada is a humming beehive of brothels, looking for girls precisely her age. A lawyer and social worker, Leon Quispe, who has dedicated himself to the welfare of the community, estimates that anywhere from 5,000 to 8,000 girls, some as young as 14, move through La Rinconada's cantinas in any given year. They are held captive as sexual slaves. Some come from as far away as the slums of Lima, but most hail from little villages around Puno and Cuzco—a sad cavalcade of gullible girls who arrive in La Rinconada believing they will wait on tables, sell food, and earn good tips; that they'll be able to send their destitute families some measure of stable income. In their enthusiasm, they hand over their identity cards to a sweet-talking recruiter. What they learn when they arrive is that it isn't food they will be selling. Their bodies will be the commodities, and the prices have been long established: sex with a bargirl costs a man a few drinks and a few extra *soles;* a young girl's hymen is worth a seed of gold.

La República, one of Peru's major newspapers, explained the racket via a single story: Two 16-year-old girls from a tiny village outside Cuzco were approached in a public park by a woman they knew, a former neighbor. She offered them $500 a month to work at a restaurant in the airport city of Juliaca—all benefits included. Since they were virtually penniless, they readily agreed. But the only time the girls spent in Juliaca was the time it took to change buses. Four hours later, they were in a dilapidated bar in La Rinconada, in time for the miners' change of shifts. It was then that they learned they were obliged to consort with men, offer them sex. They were told the rules: If a man touched their breasts or genitals, they were not to rebuff him. They would be given a ticket for every six bottles of beer their clients consumed. One ticket was worth 4 Peruvian *soles,* or $1.25. Whatever sex they might negotiate would be traded at a more favorable rate: the proprietor would only take half. The girls quickly found that they had no way to exit that nightmare: they had no papers, no means to travel; and a surly guard with a knife was at the door.

The cantinas in La Rinconada are 24-hour-a-day operations. They do business out of slipshod edifices that climb up the road willy-nilly, alongside the gold-burning shops. During the day, miners come for a beer or to have their mercury-laden nuggets fired down to pure gold. The crude furnaces sit out where everyone can see them, spewing mercury into the open air; the fumes snake through the cantinas and float out onto the glacial snow, La Rinconada's primary water source. Mercury levels in those public spaces are 5,000 percent higher than what is permissible in regulated factories. But here, no one is measuring. Women and children hurry through the murky haze, hawking their food and water. The sick struggle in and out of doorways, breathing the deadly air. At night, when the drinking establishments turn into brothels, La Rinconada descends through every circle of hell. A deafening music pounds; drunks reel through the open sewage; food vendors traipse through the phantasmagoria as if it were a happy carnival, and small children flit past, laughing and falling into the toxic mud. Downstairs in the brothels, the young girls are lined up against the walls, their faces resolute and grim. Upstairs, by the light of a thousand flickering strobes, sex is traded, violence runs riot, and buckets of urine are tossed from windows as the poor drink away their hard-won gold.

It isn't a pretty picture. But so famous has La Rinconada become for its wanton nightlife that village boys for miles around come to work in the mines, have sex with women, and drink all the beer they can. A schoolteacher from Puno explained that often the boys are never the same after their journey to the frozen mountain: they drop out, leave home, and go on to a life of profligacy and ruin.

A life of profligacy and ruin was precisely what Juan Ochochoque did not want for his children. He had worked all his life to feed them, house them, give them what he could. Although he was illiterate—although he had never stepped foot inside a school—he began to counsel Senna, who was all of five when they began to cook together over their tiny ethyl stove, that education was her only way out of the grind of poverty. How he knew it is anyone's guess. There was nothing in Juan Ochochoque's past to suggest he would value an education, except for a vague perception he seemed to have about the prevailing power structure: the engineers who ran La Rinconada read and wrote; they knew mathematics, physics. A hierarchy was at work, and it involved knowledge and intelligence. He wanted his children to have that advantage. His wife, Leonor, did not necessarily agree. As far as she was concerned, the family needed to make ends meet, and that meant immediate results—not the sort of long-term, hard-won investment that education entailed.

By the time Senna was 10, her father was dead. His bloated body—shot through with chemical toxicity—had reached the crisis point as he left a bus at the foot of Mount Ananea, trying desperately to find a cure. It gave out suddenly as Leonor helped him to struggle across the road. Juan Ochochoque's long battle with La Rinconada's poisons was over, but the lesson he left his daughter refused to die: it was he who had pointed out, as his little girl puttered about alongside him, telling him stories, making up ditties, that she was good at words, good at digging out the right ones, good at polishing them to a fine shine; she was a miner of a different kind.

Which brings me to the crux of this story.

I had gone to La Rinconada precisely because of Senna's words. I had seen a video of her telling the story of her father's illness and the wreckage it had left behind. Throughout her story, she summoned allusions to the heartbreaking poetry of César Vallejo, using his words to express what she felt. I had never heard, in all my years sitting at dinner tables with the Lima elite, such easy familiarity with Vallejo's poems. I had been charged by a film company, the Documentary Group, with the task of finding a Peruvian girl in a poor community: a child whose story might be documented by the award-winning American director Richard Robbins in a movie about poverty around the world. His advance film party had shot videos of young girls in the Amazon jungle, of girls in the icy reaches of La Rinconada and Cerro Lunar. Senna was not particularly photogenic. She was shy in front of the camera. Hunched and incommunicative, she didn't seem like a good candidate for a feature film. But when she started to speak, when she pulled Vallejo's words from the air to describe her pain—"There are blows in life, so powerful"—a flame seemed to grow within her. I was riveted. "Blows like God's fury—like a riptide of human suffering rammed into a single soul . . . I don't know."

Social science now tells us that if we can take indigent girls between the ages of 10 and 14 and give them a basic education, we can change the fabric of an entire community. If we can capture them in that fleeting window, great social advances can be achieved. Give enough young girls an education and per capita income will go up; infant mortality will go down; the rate of economic growth will increase; the rate of HIV/AIDS infection will fall. Child marriages will be less common; child labor, too. Better farming practices will be put into place, which means better nutrition will follow, and overall family health in that community will climb. Educated girls, as former World Bank official Barbara Herz has written, tend to insist that their children be educated. And when a nation has smaller, healthier, better-educated families, economic productivity shoots up, environmental pressures ease, and everyone is better-off. As Lawrence Summers, a former Harvard University president, put it: "Educating girls may be the single highest return investment available in the developing world." Why is that? Well, you can make all the interpretations you like; you can posit the gendered arguments; but the numbers do not lie.

The irony in all this is that young girls like Senna are hardly valued in La Rinconada. The girls and women of that harsh, remote mining town may well be the community's most promising resource, but the overwhelmingly male culture of the mountain leaves little choice for a young adolescent female but to follow her mother to the cliff and perpetuate a cycle of ignorance and poverty.

All the same, there are signs that the overall business of gold mining in Peru may be facing significant corrections. In 2006, residents of villages near the largest gold-mining operation in all of South America, the U.S.-owned Newmont Mining Corporation's Yanacocha Project, just outside the historic city of Cajamarca, blocked the roads and declared that they had had enough of the company's toxic and predatory practices. A bloody standoff between the mine's armed security forces and the residents of Cajamarca followed. Five protesters were killed. By the end of 2011, the mineworkers were radicalized; they called a strike against Newmont's new Minas Conga Project. Their complaints were loud and clear: the workers were operating in wretched conditions, the environment was being ravaged, the toxicity of chemical waste was proving ruinous to public health.

Indeed a German scientist claims that the once sparkling lakes that surround Cajamarca are dangerously tainted and the 2 million residents of that city are at risk. But there is more than environmental despoliation at issue here: once Peruvian ore is excavated, processed, and the gold shipped abroad, Peru retains a mere 15 percent of Newmont's annual $3 to $4 billion profits. The protesters and strikers in Cajamarca became so outraged about such injustices that troops in riot gear were called out to contain what was perceived as a larger threat to the Peruvian economy. On July 4, a priest who was an outspoken leader of the protest movement was taken by force from a bench in a public park, arrested, and roughed up before he was let go. President Ollanta Humala, who had won the presidency on a socialist vote, now said with unequivocal free-market conviction that Conga would continue to mine, albeit with stricter government oversight. Peru's boom, in other words, is sacrosanct. Gold trumps water; and world markets take precedence over people.

In June of this year, La Rinconada followed Cajamarca's suit. Although La Rinconada is an "informal" operation with no one but Peruvians to blame for its troubles, workers emptied the mines, shut down the schools, and put down a collective foot: they called for the Peruvian government to give them water, a sanitation system, paved roads, health clinics, heightened security, child care, a better school, and all the attendant benefits a producing economic sector deserves. The nonprofit organization CARE is willing to help ameliorate the situation and, after having abandoned La Rinconada as hopeless some years ago, has sent representatives up the mountain again. In April, the head of CARE Peru, Milo Stanojevich, made the difficult trip to see the evidence for himself. But it's a risky business. The inhabitants of La Rinconada are all too aware of the proverbial "Beware of what you wish for." With government gifts come government regulations, and that means federal taxes, the marginalization of *cachorreo* workers, and the very real possibility that the work from which women and children now make a subsistence living—the sweeping, the *pallaqueo,* the *chichiqueo*—will be outlawed.

To Senna, the strikes in La Rinconada, which continue even as I write, have meant something more potentially harmful: school, in which she has invested all hope for a brighter future—which she had promised her dying father she would attend—has been shuttered, its doors bolted. The teachers in La Rinconada, after all, are miners who work there for extra cash; so school, for better or worse, is tied intimately to the mines. Even in this, even in education, a child's life is contaminated by gold's offal. But it's not the first time Senna has faced adversity. One gets the feeling that the seed of survival, planted so carefully by her father, will take root and flourish anyway. If a girl is motivated enough to save her hard-earned pennies, buy a dog-eared pamphlet of poetry from her teacher, and memorize whole pages of verse, that girl stands poised to redirect her future, make Herculean changes—a woman warrior, indeed. She will learn; she will open that door to a better world. And, if the social scientists are right, a whole village will follow.

CHRISTOPHER DE BALLAIGUE

Caliph of the Tricksters

FROM *Harper's Magazine*

ON A VISIT several years ago to Afghanistan, in a Kabul restaurant of the better kind, I met a policeman named Hossein Fakhri. A laconic, handsome, tense sort of man, Fakhri had been introduced to me as a police officer whose loves were literature and the city of his birth. Speaking in Persian, Afghanistan's literary language, we discussed Kabul and the writers and poets who live there. So much had happened to the city in its recent history, I said, that it wasn't easy for an outsider like me, visiting at some arbitrary point in events, to arrive at a settled view of the place. My opinion seemed unduly contingent on the latest suicide bombing, or land-grab scandal, or my sense of the Taliban at the gates. "That," Fakhri said, "is no way to look at a city."

Before he got up to return to work, Fakhri presented me with an edition of his short stories. It was called *The Roosters of Babur's Garden*. He advised me to read the title story, adding, "I think you'll find there is something of Kabul in that." After he had gone, I ordered a pot of green tea and opened the book.

"The Roosters of Babur's Garden" is narrated by a boy whose father, a poor Kabuli, sells his patch of dry, stony land and buys a three-month-old pedigree cockerel. Cherished by his new owner, the cockerel grows into a fine adult, taut from exercise and energized by a diet of wheat seeds, worms, and almonds. The transformation extends to the owner, who seems to grow in confidence and stature along with his bird. "I've had black-flecked birds," he boasts, "spotted ones, raisin-red and white birds, and bee-colored birds. I've had birds with up-standing combs, flat combs and floppy combs. A bird is a bird. But this one is something else. Woe betide the bird that is matched with this!"

Cockfighting, I learned from Fakhri's story, is not simply about pedigree and preparation. Luck is also essential, for only in the pit will a bird's true martial abilities show themselves. Is he wild and unthinking, a "tyrant" who exhausts himself after a quarter of an hour, or a stayer, his resolve growing as the shadows lengthen and his rival starts to weaken? Does he have a particular trick, such as thrusting his head under one of his adversary's legs and forcing him to hop around, draining him of energy? It is better to strike rarely but lethally, in those very tender "death places," the eyes and chest, than to land blow upon blow on a rival's feathery armor. Finally, and most important, will the cock fight until victory, no matter how valiant his opponent? In losing, the cock dishonors not only himself but his owner, too.

So it proves in "The Roosters of Babur's Garden." One icy winter's morning, father and son take their bird to the opening bout of the season. The fights take place in the ruined garden in which the 16th-century Mughal emperor Babur was buried. The rookie clucks and crows impressively, and a match is found, with a mean-looking specimen, dirty and unkempt. But the ragamuffin turns out to be deadly, and over the course of a long and terrible fight the poor Kabuli's bird weakens and eventually takes a spur in the eye.

The cock's defeat is bloody, but Fakhri is equally interested in the demise of his owner. The crowd rains derision on the stricken bird, and the boy wishes his father were "safe inside the four walls of home, under his bedclothes, where no one but God could see him." His sympathy does not last, however, for suddenly the enraged father seizes the dying cock and slits his throat. "Stony-hearted!" someone exclaims. "Mad!" someone else calls out, and the boy runs home in shame.

Reading the story, and rereading it after returning home to England, I found myself drawn to the idea of a literary sensibility engaging in so savage a pursuit. Cockfighting is a blood sport par excellence. There is no ulterior motive, no equivocating about killing in order to eat, as there is with shooting game or fishing, or about killing vermin, as is the case with fox hunting. Cockfighting is pure vicarious violence, and the sport has been marginalized to the point of extinction. Although illegal, it endures in pockets of America, and in one or two parts of Europe it has been preserved by local laws as a relic of the old decadence. Not so in Afghanistan, where civil war of one kind or another has been waged for the past three decades and combat is for many the most salient fact of life. Cockfighting is outlawed in Afghanistan, but not for the reason it is outlawed in virtually all American states and most of Europe—that it is cruel. It is illegal in Afghanistan because its association with gambling brings it into conflict with Islamic law.

Fakhri had told me that the season gets going in December and continues to spring. I learned that the center of the sport is Kabul, with at least two regular meets each week, though there is a provincial scene as well. The sport is gaining in popularity, and attendance and bets are growing. I was amused to be told all this by a policeman. Clearly, the word *illegal* has a particular meaning in Afghanistan.

In December 2010, I returned to Kabul. I engaged a young man named Karim Sharifi as a local helper, and early one Friday, the Muslim day of rest, we drove to our first cockfight. We passed Babur's garden, which, having been beautifully restored by the Aga Khan Trust for Culture, has closed its gates to the cockfighting fraternity. Kabul's cockers have not moved far, but they have come down in the world. We arrived at a desolate, rubble-strewn lot with a ruined building in the middle. "It used to be a tile factory," Karim explained. "Now it is the headquarters of the sport."

It was just after nine o'clock. The lot was full of cars and people milling around, greeting one another and inspecting the birds that many of them held under their arms. One grizzled old-timer told me about the mythical hero Rostam and his flight after a particularly difficult battle. Rostam's disapproving father arranged a cockfight and by this device impressed on his son that no true warrior turns tail. Today, Rostam's name is synonymous with unyielding courage and valor. "But it was only after seeing a cockfight," the old man explained, "that Rostam became Rostam."

As we walked toward the building's entrance, my attention was caught by a middle-aged man wheeling his bicycle into the lot from the road outside. He wore a scruffy anorak over a long *tanbon* shirt, and a piebald *dastmal,* or scarf, over his head, and exchanged pleasantries with everyone he passed. He grinned at us and went into the derelict factory, giving off a strong smell of hashish.

Karim and I also went in, handing over the equivalent of 75 cents. The walls had been badly shot up at various times during the many years of fighting, and the winter sun strained through holes in the roof. We took our seats on the lowest of several steps running around a rectangular area of packed earth the size of a squash court. By the time the last of the spectators had filed in, there must have been around 500 of us, greeting one another, cursing cheerfully, squeezed around the pit.

The spectators were as varied as Afghanistan itself. There were ethnic Uzbeks from the far north, wearing neat little turbans over red skullcaps, as well as a sprinkling of fuller Pashtun turbans, and beards one could lose a fist in. Most common was the mujahideen look, consisting of a long shirt with an obliquely slashed hanging collar, trousers stopping above the ankle, and a soft-brimmed woolen hat over a trimmed beard. Even in winter, sandals without socks are de rigueur for the ex-muj, denoting manliness. And then, a disheveled fashion plate on the bottom step: the bicyclist with the *dastmal* over his head, his almond-shaped eyes suggestive of Turkish ancestry, listening with an amused expression to the anecdote of a neighbor.

Two men holding roosters walked to the middle of the pit. One was glowering and musclebound in combat fatigues. (He turned out to be a general in the Afghan National Army.) The other was chubby and young. His name was Sabur, and he and his brother Zilgai—Karim pointed him out, sitting behind us—were considered up-and-coming cockers.

Two handlers, called *abdars,* took the birds, and the owners sat on the lowest step around the pit. The *abdars* set the birds on the ground facing one another, beak point to beak point, hackle feathers rising to form collars around their small, concentrated features. Then there was a furious dash of wings and spurs.

It was all over very quickly. Before I had properly focused on the combatants, the general bolted from his place, his face ashen, and carried his rooster away. "I think the general's bird was hit in the eye," Karim said. "Very unlucky, after just a few seconds. I don't think he'll be able to fight on." The young brothers, Sabur and Zilgai, were jubilant.

I had not seen the deadly blow, and I missed the significance of much else that day. The birds' spurs were bewilderingly quick. The betting, with men leaping into the pit and shouting odds, and others signaling their acceptance, was chaotic. Later on, having grown accustomed to the speed of the action, I was able to follow the feints and maneuvers more easily. I was not revolted, as I had expected to be. There were several small boys among the spectators, looking on with frank enjoyment, and they may have had a disarming effect. I thought of my own seven-year-old and how he would have reacted.

Westerners have felt drawn to write about conflicts in Afghanistan ever since the British and Pashtun first crossed swords back in the 19th century. Journalists maintained the tradition in the 1980s, in many cases romanticizing the mujahideen who fought to expel the Soviets, and they carry on today, embedding with American military units that are in conflict with the Taliban. Watching events in the ruined tile factory, it crossed my mind that I, too, was embedded—in a parallel war, a simulacrum of human combat, animated by the same honor and fear, the same selfishness and pride.

The atmosphere of the pit, the racking coughs and curses and the gamblers slipping out to squat and piss over the rubble outside, did not correspond to any idea I had of wealth. Then, after one fight, Karim told me that the equivalent of $22,000 had been riding on the result, including a $2,000 wager between the owners. These are huge sums in a country where per capita income is less than $500. Karim gave me whispered biographies of the better-known personalities sitting around the pit, telling me of their past service to the jihad and of their current elevated positions in President Hamid Karzai's bureaucracy, army, and police. I would not, I realized, find a version of the poor Kabuli who had featured in Hossein Fakhri's story. That character had bought his pedigree cockerel for less than $700; nowadays he would need to pay four or five times that much. Kabul is an artificial boomtown, powered by war, crime, and foreign aid, and the price of virtually everything, including gamecocks, has soared.

Later, at the end of fights that proceeded in increments and often lasted several rounds, I saw magnificent creatures die, trembling and alone, reviled by the very men who had cheered them, and I regretted my earlier insouciance. Surely the bouts could be stopped before it came to this, and points awarded? That way, the birds would live to fight another day and perhaps enjoy a warrior's retirement. I looked around—at the flushed faces, the looks of triumph and vindication. No, death was the whole point.

As we were leaving the building, Karim and I found ourselves in step with the man with the *dastmal* over his head. We learned that he was called Hafiz and that he owned several fighting cocks. He agreed to meet with us the following day to talk about cockfighting. "The one true love of my life!" he cackled and went to fetch his bicycle. We heard someone greet him, "Hafiz! How are you, caliph of the tricksters?"

Early the next morning, Karim and I went for a walk in the center of Kabul. He told me that our route, toward Straw Sellers' Alley, would take us past Zilgai, one of the brothers whose bird had caused such a sensation at the tile factory. Zilgai's day job, as it happened, was selling fighting cocks.

Along the way I had a grand experience: my pocket was picked and then exquisitely unpicked. I was squeezing between two hawkers' carts when I felt my progress impeded by a dark, bedraggled figure at my side, also trying to get through the narrow gap. "After you," I said, and the man walked on. There had been a slight pressure on my waist, so I put my hand into my jacket pocket. My mobile phone was gone.

So was the man, who was now running through the crowds. I made mad chase, shoving people out of the way and eventually grabbing his collar and stopping him dead. "Give me back my mobile!" I shouted, guessing that a Persian-speaking Westerner upbraiding a thief would draw sympathetic interest; he stared with addled eyes while I raved and a small crowd gathered. The thief pointed at my pocket and said, "Have a look." Again I put my hand in my pocket, this time drawing out my mobile phone. It took me a few moments to realize what had happened, but by that time the dark magician was gone and the crowd had turned away in disinterest.

As we walked on, I saw Zilgai from a distance, crouching in his black leather jacket while two cocks sparred furiously, their lethal spurs clad in leather muffs, for the benefit of a dozen observers. Both combatants were red *aseels*, the celebrated Indian breed known for its small wattles and indomitable courage that is prevalent in Afghanistan, but one of the two rose higher and struck with greater accuracy at his adversary's head and neck, and it was clear that Zilgai had deliberately mismatched them in the hope of attracting buyers.

He separated the birds before they exhausted themselves, the observers drifted away, and there was no sale. "I keep the best specimens at home," Zilgai told us, grinning and cradling under his jacket one of the combatants, who clucked excitedly. "That's where the serious buyers come."

Karim and I moved on from Zilgai, passing hundreds of chickens and turkeys for sale at the side of the road, and entered Straw Sellers' Alley. The name is a misnomer—straw hasn't been traded here for years—and the first few storefronts, where knife sharpeners sit at their wheels and an old man promises a cure for rheumatism, offer no hint of what lies ahead. Then this corridor of a street narrows further, and the sounds of the city are drowned out by the warbling and chirruping of thousands of birds inside wooden cages that have been hung up in the storefronts or laid out on the ground. The bigger cages are spliced with twigs jammed between the bars—perches for quails, starlings, and mynahs. Pinstriped partridges sit with their mates, while barrel-chested homing pigeons, the color of café au lait, squabble and chafe.

Straw Sellers' Alley doesn't cater only to the refined senses— our enjoyment of the mynah's mimicry, our poetic identification with a flock of pigeons performing above our heads. The shopkeepers here deal mostly in partridges and quails, and these are sold in order to fight. In front rooms and backyards the length and breadth of the city, combat is arranged, bets laid, and birds maimed and killed. So the economy of Straw Sellers' Alley, too, is a war economy.

To the aficionado of the fighting cock, these others are inferior warriors. As Hafiz told me, "I don't like quails or partridges. They fight for a few minutes and then one of them gives up. Even fighting dogs will fight for no more than five or ten minutes before one of them gives up. But a fighting cock, that's a different matter! They fight over three days, four. They fight until they can no longer fight. God created these birds to fight."

I spent more time with Hafiz than with any other cocker. I visited his home, accompanied him to a provincial fight, and partook of the cigarettes, laced with *charas,* a local form of hashish, that he smoked when he was not tending his birds. "I am addicted," he declared without regret. He was referring to the cockfighting, not the hash. "Everything I earn, I lose!"

Hafiz stands about five feet seven and often smiles through his gray beard while his eyes twinkle roguishly. Apart from the *dastmal,* his main prop is a ring set with a milk-white agate, which he rubs against his eyes, and to whose mysterious properties he attributes his excellent eyesight. As a cocker and a *charsi,* Hafiz stands on the margin of respectable society, and this is how he likes it. He is a bucolic rejection of all the handwringing that abounds in Afghanistan—all those predictions of doom and gloom. I once asked him how he viewed the country's future, and he gave a shout of laughter and replied, "I don't think about my own future. Why should I think about the future of the country?"

Hafiz earns good money when he works as a construction foreman, but the building season in Afghanistan ends at the start of winter, when he becomes unemployed. This frees him to spend much of his earnings on cockfighting; he has lost a lot of money over the years and has had to sell family land in order to put his children through school. Hafiz is far from being one of the richest members of Kabul's cockfighting fraternity. He is the only cocker I have seen who comes by bike to the old tile factory.

As a Shia Muslim and a member of the Hazara ethnic minority, Hafiz is distinguished twice over from the Sunni, mostly Tajik elite that dominates the new security forces. The sum of his military experience was a spell as a reluctant conscript in the Soviet-run army of the early 1980s. He described the civil war that followed, when the different mujahideen factions fought one another, as a "wretched" time. Hafiz spent the Taliban period in exile in Pakistan, weaving carpets in Peshawar, returning home only after Karzai came to power in 2002.

Sitting in the house he inherited from his father, in a modest but respectable Kabul neighborhood, he showed me the bird he intended to take to the tile factory that coming Friday. The cock was a lustrous red creature with a large comb and a white-tipped saddle, and Hafiz withdrew him from his cage in a corner of the warm sitting room so that I could admire his sheen and the tautness of his breast and thighs. Even when his cage was covered, Hafiz told me, this bird unfailingly emitted his first crow of the day a few moments before dawn; it's not for nothing that the cock's first crow is known as the call to prayer.

Hafiz had exercised the bird that morning, driving him around the courtyard to build up his muscles and stamina. Now he placed him on the floor and snapped his fingers. The cock pirouetted aggressively, his dark eyes gleaming. In Afghanistan they call the onset of maturity, when a cockerel becomes an adult and will fight any adult male who comes near, his "drunkenness." Hafiz's eyes gleamed, too. "He's ready to fight! He'll cause a revolution in the pit—just see if he doesn't!"

I asked Hafiz's eldest son, Omid, a solemn 11-year-old, whether he would be coming on Friday. Omid shook his head, and Hafiz explained how, unlike many other owners, he has not encouraged his children to get involved in the sport. In this, and in his *charas* smoking, Hafiz's approach to fatherhood is to point to himself as a negative example. "Who do you learn manners from?" he asked, then supplied the answer himself: "From the ill-mannered."

Hafiz placed an iron tablet flat on the room's wood-burning stove. When the tablet was hot, he laid some lengths of old cloth on it and unscrewed a container that was full of a dark, glutinous pomade. Several times in the days leading up to a fight, Hafiz coats the heated cloths with this pomade, which he has concocted from a dozen concentrates and infusions, and wraps them tightly around the bird's head, breast, and thighs. This is intended to toughen the skin and make it harder for a spur to penetrate. Hafiz started telling me which ingredients go into the pomade: "alum, pomegranate skin, tamarisk blossom, walnut shell . . ." Then, wrapping a length of cloth around the bird's neck, he interrupted himself: "Hold on! I'm not going to tell you the rest. They are a secret that only I know!"

The following day, Hafiz was due to attend a meet in the Shomali Plain, about two hours' drive from Kabul, and he agreed that Karim and I could accompany him. Traveling is one of the aspects of cockfighting that Hafiz likes best, and the trips he has made around the country are his fondest memories of the sport. From Mazar-i-Sharif in the far north to Kandahar in the south, Hafiz has carried birds from one fight to the next, staying with fellow cockers, smoking his *charas,* and watching the young men whose dancing, in this sexually segregated society, constitutes an acceptable evening's entertainment.

Karim and I picked Hafiz up at dawn and drove northward, out of the capital. He told us that the Taliban exerts growing control over the countryside, including many main roads, and that traveling is becoming less and less feasible. If members of a Taliban roadblock find a gamecock being transported, they will confiscate the bird and fine or whip the owner.

Shortly after the Taliban took Kabul, in 1996, Hafiz was caught attending an underground cockfight. "They hung me up from the ceiling by my right wrist and flogged me on the right side. Then they did the same to the left side of my body. I was covered in wounds." But Hafiz was dedicated, and two days later he attended another meet. "Suddenly," he recalled, "someone shouted that the Taliban were coming. I ran for home, a long way away, and by the time I got back my wounds had opened and I was covered in blood." This experience convinced Hafiz that he should leave the country. A few days later he was in Pakistan.

Now we were beyond the mountains that encircle Kabul and so had escaped the city's dust and smog. We entered a broad plain flanked by mountains and headed toward the Panjshir Valley and Mazar. We were traveling along one of the few safe routes out of the capital. The people here are Tajiks with a history of loyalty to the mujahideen, and they have provided thousands of recruits for Afghanistan's new army and police. Taliban are thin on the ground.

I asked Hafiz to describe the most poignant cockfight he could remember, and he responded with a tale of humiliation. One of his birds had been losing badly, and Hafiz had wanted to concede defeat, which would have saved the bird. A fellow member of his syndicate had insisted on a different course of action. "I'll take over your bet," the man had said. "Your winnings or losses will be mine."

After this, Hafiz recalled, "my bird suddenly got a second wind. He defeated his opponent, and my partner picked up my winnings. I put the bird under my coat and went home, but when I got home I saw he had died along the way." He grinned ruefully.

The men who gamble large sums on cockfights do not regard themselves as having repudiated their religion. Hafiz's description of his encounter with the Taliban reminded me of the words of another cocker I spoke to at the tile factory. He said, "Everything we do is sinful. You walk down the street and look at a woman—it's a sin. Under Islam, traders are supposed to make no more than ten percent from their transactions, but here in Afghanistan there are people who make five-hundred-percent profits." Then he quoted an Afghan saying: "Drinking wine is forbidden; tell me something that is permitted in this world!"

We arrived at a small provincial town, came off the main road, and followed a dirt track away from the houses and in between the fields, many of them planted with vines. High adobe walls encircled even the smallest plot—a testament to the precariousness of ownership in Afghanistan. Our destination was the bank of a canal that was lined with parked cars. We walked across a bridge to a big ruin, also made of adobe, which had once been the home of a prominent local family before it was colonized by the cockers. By now the sun was up, warming our backs.

A dozen owners were in the pit, sorting out which bird should fight which. Hafiz saw friends and went off to say hello, kissing cheeks and exchanging the usual profanities. A coal-fired samovar chugged away in one corner, and Karim and I breakfasted on green tea and greasy french fries wrapped in bread. A couple of armed men wandered around. Spotting me, the only foreigner in the place, one of them asked whether I was a suicide bomber. I said no, and he accepted a cup of green tea.

During an interval between fights, we sat by a stream and chatted with a local commander, a youngish man wearing a dun-colored shawl. He had joined the mujahideen as a 13-year-old, he said, and after a few years came to lead a force of 2,000 men. Now he was a high-up official at the Culture Ministry in Kabul, with responsibility for museums across the country. It crossed my mind that this culture czar might not be able to read or write. And that the cost of his sleek black SUV and of maintaining his various flunkies could not have come out of a government salary.

The commander told me that the essence of cockfighting was *showq,* or love—love of the fight, of the fraternity, and of the valiant birds themselves. I had heard similar sentiments from owners and gamblers back in Kabul. The grandees of the pit, distinguished white-bearded gentlemen, had called for enough *showq* to "turn our woes into flowers!"

Hafiz survived on *showq* that day. He lost more than $200, which was split among the five-man syndicate of which he is a member. Still, he had Friday to look forward to.

*

The old tile factory filled up. The owners gathered in the pit, setting their birds on the ground, sizing up prospective adversaries, arranging the fighting order. Bets were placed. Someone exclaimed, "Whoever is not true to his word is a pimp and a cuckold!" A younger man protested: "If I am not true to my word, stone me to death!"

A bear of a man named Bagho got impatient. He seized a stick and began circling the pit, whacking the ground and sending up clouds of dust, shouting at people to take their seats. Bagho is a fixture of the Kabul cockfighting scene. He used to be an *abdar,* but the birds he was allotted generally lost, and it was said that Bagho had brought them bad luck. In the end, people stopped asking Bagho to be an *abdar.*

Abdar means "he who has water," a name that evokes one of the *abdar*'s key functions, which is to ensure his bird does not overheat. At regular intervals he fills his own mouth with water, separates his bird from his adversary, and sprays the bird's head and anus. Using a cloth that he keeps slung over his shoulder, he fans the bird and wipes him clean of sweat and blood. Curling the cloth tightly, he puts it down the bird's throat and retrieves potentially hazardous feathers that he has swallowed while pecking his rival. The *abdar* replaces broken spurs and beaks with spares that have been lifted from dead warriors. He uses his tongue to clean bloody eyes, and he stitches up chest wounds. His job is not for the squeamish.

The first and second fights began, proceeding in alternating 20-minute periods. Every so often I glanced at Hafiz, who was sitting on the lowest step, his bird under his coat, conferring with other members of the syndicate. Hafiz had been paired against Zilgai and Sabur and was more pensive than I had seen him up to this point.

The second fight ended with the withdrawal of one of the birds. I went out for tea, and when I came back the third fight was underway. There was much excitement, not only because the contestants were evenly matched but because one of the cocks, a sturdy, black-flecked creature, was owned by the nephew of one of Afghanistan's most powerful warlords. The nephew in question, a thin man of about 40, sat impassively, but his young companions were less inhibited. Their faces became ugly and contorted as the fight grew bloodier, and they ran into the pit to shout bets and punch the air.

By the end of the second round, both birds were exhausted and bleeding. They hung off each other, their necks entwined, before stepping back and launching themselves into the air, kicking furiously. Some way into the third round, the black-flecked bird suddenly stumbled. One of his wings rested on the ground. The men around me yelled, "He's blinded!"

I turned to Karim and asked, "Surely they'll stop the fight now?"

He shook his head. "Do you know how much money is riding on this? More than thirty thousand dollars! They'll do anything to make sure he can fight on!"

There was pandemonium as the spectators milled around the pit and the *abdar* locked the stricken bird between his legs and stitched a gash that had opened under the bird's darkened eye socket. Then he rummaged through his pockets for a replacement for the bird's shattered beak. Someone loudly accused the *abdar* of improperly interrupting the fight. Others retorted that he was behaving within the rules.

The *abdar* cradled the black-flecked bird, who it was now clear had been paralyzed. His single eye stared, dying and uncomprehending. Money started changing hands—more money than I had ever seen in Afghanistan. The nephew of the famous warlord went off in his Land Cruiser with his bodyguards.

At the end of the fight, Hafiz rose from his place at the side of the pit. It was getting dark; his fight and several others would have to wait until the following day. He put his bird into a box on the back of his bicycle and pedaled off. But when he reappeared the next morning, the bird's face was a shade darker than it had been, and his eyes were listless and dull. Whether from being kept the whole of the previous day in the chilly factory or from being moved around in Hafiz's drafty box, he had caught a chill.

Later I learned that Hafiz's partners in the syndicate had urged him to withdraw the bird and pay Zilgai the standard forfeit, but he had insisted the fight go ahead. Was it a kind of madness, or the need to gamble, that led him to field a bird that was sure to lose? At times, over the course of the three rounds he fought that day, Hafiz's bird came to life, and Hafiz with him, jerking his little limbs, his *dastmal* over his head—a fighting cock in a man's body.

But the bird with the white-flecked saddle landed only a few good hits. It was a battle of attrition, which only the brothers' stronger, fitter bird could win.

That night Hafiz stayed up, sweating him, murmuring to him. At dawn he failed to crow. It was a terrible omen. Hafiz brought him back to the tile factory. The bird's face was almost black. The fight restarted.

A more futile, avoidable death cannot be imagined. The decisive blow, inevitably, was a spur in the eye. Hafiz's bird staggered backward, and the assembled cockers turned on him with their usual vitriol. The *abdar* brought the bird over to Hafiz, who looked down and exclaimed, "No! God! It's all gone bad!" Zilgai and Sabur smiled.

Hafiz conceded defeat. The syndicate paid out around $1,000, a third of which came from Hafiz's pocket. "I got him as a cockerel and raised him," Hafiz said, to no one in particular. "What can I do if he turns out to be impotent on his wedding night?" Then he rode away on his bicycle. Two days later, Hafiz's bird died of his wounds.

IAN FRAZIER

A Farewell to Yarns

FROM *Outside*

A TRUTH ABOUT the outdoors is that it causes people to lie.
Strange forces out there in the wild have always conspired to cor-
rupt human honesty. Over time, intelligent listeners and readers
came to accept that an adventurer's reports would not consist of
one-to-one representations of fact but instead would contain exaggerations, distortions, omissions, additions, events that foolish
people wanted to believe had happened but hadn't, and deliber-
ate, implausible, fantastical lies. Maybe that was even a reason the
restless and sketchy among us ventured into the wilderness in the
first place: because if we claimed we did or saw something amazing there, who could prove the contrary? Returned from our journeys, we could brag all we wanted without fear of contradiction.
An enormous attraction of far places has always been that no one
else was inconveniently in the neighborhood to check.

"Here Be Monsters," the old maps announced, next to drawings
of walking leviathan-fish with huge maws and claws and fangs. The
pictures must have been accurate; how would the mapmakers have
known what to draw unless eyewitnesses had told them? Somewhere out there, travelers said, lived blue-eyed Indians who spoke
only Hebrew—a Lost Tribe of Israel, miraculously transported to
remotest Asia or the American West. Those who revealed this discovery had not, it turned out, met the blue-eyed (*blue-eyed?*) He-
brews themselves but once crossed paths with parties who had.
Inventive wanderers said they had seen snakes that had bit their
own tails and made themselves into hoops and rolled across the
ground, cannibals with three heads, Arctic dwellers who covered

their ears against the sound of the sunrise, and beautiful Amazonian women warriors who held healthy young men (often the wanderers themselves) captive for sex. Explorers claimed they had climbed mountains they hadn't climbed and had reached the North Pole when in fact they never reached it. Apparently sober individuals gave firsthand accounts of seeing yetis in the Himalayas and Nessie in her loch and jackalopes on the prairies. Old-time sailors boasted of sleeping with beautiful mermaids, annoyingly omitting the precise physical details, and according to certain fishermen, mermaids offering to grant them three wishes had come up in their nets. The words *fisherman* and *liar* are linked in our brains for good reason. And in the interest of brevity, I will pass over the many stories involving logging roads, elk hunters, space aliens, and intergalactic crossbreeding. There are some doors man was not meant to open.

Lies made the wild scary and alluring. When I was a boy, local places I knew about buzzed excitingly with crazy tales. In rural Illinois, Argyle State Park was said to be inhabited by a creature called the Argyle Monster—a huge cougar that had lost its front feet in a trap and ran through the forest on its hind legs at dusk and "screamed like a woman." Or so said Billy somebody, who told his friends, who were friends of mine, who told me. I never saw the Argyle Monster myself, but it ran on its hind legs through my imaginings and colored the dusk of this unremarkable state park a deep and thrilling sepia when I walked back to the picnic area after fishing. It's been decades since I went there; I regret that I quit being afraid of the Argyle Monster long ago.

More recently, as a grownup supposedly immune to phantasms, I learned from Russians when I was traveling in Siberia that somewhere in its remotest parts is Coca-Cola City (Gorod Koka-Kola), which was built during the Cold War as a reproduction of an American city. The residents of Coca-Cola City speak perfect English and use American products and behave like Americans, providing a realistic setting in which the Russian spymasters can train special operatives who will be sent to the U.S. Coca-Cola City is alleged to be the topmost of top-secret sites, and it is closed, of course, to all visitors. I'm not sure if that's why I never could pin it down on the map. I suspect that it does not exist and never did—but who can say? The rumor of it made Siberia more Siberian for me.

*

You might not think that any human creation as hardy as lies could be in danger of dying out, but I'm afraid that, at least outdoors, they are. Nowadays, a good outdoor what-if story has a much smaller chance for survival. Some years ago, you may remember, observers in the deep woods of eastern Arkansas said they had seen an ivory-billed woodpecker, the wonderful and near-mythic bird that black people called the Lord God Bird because of its soul-shivering appearance. There had been no confirmed sightings of the ivorybill in decades, and its possible extinction was and is bad news. The observers who said they had seen it weren't trying to deceive, just being wishful, and because they recorded it with a video camera their wishfulness was eventually dashed—close analysis of the video revealed that the bird was not an ivorybill.

It would have been nice to think that the bird still survived someplace far away in the forest. But truth is always better than error, I suppose. Consider the recent case of the giant wild hog Hogzilla. A Georgia man said he had shot it while it was running around someplace in the woods, and he posted pictures of it online. This 8-foot-long, 800-pound animal was as monstrous a creature as the Georgia swamps had ever seen. The man added that he had buried the hog in a grave marked with a cross (though feral, it had been a Christian hog, apparently), and because of the excitement stirred up on the Internet the man eventually had to submit the corpse for examination. Through DNA testing, experts determined that it was a mix of wild hog and domestic pig. Its size suggested it had eaten a lot of hog feed. Such a disappointment—Hogzilla, a pen-raised fake. How much more stimulating to believe that there are 800-pound wild hogs infesting the swamps of Georgia. One hates to think what a radio collar and a wildlife-management team would have done to William Faulkner's bear.

The Hogzilla debunking was another example of the pesky trend toward factuality currently sweeping the out-of-doors. Technology, of course, is at the root of it. The global landscape used to be a theater of various shadings—sunlit fields and canyons of dark obscurity, trackless jungles, and misty Shangri-las. Now the whole world is like a cineplex when the lights have come on. Almost no place on the surface of the planet is really obscure anymore. Satellites watch it all and can let you know to the millimeter how far continental drift moved your swimming beach last year. What's up along the banks of the great, gray-green Limpopo? How's traf-

fic on the road to Mandalay? What's the snowpack like across the
wide Missouri? The Internet or Google Earth will tell you.

Traveling in Siberia a decade ago, I thought I was pretty much
beyond the reach of checkability; in fact-checker shorthand, anything I wrote would be "OA," which stands for "on author," meaning "unverifiable by anything other than the author's say-so." I did
not need to worry that any checker would visit where I had been,
nor was it likely that an irate reader would write in claiming I had
got something wrong about the tundra zone of the Chukchi Peninsula, given the difficulty of getting there and the absence of any
reason to go. But then time and advancing technology proved me
wrong. During the many years my Siberian research took, satellite
imagery of the earth's surface became available online, and my
claims about the lay of the land in Siberia proved to be checkable
after all. Even in far-flung places, descriptions could be verified. If
I said there was no bridge over a remote Far Eastern river that I
had crossed by ferry, the checker could look on Google Earth and
see that, in fact, no bridge showed up in the satellite photo, and a
small boat much like a ferry could be seen crossing there.

Today the adventurer's tale-telling days are over and his crooked
ways have been made straight, and every untruth can be revealed.
No point in lying: we've got it all on tape, as the TV detectives say.
If you claim you drove to Nunavut and we think maybe you didn't,
we'll just look at the E-ZPass records for the toll roads along the
way. And if they don't tell us, the cell phone towers will. Formerly,
a cell phone tower could follow a phone only when the phone
was on, and smart criminals knew to turn it off before committing crimes. Now phones ping the towers and the towers record
the presence of the cell phones in the vicinity, often whether they
are on or not, and to escape the network's observation you must
remove the battery entirely. Almost everywhere, some degree of
electronic connection can be assumed.

I never took much notice of the satellites going over constantly
until I was out in the night in Siberia, with its grand darkness.
In the middle of the Barabinsk Steppe or some other nowhere, I
always studied the night sky before getting into my tent. Amid the
stars' wild randomness, the little dots of light crossed the heavens
on routes as purposeful and direct as a cue-ball shot. I carried a
satellite phone myself. Sometimes I would pick a likely looking satellite and shoot a call to it (I thought; actually, the link was more

complicated, and to a satellite I didn't see) and then do something ordinary like make an appointment with my dentist back in New Jersey or talk to my daughter about her week at school. And all this from a region where exiles in former times used to disappear, never to be heard from again.

A favorite word for the technological fishbowl effect is *transparency*. Anything you do in far places, and anything that exists out there, can, in principle, be seen. *Transparency* is one of those words whose real meaning is its opposite, the way that countries with ministries of culture haven't any. Of course, all the technology known or yet to be known won't see even a part of everything or stop people from making things up. It's just that the realm of colorful prevarication has moved inside, where the heart does its sneaking. Most of the gods and demons and fairies and windigos who used to inhabit their own particular outdoor places died off long ago, and modern technology has zapped the survivors. If you want to spin a yarn, it will be about something inward and private, like whether you took steroids.

During the days when the Argyle Monster still seemed a possibility in my mind, one of the books I liked to read told about the life of a German hunter and sportsman named Baron Münchausen. This baron lived in the Black Forest in some former time—the stories date to the 1700s—and journeyed through the fastnesses of the forest having adventures. A typical one was his encounter with a young stag he surprised one day in a dark glen. Grabbing his rifle, the baron found he was out of bullets, but he happened to be eating a cherry at the time, so he spat out the cherry pit, loaded the rifle with it, and fired, hitting the stag squarely between the eyes. The stag fell down but then quickly leaped up and ran away. Years later, the baron was again in that part of the woods. All at once, to his astonishment, he came face-to-face with a huge stag that had a small but healthy cherry tree growing between its antlers.

As a boy I did not believe that had really happened, but I kind of suspended final judgment, because maybe it could, you know? Because it was cool, I didn't altogether rule it out. Today the baron would be a video game. Progress has cleared the outdoors of its tall stories and imaginary beings and redeposited them on screens. Cyberspace is full of invented monsters, and movies seem to be about nothing but winged horses and multiheaded dragons and rivers of snakes. In the first Harry Potter movie, a "full-grown mountain troll" appears in a Hogwarts bathroom and tries to smash Harry with its huge club before Harry manages to kill it by sticking his wand up its nose. Not too long ago, many people believed there really were such things as trolls in the mountains. I mourn the loss; the mountains are poorer without their trolls. As far as I'm concerned, not every last troll has left, and a stag with a tree growing between its antlers is an unlikely sight, but not out of the question completely.

The point is, wonders are out there still. If you don't on some level believe that, you're going to stay home with the TV, and "remote" will be what's lost between the cushions. Technology or no, I expect to see miracles and portents any time I leave the pavement. A while ago, I was fishing for snook in the Florida Everglades. My guide and I had made our way far back in a gin-clear avenue between stands of mangroves when two manatees swam right beneath the boat. I had never seen a manatee before. They went past faster than Usain Bolt and executed a right turn with marvelous agility and were gone, and I swear I saw mermaids. Naked, brown, extremely sexy mermaids, like the fishermen said.

RICH COHEN

Pirate City

FROM *The Paris Review*

LONG BEFORE THE foundations of New Orleans were laid, the
river existed as a legend and a rumor. It was the monster to the
west, just beyond the next hill, stand of trees, prairie, horizon. It
was the mother of all waters, the torrent that flowed out of the
garden to touch the desolate earth. It flowed through the Indian
imagination as it flows through the American mind, through music and literature, carrying the shipwreck and the bloated body
of the fool who went missing after a party on the levee. The river
starts as a stream in Minnesota and picks up volume as it heads
south, meandering through the country—"It seems safe to say that
it is also the crookedest river in the world," Mark Twain writes in
Life on the Mississippi, "since in one part of its journey it uses up
one thousand three hundred miles to cover the same ground that
the crow would fly over in six hundred and seventy-five"—before
shattering into a network of bayous, swamps, and estuaries below
New Orleans. This is the delta, and it's a mess. For generations,
sailors could not find a reliable channel to follow into the river,
as the mouth of the Mississippi constantly silted up with debris
from the north. "The river annually empties four hundred and six
million tons of mud into the Gulf of Mexico," writes Twain. "This
mud, solidified, would make a mass a mile square and two hundred and forty-one feet high." Simply put, the country is vomiting
its innards into the Gulf.

The mouth of the Mississippi appeared on Spanish maps years
before it had been seen by a white man. I'm thinking of a particular map: *Tabula Terra Nova,* drawn in the early 1500s. This is one

of the first renderings of the world as it would come to be known: two hemispheres—Occident, Orient. America is a shapeless mass, the Tropic of Capricorn cleaving the New World in two. Due west of Ethiopia, adrift in Oceanus Occidentalis, the Southern Hemisphere is crowded with the names of settlements. But a generation after Columbus, North America is punctuated by few landmarks, the river among them. It emerges from beyond the left border of the map and branches as it touches the sea. It was drawn before the voyages of Ponce de León, meaning it had not been seen by the mapmaker, or by anyone who might have spoken to the mapmaker.

The Mississippi was navigated by white men in 1519. So here's the first tall ship, with its sails and steel-plated men, cruising the archipelago of grass islands. The ship was captained by Alonso Álvarez de Pineda, famous in Seville, an explorer who returned home with miraculous tales of the New World. He traveled 20 miles up the Mississippi that first trip. He said he had seen a city on a hill beside the river, and in that city little men, pygmies, covered in golden ornament. Pineda, killed by Indians on a later voyage, left behind the first accurate map of America's Gulf Coast—a scrawl, like something written on a cocktail napkin after the second drink.

Luis de Moscoso was the first European to see the future site of New Orleans, a strip of land between the Mississippi and the great salt estuary later named for the French minister of the marine Louis Phélypeaux, Count of Pontchartrain. He was a member of de Soto's last expedition. This trip was later recalled as a delirium, a terror: the men marching in armored ranks through the swamp, the sun beating down, the stink of the marsh, the misery of the waste places. They searched out the natives, killed whomever they met, then took notes on each killing. (As John Wayne says in *Red River,* "I'll read over him in the morning.") In March 1541, the party, which began with 600 men and 200 horses, was attacked by Chickasaw Indians. Horses slaughtered, Spaniards killed. Those who escaped did so by running. De Soto died on a raft in the river, which is perfect, a consecration, his flesh devoured by catfish with black eyes and long whiskers. Moscoso led what was left of the party south. It was from this vantage point—on rafts in the river—that Moscoso and a dozen others saw the swell of land that would become New Orleans. It was the summer of 1543.

The site was not visited again for over a hundred years, and then by Robert de La Salle. The French explorer traveled the length of the Mississippi, planting a cross near what is now Jackson Square in 1682. The city foundations were laid in 1719 by Jean-Baptiste Le Moyne de Bienville, a diplomat charged with establishing a town near the mouth of the Mississippi, which was to give Paris control of the interior. In his diary, Bienville said the site was selected for its natural advantages. At 10 feet above sea level, it seemed unlikely to flood. In this, the founder set the general pattern of municipal leadership: totally confident and completely wrong. The waters inundated the city, then just wooden stakes and foundation holes, less than a year after the cornerstone had been laid. The outline of the town was already visible: a parallelogram, which is just a drunken square, 4,000 feet along the river, its ass protruding 1,800 feet into the swamp country that continued to Lake Pontchartrain.

This was divided into sixty-six 300-square-foot lots, which, covered in houses, hotels, stores, and such, would eventually be known as the French Quarter. A parade ground was set aside on the riverfront: Jackson Square. The early years of the city were just disaster after disaster: hurricanes, floods, Indian attacks, outbreaks. In 1735, the city was set upon by wild dogs. Yellow fever and cholera rampaged through the beginning of the last century. In 1905, the windows of the French Quarter were shuttered, the streets filled with funeral processions, the horse-drawn hearse carrying victims of yellow jack to the Saint Louis Cemeteries beyond the ramparts. According to historians, the jazz funeral is probably a remnant of that plague year, when burials were so frequent that turning the dour processions into a parade was a means of survival, the march to the ground being a dirge because death is terrible and great, the march back to town being a parade because life is greater still.

As soon as there were streets, they were lined with whorehouses. The early inhabitants were a ragged crew of gamblers, vagabonds, criminals, and drunks. The first women were prostitutes sent to pacify the ne'er-do-wells. In 1724, Bienville enacted the infamous Code Noir, which called for the expulsion of all Protestants and Jews, but this order was largely ignored. In fact, if you were a Jew in North America in the 18th century, you would have had a hard time finding a better place. In 1788, the city, then under Spanish rule, burned down and was rebuilt, which is why the French Quarter looks less French than Spanish. Only two original French buildings survive. One of these, at 632 Dumaine Street, is mark-edly different from the others—blank-faced with few windows, oblong, closed off, shuttered, lonely, strange. The French retook control in 1803, holding it just long enough to sell the entire territory to the United States. New Orleans was a small city, 10,000 or so people crowded into streets lined with beaneries, each an imitation of a grander establishment in the French capitals of the West Indies, such as Santo Domingo, which themselves were filled with imitations of Paris.

The United States took over on December 20, 1803. William Claiborne was Louisiana's first American governor—that's why his name is on everything. As the years went by, New Orleans, which experts believed would be normalized by an influx of Americans, only became more exotic. By the mid-1800s, its population was a hodgepodge: there were descendants of the French who first settled on the land; there were descendants of the Spanish who had ruled a generation later; there were descendants of the French who moved in when Quebec fell to the British (because they came from Acadia in Canada, they came to be known as Cajuns); there were Americans who came in the wake of the Louisiana Purchase, farmers and rivermen from Kentucky; there were French nationals who came when the slaves rose in Santo Domingo, driving out colonial property owners; there were others who emigrated from this or that island when the wrong nation came to power—French speakers from Cuba, Dutch from Curaçao. New Orleans was a big drain, pulling in the debris of the river and ocean trade, with great forests and lumber mills to the north and the Gulf of Mexico to the south, Cuba, Jamaica, the Spanish Main.

Once upon a time, men in New Orleans carried charts that classified the product of every conceivable coupling:

1. black + white = mulatto
2. mulatto + white = quadroon
3. quadroon + white = octoroon
4. octoroon + white = quinteroon
5. mulatto + black = griffe
6. Indian + white = mestizo

And so on . . .

By the mid-1800s, the city was known for its quadroon balls, opulent affairs where local dandies went stag to dance halls on Saint Philip Street and watched through opera glasses as young women of mixed race, the offspring, usually, of a white father and a half-black mother, were marched across the floor in extravagant gowns. When the moment was right, a man selected a quadroon. Dolled her up. Established her in luxury in a house in a section of the city set aside for the purpose. Loved her. Impregnated her. A duke from Saxe-Weimar, Germany, who attended a ball described the quadroons as "almost entirely white: from their skin no one would detect their origin; nay many of them have as fair a complexion as many of the haughty creole females." A quadroon, once established, was referred to as a *placée*. She took her man's name, as did her children. In this way, the wealthy men of New Orleans could lead a double life, one above ground with a white wife and white children, the other subterranean with a quadroon *placée* and octoroon children. The practice continued till the Civil War, in the wake of which racial distinctions hardened. No more balls. No more secret families. Most of the quadroons (who, after generations of intermarriage, were more white than most white people in the city) went north, where they vanished into the fabric of America.

The city owed its importance to the river. The Mississippi was the first American superhighway, *Huckleberry Finn* the first American road novel. The wealth of the farms and forests, the factories and mills, everything west of the Alleghenies—all of it floated down the river. New Orleans was the city at the end of the run, where the produce was counted, tagged, stacked, and shipped. The life of the city was the waterfront, the docks, the boats. The first were pirogues, or canoes, fashioned, Indian-style, from tree trunks. These were followed by keelboats, mackinaws, flatboats, scows, the grandest of them 300 feet long and as tall as a house. There were barges known as arks; broadhorns, or Kentucky flats; and ferries, called sleds, with roofs and passenger cabins. Before steam power, the challenge was getting back upriver—to Cairo, to Saint Louis. After the flatboats were unloaded in New Orleans, they were broken into pieces and sold as scrap wood. For years, the sidewalks of the French Quarter were made from the debris of the riverboats. The crews then walked home—a trip through wild country that took months. When he was young, Abraham Lincoln made the trip from Illinois to New Orleans by raft. It was in the course of this journey that he first saw slaves, sold in the French Quarter markets.

It was a rough life on the river, a story by Robert Louis Stevenson or Jack London. The crews slept on the decks of the boats, months in the open, watching the shore—punishing in its sameness—drift by at two or three miles an hour. The men were unshaven and dirty; they washed in the river but were never clean. They were bare-chested all summer or donned brogans studded with spikes. In the winter, when the temperature dropped below freezing, they wore fur so fresh it had claws. There was always a card game going, men hunched over a deck, betting by firelight: faro, poker, blackjack, seven-up. They subsisted on bread and meat set before them in communal pans twice a day. They were drunk all the time. They referred to their whiskey as "good old Nongela," as it was distilled on the banks of the Monongahela River. These men were tall and short, fat and thin, fair-skinned and swarthy, the same sorts who once filled the galleys of Roman ships. It was a male society, where the rivermen constantly fought to establish position. Each boat had a champion, a man who bloodied all the others. He wore a red turkey feather in his hat, which told the world, *I'm the baddest motherfucker on the Mississippi*. At night, when the ships tied up at the landings, crews intermingled. When the holder of a red feather came across another red-feather holder, a circle formed and a battle commenced. The names of the great fighters live on: Mike Fink, the toughest man on the Ohio; Bill Sedley, who whipped everyone on the Mississippi then went mad in New Orleans, killing two people in a dive bar before fleeing into the Indian Territory.

It's a culture lampooned in *Huckleberry Finn* when two flatboat toughs circle each other while sharing their bona fides. In this passage you have, in nascent form, the best of the blues and hip-hop, as well as the trash talk of Muhammad Ali:

Whoo-oop! I'm the old original iron-jawed, brass-mounted, copper-bellied corpse-maker from the wilds of Arkansaw!—Look at me! I'm the man they call Sudden Death and General Desolation! Sired by a hurricane, dam'd by an earthquake, half-brother to the cholera, nearly related to the small-pox on the mother's side! Look at me! I take nineteen alligators and a bar'l of whiskey for breakfast when I'm in robust health, and a bushel of rattlesnakes and a dead body when I'm ailing! I split the everlasting rocks with my glance, and I squench the thunder when I speak! Whoo-oop! Stand back and give me room according to my strength! Blood's my natural drink, and the wails of the dying is music to my ear! Cast your eye on me, gentlemen! —and lay low and hold your breath, for I'm bout to turn myself loose!

For men on the river, every trip ended in New Orleans. That is where they were paid and spent what they were paid. It was the goal, the place they would finally drive out the boredom of all those weeks on the water. It was the adventures accumulated in the course of all those sprees that turned New Orleans into a party town. All those tchotchkes (the nipple-shaped shot glass), T-shirts (*What drinking problem? I get drunk and fall down. No problem*), and stories ("and the funny thing is, I don't even remember driving home, but there was the car, in the middle of the lawn") started on the keelboats, where the deck hands shouted as the spires came into view. Even in the 1800s, rivermen referred to New Orleans as the City of Sin. The culture of the docks spilled into the streets and became one aspect of the town. The violent mood in the dives, the Mardi Gras of stoned outsiders filling the squares and driving the locals indoors, the way the town can seem like two towns—the one seen by the drunken conventioneer who gets in a fight on Bourbon Street; the other seen by the native, secret and protected—was established during the first river boom, when the keelboats crowded the water bank to bank, and the deck hands took their restless ennui as a cause to raise hell in the Vieux Carré.

Any river city whose wealth is concentrated and dispersed on ships is going to be lousy with pirates. New Orleans attracted them from its earliest days. The geography invites it. A dozen miles outside of town, the land gives way to swamp, bayou, bay. Lake Pontchartrain, north of the French Quarter, dumps into Lake Borgne, which dumps into the Mississippi Sound, which is protected from the Gulf of Mexico by barrier islands. If you designed a seascape for piracy, this would be it. There were big islands—Grand Terre, Grand Island—in the sound, but also lonely outcroppings where the seagrass waved and the earth vanished if you stepped on it. There were islands covered with dwarf oaks and Spanish moss, a screen from outsiders. There were groves in the water, trunks rising from the waves. There were low-lying islands that disappeared in flood tide. There were inlets and swamps and landmarks that served as rendezvous points for pirates, the most notorious being the temple, a mountain of clamshells that had dominated a barrier outcrop as long as even the oldest Indian could remember. There were channels between islands, some deep enough to float a ship, some so shallow only a raft could get through. If being chased by a British man-of-war, a pirogue-riding pirate could vanish into a narrow, weed-bedecked channel, then emerge into a lost bay. The entire area was a tangle: reefs, storms, sea surges, tides, roots, alligators, shells, catfish, and turtles as old as the world. Turn around twice and you're lost forever.

Old Spanish maps identify it as Barataria. The origins of the name are mysterious. Some say it comes from part two of *Don Quixote,* in which Sancho Panza is appointed governor of an island called Barataria, a name that rings mock heroic in the original. It echoes the Spanish word *barato,* which means "cheap." In other words, Barataria is Bargainland, a Filene's Basement for the pirate set, where all items have just fallen off the back of a truck. The bayous were a smuggler's paradise, where good deals could always be found. Over time, Barataria became the subconscious of the city, New Orleans reflected in a dark mirror, a refuge for all those who'd been driven out or had chosen to live beyond the law. Thieves hid stolen goods there; fugitives vanished into the weeds. There was a permanent population of runaway slaves. It was a warehouse where the criminal inventory was stored. (Blackbeard took refuge in Barataria in 1718, drifted and dreamed as bounty hunters searched in vain.) It grew alongside the city. The bigger the warehouses on Tchoupitoulas, the better the business in the bay.

By the 1800s, Barataria was attracting buccaneers. It was everything a pirate wanted: far away yet close at hand, convenient, within reach of shipping lanes that carried the wealth of the New World. The men who lived there were not pirates in the traditional sense—they were privateers. In strongboxes they carried letters of marquesses, documents that deputized them into foreign navies, giving them the right to prey on ships flagged by enemy nations. In the age of Napoleon, everyone was at war with someone, making these letters easy to come by. The most notorious privateers were Frenchmen chased out of Santo Domingo or Cuba, sailors who preyed on Spanish galleons. Such men—many burned with hatred for Spain—could secure letters from a half dozen countries, but most sailed under the flag of Colombia, where Simón Bolívar was in revolt.

Barataria boomed in 1808 when the American Congress banned the importation of African slaves. From then on, all slaves would be bred (terrible verb) domestically. This was done partly to curb the nation's addiction to slavery and partly to protect America from foreign ideologies, the notions of freedom and revolt that might, accidentally, in the way of cholera, be imported from a state like Haiti. But there were many in the South who preferred African-raised slaves for reasons that strike us as obscene: because they were more docile, stronger, darker; because, uncorrupted by America, they worked harder.

It's not unlike what happened in America during Prohibition. Here was a group of criminals—gangsters in one case, buccaneers in the other—who were disorganized, smalltime, in it for a quick score. And here was a business, legitimate and thriving one minute, then, with the stroke of a pen, turned over to crooks. Anyone who partook in the African slave trade was now an outlaw. In this way, an aboveboard business became the province of pirates. Men who might have otherwise reformed or faded away—many of the gangsters of New York were on their way out, too, before Prohibition—now had a big-time industry to run. Soon after the law's passage, privateers began preying on slow, fat-bellied ships heading for Cuba. They attacked, then carried the human cargo back to Bargainland. This meant serious money: sable coats, silk eye patches, a diamond stud for each ear. The result was more pirates, more pirate ships, more pirate guns, more pirate violence. It was a gang war like the gang war between Al Capone and Bugs Moran. Who will control the North Side? Who will control Barataria? It was hurting business. Planters and merchants were afraid to go to the bayous to make a purchase. This was a moment that demanded a leader, a strongman who could bring order to the pirate islands.

The origins of Jean Lafitte are difficult to pin down. Like a hero in a folk song, he seemed to arise from nowhere, fully formed, with teeth and claws, his mind buzzing with ideas. Some believed him the son of a sailor who stowed away to see the watery places when he was 15; some believed him the son of a nobleman whose parents were rounded up in the terror of the French Revolution; he went to the Caribbean because it was as far away as he could go. Some said he was raised in the Pyrenees. Some said he was raised in a French town on the Spanish border. According to William Davis, who wrote a book on the subject, Lafitte was born in 1782 in a fishing village on the Atlantic. As a young man, he traveled with his older brother, Pierre—they were as close as brothers get—to the colonies as part of the migration of French who fled the Revolution. In one story, they alight in Santo Domingo, where they thrive in business until the slaves revolt. The houses burn; smoke rises from the outskirts. Everything is on fire. The slave armies march through the fields, the standard-bearer carrying a pike topped with an impaled white baby—the flag of the rebellion. The brothers were separated in the chaos. Pierre was on the last ship out—the helicopter that rises slowly from the rooftop as the Vietcong come over the wall.

Jean was waiting for his ship on the wharf in New Orleans, the great city spreading away like a stain, narrow streets, iron balconies, boulevards and taverns, a French city where the Lafittes were at home. Jean and Pierre made a name with the social set. Jean especially, who turns up in articles: a phrase, a bit of dialogue, accompanied by a physical description, a mention of his good looks. A shade over six feet tall, slender as a string, with dark hair, sidewhiskers, and eyes that shade of blue known as robin's egg. He had delicate hands and long fingers. His fingernails were clean, unusual for a pirate. Dandyish in dress, he preferred silk shirts, velvet tailcoats, ankle boots with brass clasps, a ruby ring on his pinky. He loved all women but had a weakness for those of mixed parentage, mulattoes and quadroons, and was often seen late at night wandering in the worst part of town. There is only one known likeness of Jean Lafitte, a quick sketch done by a man named Lacassinier, who worked for the Lafittes in Galveston. It shows a pirate with mournful eyes, his hair swept across his forehead. It could be Rimbaud or some other poet gone to seed in the bohemian taverns.

Pierre was not as good-looking as his brother—smaller and bigger, shorter and fatter, with a round face and thick brown hair. Here's how he was described on a wanted poster put up in the city in 1814: "Five feet ten inches in height, stout made, light complexion, and somewhat cross-eyed." Pierre had a stroke when he was 40 and suffered occasional trembling fits as a result. He had a lazy eye, which explains the description in the poster.

The Lafittes opened a blacksmith shop in the French Quarter. You can still visit: 941 Bourbon Street on the corner of Saint

Philip, dilapidated in the best way, a hymn of sagging wood and brick, nondescript on the outside, a crayon drawing done by a child, warm on the inside with uneven floorboards and a staircase leading to unknown recesses. Now called Lafitte's Blacksmith Shop, it's said to be the longest-operating bar in the United States. For the Lafittes, it was a front. The brothers were in a tradition that includes the Bonannos and the Gambinos: criminals in the beginning, middle, and end. Jean and Pierre were go-to guys: If you were a thief with something to sell, they would find a buyer and take a cut. If you were a consumer looking for a hard-to-acquire or possibly illegal product or piece of property—they could help there, too. They had connections to the black marketers and pirates of Barataria, most of whom, like the Lafittes, were French. In 1808, they went into the business of African slaves. First as a fence. The guy who knows the guy, could arrange the thing. Then, more and more, as a dealer: the guy who had the thing. That's where the money was.

For a minute, it looked like the Lafittes would get rich. Then it didn't. The chaos of the trade—the competition among privateers—was bad for business. The violence and crooked dealing in the swamp had driven away customers. You cut a deal with a pirate, load the cargo, set sail, but don't make it beyond the channel before you're hijacked by another pirate. It's a question of ethics, the integrity of the marketplace. When a man can't make a deal with a criminal without being robbed by another criminal, well, that's the end. Jean Lafitte must have waited for a strongman to step forward, some Arnold Rothstein who, understanding what was at stake, would impose order. When none emerged, he set off to impose order on the islands himself.

Lafitte had been a sea captain. He understood how to sail, pursue, take a ship. He was well known in the criminal dives, was familiar to the important underworld players. Yet this was still a mad plan, a defining gesture. Charlemagne reaches for the crown. Gotti heads for Sparks Steak House. It took two days to reach the big islands of Barataria. He traveled by pirogue, through bayous and swamps, where the crocodile smiles on the sun marsh. It reminds me of the trip the boy takes in Maurice Sendak's *Where the Wild Things Are.* His name is Max. He misbehaves, is sent to his room without dinner. While wearing his wolf costume, he lies in bed. His room grows over with weeds. It turns into a jungle as he sleeps. It resembles Bayou Lafourche in Louisiana. He wakes to find a small boat on the shore of an ocean. He crosses the water—small boy, big sea. He lands on an island populated by wild things, who are nothing but pirates. When they try to scare Max, he tames them with a cold, steady eye. He has soon subdued the monsters, secured his rule. That's when the wild rumpus begins, the pirates dancing, parading, swinging from trees, Mardi Gras, Jazz Fest, a party that goes from can till can't. In the end, depleted by his exploits, Max sails away, leaving the island just as he found it.

I will now tell you exactly how the adventures of Jean Lafitte mirror those of Max:

As Lafitte dozes in his blacksmith shop on Bourbon Street, the bayous grow over with bad men, become wild. When he wakes, he finds a boat waiting at an inlet. He sails across the water. After two days, he reaches Grand Terre Island, where wood huts face the open sea. He is met on the shore by the wild things. In Sendak's story, the monsters have dagger nails, tangled manes, huge eyes. In Lafitte's story, they have pointy boots, hoop earrings, peg legs. There were a few hundred men living on Grand Terre when Lafitte arrived: crooks, runaway slaves, fugitives, privateers, deserters, traders, trappers, and smugglers who were in a state of war. Several had served in the armies of Napoleon, fired artillery at Austerlitz, stood beside big field guns. The most notorious were Vincenzo Gambi, Dominique You, and Louis Chighizola, known as Nez Coupé, or "Cut Nose." In the way of Max, Lafitte fixed them with his cold, calculating stare. He told them he'd come to bring order to the wild places. No more stealing what's been stolen, no more selling what's been sold. From now on, the pirates will work under a single flag. It's about the greater good. Most of these men had known Lafitte for years: as a fellow traveler, the fence. Most liked him; others feared him. Those who neither liked nor feared began dying soon after Lafitte crossed the water: dead in a crick on the edge of the settlement; killed by a boom swinging across the quarterdeck.

Lafitte soon had the pirate islands under control. Business would now be conducted in the efficient way of the marketplace. The pirates took to sea, scouting for targets, bringing captured ships through the channel into Barataria. Crew and passengers were held captive in comfort until a ransom was paid. Stolen goods were inventoried and stored in island warehouses. If the pirates were lucky enough to come across a slave ship—the big prize, easiest pickings with the best return—the cargo, which was human misery, was moved to slave quarters built on Grand Terre. After arranging matters with Pierre at the blacksmith shop, plantation owners sailed out for the weekend. They would stay for two nights, drinking and eating, a party, a feast, before walking the aisles, saying, *That one looks sickly, but I will take that one, and that one, and that buck over there.* A few days later, the pirates would load the slaves onto pirogues and flatboats and carry them to plantations up the river.

If the pirates came into possession of an especially large cargo of African slaves, an auction was held, the location kept secret until the last moment. These events—the biggest took place at the temple, the huge pile of clamshells—were advertised in handbills scattered around the quarter: "Come One! Come All! To Jean Lafitte's Bazaar & Slave Auction. Tomorrow at the Temple, for Your Delight, Clothing, Gems and Knick-Knacks from the Seven Seas." On one such occasion, 400 Africans were sold. Within a year of Lafitte's arrival in Barataria, even the wildest pirates were calling him Old Man, Boss, Governor. To friends, he was Fita, the king of the badlands. Grand Terre became a kind of city-state, a capital of a pirate nation. It was egalitarian, each criminal taking an equal share of the loot and sharing in the responsibility of guarding the channels and the bay.

Lafitte set up a court of admiralty, where he judged the legality of each mission and the fate of each prize. As in the case with most underground economies, this one existed with the silent consent of the nearby population—it existed, in fact, because of that consent.

The majority of New Orleanians believed the ban on African slaves was foolish, and thus saw Lafitte less as a pirate than as a businessman supplying a desired product. What's more, Lafitte was a Frenchman in a French city that had recently come under American rule. He became a popular hero. Like Jesse James in the vanquished South, he personified the fantasy of defiance. Many of his practices—the comfort in which he held hostages, the return of runaway slaves—were followed with this reputation in mind. Like all dictators, he wanted the love of the people.

Lafitte remade Grand Terre, turned it from a mean camp into a criminal metropolis, the nightmare city of buccaneers. (When you were a kid riding Pirates of the Caribbean at Disney World, shuddering as an animatronic Blackbeard pulled a woman screaming into a house, did you know that all the animatronic women were being raped?) By 1809, perhaps a thousand pirates were living on the island, a sandy barrier, its back to the bayou, its face to the sea. Six miles long, three miles wide, five feet above sea level, a swell covered by scrub trees. The wind never stopped blowing, leaving the island gloriously free of bugs. If you had gone in 1810, you would have found a well-planned town in the middle of a swamp: dirt streets lined with thatch houses; mansions on stilts that seemed to float when the sea surged; clapboard storefronts, markets, hotels for plantation owners; bordellos, taverns, a casino where men sat 10 to a table; warehouses filled with merchandise—carpets, cotton, grain, gin; a scaffold where slaves were auctioned. It was strangely temporary, makeshift and ramshackle, blown together by the trade winds, a mirage, a trick of light, a driftwood empire, a parody of New Orleans reflected in the black water.

Ships traveled to Grand Terre on a regular schedule. To people in New Orleans, it was a vacation, a week at Sandals. The best house belonged to Lafitte. Built around 1808, it sat on high ground overlooking the channel. It was Spanish-style, made of pulverized oyster shells, the windows crossed by iron bars. From the veranda, dozing in his red hammock, Lafitte could keep an eye on the incoming ships.

It was not long before the authorities—tax officials, shore patrol—decided Lafitte had to be stopped. Though he would rule for a decade, Lafitte spent half those years in battle with Governor Claiborne. At times, this struggle took on the spirit of a comic opera. You chase, he runs, we laugh. Again and again, Claiborne sent ships to chase the pirates, but each time the pirates vanished into the channels, only to reappear hoisting the black flag. Claiborne finally arrested Pierre on July 2, 1814. He locked him in the old colonial jail. Jean hired two attorneys to defend his brother, but their arguments failed. And so Pierre simply escaped. Vanished. Walked through the bars. The governor plastered the city with wanted posters. It offered $500 to anyone who delivered Jean Lafitte to the sheriff of New Orleans. It was signed, "By the order of William Claiborne." It was posted at dinnertime. Before breakfast, a second sign had been placed beside the first: "A One-Thousand-Dollar Reward is offered anyone who can deliver Governor

Claiborne to Cat Island for Trial," signed Lafitte. It was the sort of gesture that turned the pirate into a cult figure. Crimes make a criminal; style makes a criminal hero. Lafitte was nothing but style. He knew how to dress, how to carry himself. History is not what's remembered, but what remains when everything else is forgotten: the kidnappings and the killings, the slave trading, the smoke rising from the plundered coastal towns.

Lafitte knew he could not win forever. He depended too much on luck. Even the king of hearts knows the ace of spades is somewhere in that deck. He was looking for an escape, a ladder to the street. He spotted it on September 3, 1814. That morning, HMS *Sophie*, a British warship, dropped anchor off Grand Terre. Lafitte rowed out in a canoe. He was greeted by Nicholas Lockyer, captain of the *Sophie*. The men exchanged pleasantries before Lafitte, unrecognized by the British, asked the captain the nature of his business.

"I have a message for Mr. Lafitte."

"Get in the canoe," said Lafitte, "I'll take you to him."

The captain and a few of his men climbed in. Lafitte talked as he ferried them across the bay. He had a florid manner of speech that worked a kind of magic. He spoke of sea battles and fog, of man's fate and treasures worth pursuing in this too-short life. The conversation turned to the terrific battle then underway. Later called the War of 1812, it pitted the British against their former American colonists. For the British, New Orleans would be a great prize, economically important and weakly defended, with a large French population whose loyalty to America was questionable. As Lafitte ran the canoe aground, he reintroduced himself with a flourish, saying, *"Lafitte c'est moi!"*

The British were surrounded as pirates came down to the shore to greet their leader and his guests. Several men in the crowd wanted to kill the British, run 'em through, string 'em up. The British navy was hated. No, said Lafitte, these men have come on parley, as our guests. We don't hang guests.

The men sat on the veranda of Lafitte's house, eating lunch within sight of the sea. Red snapper, oysters, wine. After much drinking, the British captain stated his business: he wanted Lafitte and his men to join the British in an attack on New Orleans. If Lafitte agreed, he would be rewarded with 30,000 pounds and a captaincy in the Royal Navy. If he refused, the British would destroy Grand Terre. Carrot, stick. The specifics were explained in letters that were left with Lafitte: the first included the promise (money, rank), the second included the threat (cannonball, ruin). Lafitte said he needed time—he would have to explain the offer to his followers. As a Frenchman in the age of Napoleon, Lafitte hated the British. He was, in fact, something of an American patriot, had come to love his adopted country, though he lived outside its laws. To him, the British offer was just an opportunity. He'd recently heard the U.S. Navy would dispatch an armada to destroy Grand Terre. Here was a way to save his island.

The next morning, Lafitte sent a message to Governor Claiborne, including the letters from the British. These had great intelligence value, as they spelled out Britain's plans. This resulted in a correspondence between Lafitte and Claiborne, in the course of which Lafitte offered the services of his men in the defense of New Orleans in return for a pardon, which Lafitte described as "an act of oblivion for all that has been done hitherto." "I may have evaded the payment of duties to the custom house," wrote Lafitte, "but I have never ceased to be a good citizen; and all the offence I have committed I was forced to by certain vices in our laws."

When Governor Claiborne discussed the proposal with city leaders, the response was mixed. Some feared the British more than they feared the pirates. What's more, as Lafitte and his followers were French, such a pardon would help unify a town that was an uneasy mix of French and American. In making this case, Claiborne—he was married to a French native of New Orleans—quoted a passage from Lafitte's letters: "I am the stray sheep, wishing to return to the sheepfold. If you were thoroughly acquainted with the nature of my offences, I should appear to you much less guilty, and still worthy to discharge the duties of a good citizen." But the final decision had to be made by Andrew Jackson, the general responsible for the defense of New Orleans—he would soon take over as military governor. Jackson was already on record regarding Lafitte and the Barataria pirates, whom he described as "hellish banditti." The proposal was rejected.

This was the state of affairs on September 16, 1814, when nine U.S. Navy ships appeared off Grand Terre. Sailors manned the cannons, the big black mouths like portals to the next world. The first shell was fired around 8:30 A.M., dawn buccaneer time, as Lafitte's men were sitting at tables enjoying a pirate breakfast: rye whiskey and gruel. First the big guns, *ka-boom! ka-boom!* Then the rat-a-tat-tat of small arms, muskets and rifles, then more from the big guns. Cannonballs whistled across the sky, lit up the driftwood houses, set the warehouses ablaze, opening craters on the main street. The slave scaffold fell in a heap. The Planters Hotel was destroyed. The casino collapsed. The pirates had been a gang, but when the on-slaught came it was every man for himself. Some stood around, stunned. Some hurried to the warehouses to take whatever they could carry. Some hid. Some unsheathed their swords and ran into battle. Everywhere the uniformed military men, with their starched collars, shiny boots, and shaven faces, fought the pirates, it was classical music versus rock-and-roll. The pirates were long-haired, jewel-bedecked, tattooed, and drunken. Now and then, they fought with an abandon that terrified the regular army, but most of them ran. Away to the flatboats and canoes, to the streams and bayous where the big navy ships could not follow. Grand Terre burned at their backs, got smaller as they went away. First it was the whole world on fire, the sky colored like a bruise, ash falling on the forehead like a benediction, then it was smoke in the distance.

Pierre Lafitte had been staying with his brother at the time of the attack. They fled together, raced through the streets of burn-ing houses, climbed into a pirogue, paddled like mad. Jean was in his midthirties, still handsome but gone a bit soft—too much of the high pirate life. He cursed as he left, exiting his kingdom like Sendak's Max—all this time, and he was still wearing the wolf costume—driven from the island of the wild things across a sea of flames. They navigated the confused network of rivers and swamps, traveling through afternoon and evening from Little Lake to Lake Salvadore, along channels and estuaries without name, landing, after two days, at a friend's farm on the German Coast, a dozen miles above New Orleans. The area, which took its name from an early group of settlers, had became a refuge for Frenchmen who fled Acadia when the British took over. Cajun country. The Lafittes hid on the farm for weeks, gangsters on the lam. The other mem-bers of the pirate band had been killed, scattered, or captured. Dozens took shelter on Last Island, a sandbar between the Mis-sissippi Sound and the Gulf. Eighty more were in jail in New Or-leans. The loot that survived—the goods as well as the ships—was sent back to the city, where it was catalogued, counted, and divvied up among the navy officers. The pirate capital was sunken in the way of Atlantis, turned into a story.

Jean Lafitte continued to scheme. Every trap has a catch, every cell has a secret door. He sent letters, via courier, to the leaders of the city. *Grand Terre is dead and gone. The loot has been retrieved, the privateers killed or jailed. What matters now is the city, which will soon be attacked by the British. And for that, you need the men of Grand Terre.* Lafitte made this case to Claiborne, and Claiborne made it to Andrew Jackson when he arrived in New Orleans in December 1814. By then, Lafitte had become a popular cause. French residents demanded the inclusion of the pirates in the defense of the city. Jackson finally came around when he got a look at the situation on the ground. New Orleans was vulnerable. The defenders were inexperienced in combat, and there were not nearly enough of them. Few were native to the region—they would be as lost in the bayous as the British. But the pirates had lived in the swamps as a man lives in his mind. For every path, they knew a dozen shortcuts, caves, hidden coves. They could serve as scouts, helping General Jackson and his officers understand the maps and the confused ways of the land. They could stand sentry at the heads of the channels, block the British from slipping into the city. Since several of the pirates had served under Napoleon, they could offer hardened battle experience to an army of raw recruits.

There was also the matter of the flints—probably the deciding factor. To fire, the rifles in use at the time needed a flint. This was like the reed used in a wind instrument. No reed, no music; no flint, no bang-bang. As he prepared for the city's defense, Jackson realized his army was dangerously short on flints. Even if they could outmaneuver the British, the Americans would not have enough working guns. It just so happened Jean Lafitte had thousands of flints hidden in Barataria. It was his insurance policy, his 100k in an unmarked safe-deposit box.

Lafitte traveled to the city to work out terms. He came by canoe, tied at the foot of the parade ground, walked the streets. He met General Jackson in the French Quarter that night. It's a famous scene. Old Hickory from backwoods Tennessee, the lover of the common man and the wild-haired face on the $20 bill, sharing a brandy with this duded-up gangster in pirate finery, the men chatting as casually as a capo and a Mafia don in folding chairs on Mulberry Street. The terms went as follows: Any pirate who joined the Americans would be freed from jail or welcomed back from Barataria, then assigned a role in the defense of the city. At the end of the war, if the pirate's service had been honorable, Jackson would request an official pardon from James Madison, the president of the United States.

Jean spent the Battle of New Orleans in the bayou. Though he did not see much action, he played an important role. He was like the bouncer at the side door. His presence pushed the British into the position desired by General Jackson. Pierre was more active. He was a scout, advising the American commanders where to place their ships. Looking at the charts, he told the navy officers which islands were islands and which only looked like islands but were in fact marsh. When the British attacked on January 8, 1815 — two weeks after a treaty had been signed and the War of 1812 officially ended — Pierre was at the front. A heavy fog came off the river, making Pierre's deep knowledge of the terrain invaluable. In the end, this fog, along with luck, led to the rout of the British. It was the Battle of New Orleans, more than anything, that made Andrew Jackson president. And it was President Jackson, with his love of native trash culture, that made America modern. In this hidden, backchannel way, the pirates of Barataria played a role in the creation of modern America. Jean and Pierre Lafitte are black-sheep relatives everyone relied on but few acknowledge.

The pirates were pardoned for their crimes in the afterglow of victory. For a moment, it seemed the Lafittes might settle down to a normal life, open a shop, grow fat and old, and entertain the neighborhood kids with exotic tales of yore. What drove them away? What returned them to sea? Some attribute it to a single slight, a bit of indecorum suffered at the victory ball hosted by Andrew Jackson after the war. It was in a ballroom in the French Quarter on January 23, 1815. For Jean Lafitte, it was a kind of debut, his first affair as a legitimate citizen. The room was crowded with uniformed soldiers. Lafitte approached a group of big shots that included Governor Claiborne, General Jackson, General Coffee, and General de Flaugeac. As Lafitte reached out a hand, de Flaugeac, seeming to notice a friend, turned his back. Claiborne came to the rescue, pulling Lafitte into the circle and introducing him to General Coffee, who blanched when he saw the notorious Lafitte, held out a hand tentatively, then, as if not knowing what to call Lafitte, said something like, *You are uh, uh, uh, uh . . .*

Jean frowned, said, "Lafitte, the pirate!" and turned and went away, never to be seen in society again.

In the spring of 1816, when the azaleas bloomed and the wind carried the taste of hibiscus and palm, Jean Lafitte borrowed some money, purchased a ship, and went back to the life. Through the summer, several of the pirate's old mates, men who'd been living increasingly settled lives as merchants and bartenders in the French Quarter, slipped away from everything (wives, children) that nailed them to terra firma—you wake up and the pirate is gone and the promises were lies. From there, Lafitte's life plays out like a sea shanty in which the hero loves every woman and whips every man. He sailed to Port-au-Prince, where he tried to re-establish his pirate navy but was chased off. He went on to Gálvez-town, a gulf island off the coast of northern Mexico. He built a kingdom that rivaled Grand Terre. His house, which commanded the northern approaches of the island, was tall and clean in the sun. He returned to his hammock and his buccaneer ways, and soon the island filled with rum and pirates and the evils of the barbaric trade—Africans smuggled in chains to New Orleans. When Gálvez-town became famous for its depravity, an American navy ship sailed into view, its crew and big gun driving Lafitte away like a fly driven off by the back of a hand. Out of safe havens, he stayed on the water, guiding a small armada on a mad dash along the Mexican coast. He lost one ship to mutiny, was separated from another in a storm. While Jean was off on an errand, a Spanish galleon spotted Pierre's ship and gave chase—Pierre, Jean's only real friend in the world.

Pierre escaped in a skiff with a few others. These men headed ashore, ditching in a desolate cove. Their skiff was recovered later in a lagoon known as Las Bocas. Pierre came down with a fever, was terribly ill. He made his way on foot, wandering to a village called Santa Clara, then to a village called Telyas. The pirates carried him to a hut, where he lay as his fever climbed. Perhaps he saw things in those hours, understood things for the first time. Palm fronds, green and blue, the colors of the pirate life. He died on November 9, 1821. Pink flamingos rising from the bay—was that the last thing he saw? Two men were with him. They carried his body back to Santa Clara, where he was buried in the churchyard. A priest named José Gregorio Cervera performed the ceremony. According to his friends, Pierre was given a headstone with his name and the date of his death—no one knew exactly when he'd been born—but it's since vanished. Much later, Mexican officials placed a stone cross at the spot where Pierre Lafitte is believed to be buried.

Jean sailed on, unaware of his brother's death. The news reached him months later when he came ashore in the Virgin Islands. It had been carried in the way of a rumor, port to port. It nearly killed Jean. He went to the wharf, where the ships stood at anchor, and the men drank in the rigging, and the sky was black, and the wind never stopped blowing. Jean vanished after that; the episodes of his later years and death are largely unknown.

In his disappearance, as in so much else, Jean Lafitte the pirate is the spiritual father of New Orleans. This is a city where a friend tells you he's going to get a drink and never comes back; you see him 30 years later, in the same clothes, wandering with a go cup, face lighting up when he spots you, and he points and says, *There you are!* Boston or Chicago can have a Ward Cleaver–type patriarch who dispenses conventional wisdom, but New Orleans needs a father as crooked and mysterious as the town. George Washington was from Virginia. Abe Lincoln was from Kentucky. Teddy Roosevelt grew up in Manhattan. But no one knows where Jean Lafitte came from or who he really was. Some said he was a Catholic from Spain. Some said he was cured of religion as a boy in France. Some said his father was a noble killed by the guillotine. Some said his father was a fisherman, his fingers scarred by nets. Some said he was raised in wealth; some said he was the pauper who grew into a pirate king.

Others have claimed him as a Marrano, a descendant of Spanish Jews forced to convert to Christianity but who continued to practice their faith in secret—or, if not practice, then at least be aware of the secret thing that made them different. According to *The Early Jews of New Orleans* by Bertram Korn, Jean and Pierre's parents died young, leaving the boys to be raised by a maternal grandmother, Maria Zora Nadrimal, whose own husband had been killed during the Spanish Inquisition. It was this grandmother who "planted the seed of hatred in her grandsons," which would manifest itself at sea, when the Lafittes took delight in plundering

Spanish ships. The name Lafitte may be a variation of the Hebrew name Levi. A few decades after the pirate vanished, a historian turned up an old Lafitte family Bible, in which the following note, seemingly written in the pirate's own hand, was found: "I owe all my ingenuity to the influence of my grandmother, a Spanish Jewess, who bore witness at the time of the Inquisition."

The mystery of Lafitte's final years gave rise to legends. In some, he settled down to a quiet life in New Orleans. In others, he changed sides and fought for Spain. Few believed he died, or could be killed. In one story, he rescued Napoleon from exile on Saint Helena and spirited him back to Louisiana, where the two men lived for years, dying in their sleep, buried side by side. A more likely version was reported by William Davis in *The Pirates Laffite*. According to Davis, Jean headed south after getting the news of Pierre's death. He landed in Colombia, where, in the way of the kid who joins the marines when a girl has broken his heart, he enlisted in the navy. For months he followed the rules, patrolling the shores of Cartagena. But on the morning of February 4, 1823, spotting what seemed to be a merchant ship, he felt the old itch. He gave chase and attacked, but he was wrong. It was not a merchant ship but a Spanish man-of-war. It's a familiar nightmare: you believe you're the hunter but soon realize you're the prey. That afternoon, as Lafitte gave orders, a burst of gunfire swept across the deck and cut him in half. He was 41, died instantly, and was buried at sea, 40 miles off Honduras.

The report of his death, as carried in the newspaper *Gaceta de Cartagena*, like so much of New Orleans history, reads like a cover, the version given to the people so they'll never learn the truth: "The loss of this brave naval official is moving. The boldness with which he confronted the superior forces which hit him manifests well that, as an enthusiast of honor, he wished to follow it down the road to death rather than abandon it in flight."

Contributors' Notes
Notable Travel Writing of 2012

Contributors' Notes

Sam Anderson is the critic at large for the *New York Times Magazine*. His work has appeared in the *Paris Review, New York* magazine, *Slate*, the *American Scholar, Creative Nonfiction*, and *The Best Technology Writing 2010*. In 2007, he won the National Book Critics Circle's Nona Balakian Citation for Excellence in Reviewing. He is currently working on a book about basketball, civics, and Oklahoma City.

Marie Arana was born in Peru and moved to the United States at the age of nine. She is the author of a memoir about her bicultural childhood, *American Chica: Two Worlds, One Childhood*, which was a finalist for the 2001 National Book Award and the PEN/Martha Albrand Award for the Art of the Memoir, and which won the Books for a Better Life Award. She is the editor of a collection of *Washington Post* essays about the writer's craft, *The Writing Life: Writers on How They Think and Work* (2002), which is used as a textbook for writing courses in universities across the country. Her novel *Cellophane*, about the Peruvian Amazon, was published in 2006 and selected as a finalist for the John Sargent Sr. First Novel Prize. Her most recent novel, published in January 2009, is *Lima Nights*. She has written the introductions for many books on Latin America, Hispanicity, and biculturalism. She was the scriptwriter for the South American portion of *Girl Rising*, a full-length feature film on education in pockets of poverty, which was released in March 2013. Her latest book is *Bolívar: American Liberator*, a biography of the South American liberator Simón Bolívar, published in April 2013. Arana has served on the board of directors of the National Book Critics Circle and the National Association of Hispanic Journalists. She is the former editor of the *Washington Post*'s Book World section, and her commentary has been published in the *New York Times, USA Today*, the *International Herald Tribune, The Week, Civilization, Smithsonian, National Geographic,* the *Virginia Quarterly Review, El Comercio, El País,* and numerous other publications throughout the Americas.

Bernd Brunner is the author of *The Art of Lying Down: A Guide to Horizontal Living, Bears: A Brief History, Moon: A Brief History, Inventing the Christmas Tree,* and *The Ocean at Home: An Illustrated History of the Aquarium.* His books have been translated into several languages, and his writing has appeared in *Zeit Geschichte, Die Welt, Cabinet,* and *Neue Zürcher Zeitung,* among many others. A native of Berlin, Germany, he lives in Istanbul, Turkey, where he delves deeply into a very different language.

Kevin Chroust lives in Chicago and is a 2005 graduate of Colorado State University. His sportswriting has appeared in publications from Chicago to San Francisco to Japan. He contributes to Yahoo! Sports and the online magazine the *Nervous Breakdown,* which published an excerpt of his recently completed memoir, *Fix.* Find him on Twitter @kevinchroust.

Rich Cohen is the author of nine books, including *Tough Jews, Sweet and Low,* and *The Fish That Ate the Whale.* His latest, *Monsters: The 1985 Chicago Bears and the Wild Heart of Football,* was published in October 2013. He lives in Connecticut.

Judy Copeland's travel essays have appeared in *Alaska Quarterly Review,* the *Florida Review, Legal Studies Forum, Literal Latte,* the *Malahat Review, Water~Stone Review,* and Travelers' Tales anthologies. Since 2005, she has taught creative nonfiction at the Richard Stockton College of New Jersey.

Christopher de Bellaigue is a writer and broadcaster on the Middle East and South Asia. His most recent book is *Patriot of Persia: Muhammad Mossadegh and a Tragic Anglo-American Coup.*

Jesse Dukes is an independent writer and documentary filmmaker. For many years, he worked as a wilderness trip leader in Maine and California. He studied radio at the Salt Institute for Documentary Studies, worked for *With Good Reason* at the Virginia Foundation for the Humanities, and is a principal at Big Shed Media. In 2011, his *VQR* essay "Consider the Lobstermen" was selected as one of Byliner's Spectacular Nonfiction Stories. He recently produced the radio documentary *The Great Moonshine Conspiracy,* which aired on American Public Media's *The Story* and public radio stations. He is a contributing editor at the *Virginia Quarterly Review* and the founder of and principal at Pioneer Media Grantwriting.

David Farley is the author of the award-winning travel memoir/narrative history *An Irreverent Curiosity: In Search of the Church's Strangest Relic in Italy's Oddest Town,* which is currently being made into a documentary, and coeditor of the anthology of essays *Travelers' Tales Prague and the Czech Republic: True Stories.* He's a contributing writer at *Afar* magazine and frequently writes for the *New York Times,* the *San Francisco Chronicle, National Geographic Traveler, World Hum,* and *Gadling,* among other publications. He teaches writing at New York University. His online home is www.dfarley.com.

Ian Frazier is the author of *Great Plains, The Fish's Eye, On the Rez, Family,* and *Travels in Siberia,* as well as *Coyote v. Acme, Dating Your Mom,* and *Lamentations of the Father.* A frequent contributor to *The New Yorker,* he lives in Montclair, New Jersey.

Dimiter Kenarov is a freelance journalist and contributing editor at the *Virginia Quarterly Review.* His work has appeared in *Esquire, Outside, The Nation,* the *International Herald Tribune,* and *Foreign Policy,* among others. He currently lives in Sofia, Bulgaria.

Colleen Kinder has written essays and articles for the *New Republic, Salon, National Geographic Traveler,* the *New York Times, Gadling,* TheAtlantic.com, the *Wall Street Journal, Ninth Letter, A Public Space,* the *New York Times Magazine,* and *Creative Nonfiction.* She is the author of *Delaying the Real World* and currently teaches travel writing at Yale.

Peter Jon Lindberg is a New York–based travel journalist and essayist and the editor at large for *Travel + Leisure.* He is a two-time James Beard Award finalist for his food writing, was named a Travel Journalist of the Year by the Society of American Travel Writers (SATW) in 2005, and was nominated for a National Magazine Award in 2010 for his columns and commentary in *Travel + Leisure.* He can be reached via his website, www.peterjonlindberg.com.

David Sedaris is the author of the books *Let's Explore Diabetes with Owls, Squirrel Seeks Chipmunk, When You Are Engulfed in Flames, Dress Your Family in Corduroy and Denim, Me Talk Pretty One Day, Holidays on Ice, Naked,* and *Barrel Fever.* He is a regular contributor to *The New Yorker* and BBC Radio 4. He lives in England.

Sex, pop culture, nascent trends, and eccentric characters are all grist for **Grant Stoddard**'s mill. With an eye for the surprising and ridiculous, the

British-born Stoddard often reports from a participatory perspective, imbuing his stories with an engaging, visceral, dynamic feel and a humanistic focus. Stoddard has had two books published, *Working Stiff: The Misadventures of an Accidental Sexpert* and *Great in Bed*, which he coauthored with Dr. Debby Herbenick of the Kinsey Institute.

John Jeremiah Sullivan is a contributing editor for the *New York Times Magazine* and the author of *Pulphead: Essays* (2011).

Sarah A. Topol moved to Egypt in 2008. Her writing has been published in the *Atlantic, Businessweek, Esquire, GQ, Harper's Magazine, Newsweek*, the *New York Times*, and *Slate*, among others. She has reported from Bahrain, Egypt, Israel, Jordan, Libya, Pakistan, Russia, Turkey, the United Arab Emirates, and Yemen as well as Gaza and the West Bank. She won the 2012 Kurt Schork Award in International Journalism for her coverage of the civil war in Libya. She lived in Cairo for four and a half years and recently relocated to Istanbul.

Daniel Tyx teaches English at South Texas College in McAllen, where he lives with his wife, Laura, and their two young children. He is at work on a collection of essays about the U.S.-Mexico border, several of which have appeared in *Gulf Coast*, the *Gettysburg Review, CutBank*, and *Blue Mesa Review*.

Lynn Yaeger is contributing editor to *Travel + Leisure* and *Vogue* and also contributes to many other publications. She lives in New York City.

Notable Travel Writing of 2012

SELECTED BY JASON WILSON

LISA ABEND
   Spain Lets Loose. *Afar*, May/June.

ROSECRANS BALDWIN
   Our French Connection. *The Morning News*, May 29.
AIMEE BENDER
   Another Angle on L.A. *Afar*, February.
KEN BENSINGER
   The Frequent Fliers Who Flew Too Much. *Los Angeles Times*, May 5.
JANE BERNSTEIN
   Desperately Seeking Subtext. *Creative Nonfiction*, Spring.
RITA WELTY BOURKE
   The Larry Brown Discovery Tour. *Chattahoochee Review*, vol. 31, no. 3.
JOHN BRANCH
   Snow Fall. *New York Times*, December 23.
NATHANIEL BRODIE
   Sparks. *Creative Nonfiction*, Spring.
FRANK BURES
   The Crossing. *Nowhere*, September.
   The Reunion. *The Washington Post Magazine*, March 11.

JESSICA COLLEY
   Catching the Gist. *World Hum*, August 7.
LAUREN COLLINS
   The British Invasion. *The New Yorker*, April 16.

BILL DONAHUE
Into the Woods. *Afar,* December.

WILLIAM FINNEGAN
Slow and Steady. *The New Yorker,* January 23.

DEVIN FRIEDMAN
The Best Night $500,000 Can Buy. *GQ,* September.

RACHEL FRIEDMAN
Discovery. *Creative Nonfiction,* Summer.

RIVKA GALCHEN
Wild West Germany. *The New Yorker,* April 9.

KEITH GESSEN
Polar Express. *The New Yorker,* December 24 and 31.

LENORE GREINER
Translating Respect. *World Hum,* June 27.

PETER GWIN
Rhino Wars. *National Geographic,* March.

A. E. HOTCHNER
A Legend as Big as the Ritz. *Vanity Fair,* July.

RAFI KOHAN
From Beads to the Big House. *GQ,* February.

JANE KRAMER
A Reporter at Odds. *The New Yorker,* July 23.

PETER LaSALLE
With Nathanael West in Hollywood. *Memoir,* issue 11 (December).

EVGENY LEBEDEV
Beyond Black Hawk Down. *Vanity Fair,* May.

BRUNO MADDOX
I Was a Las Vegas Concierge. *Travel + Leisure,* June.

JOYCE MAYNARD
On the Road Again. *T Magazine,* Winter.

LINDA WATANABE McFERRIN
Bali Belly and the Zombie Apocalypse. *World Hum,* May 17.

TONI MIROSEVICH
The Deposit. *Bellevue Literary Review,* Fall.

JASON MOTLAGH
Irrawaddy. *Virginia Quarterly Review,* vol. 88, no. 3 (Summer).

CHRIS NORRIS
    The Real World. *Travel + Leisure,* February.

LAWRENCE OSBORNE
    Tourist-Free Thailand. *Afar,* June.

STEPHANIE PEARSON
    The Undisputed King of Dogsled Tourism. *Outside,* January.
BASHARAT PEER
    Modern Mecca. *The New Yorker,* April 16.
JULIA PHILLIPS
    Twilight on the Tundra. *The Morning News,* November 27.
WILLIAM POWERS
    Finding the Perfect Wave in Liberia, *The Atlantic,* July/August.
TOM PRESTON
    Where Everybody Knows Your Name. *Vanity Fair,* March.

EMILY RABOTEAU
    The Throne of Zion, *The Believer,* October.

AMY SERAFIN
    Oyster Safari. *The Smart Set,* December 14.
GRETA SCHULER
    Empty Boxes. *Chattahoochee Review,* vol. 32, no. 1.
GARY SHTEYNGART
    Hungry for Madrid. *Travel + Leisure,* May.
AARON LAKE SMITH
    Death of the American Hobo. *Vice,* vol. 19, no. 10 (October).
CHRISTOPHER SOLOMON
    Grand Slammed. *Outside,* July.
ILAN STAVANS AND JOSHUA ELLISON
    Reclaiming Travel. *Opinionator,* July 7.
JOHN JEREMIAH SULLIVAN
    Where Hope and History Don't Rhyme. *The New York Times Magazine,*
        February 12.
PATRICK SYMMES
    The Beautiful Game. *Outside,* October.

NATHAN THORNBURGH
    Something Wicked This Way Larps. *Roads & Kingdoms,* July 19.
GUY TREBAY
    Mysteries of Milan. *Travel + Leisure,* February.

CALVIN TRILLIN
    Land of the Seven Moles. *The New Yorker,* December 3.

JASON WILSON
    Food for Thought. *The Washington Post Magazine,* September 16.
ELLIOTT D. WOODS
    The Last Happy Skull. *Virginia Quarterly Review,* vol. 88, no. 3 (Summer).